COOKING FOR HER EYES

Cooking For Her Eyes

TRANSCRIPTION OF A SONATA

≀

A STORY OF MUSIC, FOOD,
LOVE, AND DEATH

Pamela, wishing you and your family good health & happiness. I hope you enjoy the book! Warmly, Susan Rakstang

Susan Uehara Rakstang

Cooking For Her Eyes: Transcription of a Sonata
©2020 Susan Uehara Rakstang

All Rights Reserved. No part of this book may be reproduced, stored in a retrieval system, or transmitted in any form or by any means, electronic, mechanical, photocopying, recording, or otherwise, without the prior written permission of the author, except as provided by U.S.A. copyright law.

PHOTOS CREDITS
Page 227–230: The author
Page 245 and author photograph: John Thoeming

Book design: John W. Hubbard / emks.fi
Typeset in Monotype Centaur

 Published by Quarter Rest Publications, LLC, Chicago, Illinois
inquiry@quarterrestpublications.com

ISBN: 978-0-578-67277-9

"Authors like to talk vaguely of structuring their books 'like music,' but they should all look to Susan Uehara Rakstang for how to do it right! Basing *Cooking For Her Eyes* on her own harmonic analysis of Beethoven's Pathetique sonata, she subtly but unmistakably weaves her own themes and key changes into a memoir that is deeply personal and filled with life's tiny details. A sprawling Part I filled with exposition and development, a dreamy, meditative Part II, and as Part III a series of vignettes touching lightly on all of the essential elements that came before. It's a wonderful, subtly crafted accomplishment of a memoir. It is about the quiet, heartbreaking beauty of the mundane details. The everyday and ordinary made extraordinary and precious."

—Dr. David Arbury, PhD
Composer and professor of music theory,
Los Angeles City College

"This book has so many wonderful different layers to draw in the reader. A beautiful memoir of life, death, and relationships, Susan's is an empowering story of finding one›s place in the world and shows her personal Japanese American experience—a powerful thing for the community, and a valuable glimpse into that community for all audiences. Like all good books, it was bittersweet to arrive at its ending!"

—Michael Takada
CEO of the Japanese American Service
Committee, Chicago, IL

"*Cooking For Her Eyes* is a generous invitation, a moving walk through time revealing Susan's intelligence in terms of character development and attention to the right details. A passionate reading experience is the result: between essential vicissitudes and raw power of the senses, this book is proof of life, undisputably."

—Marc Louis-Boyard
Editor and Founder, *Slow Culture* Magazine,
Lille, France

CONTENTS

9 AUTHOR'S NOTE

13 PART I — *Brilliant Moon*

203 PART II — *Evening Cherry Blossoms*

225 PART III — *Exhausted*

237 EPILOGUE

239 ACKNOWLEDGMENTS

242 REFERENCES / BIBLIOGRAPHY

243 APPENDIX
245 *Analysis of Sonata No. 8 C minor Op. 13 (Pathetique)*
255 *Description of Mother's New Year's Feast*

257 ENDNOTES

262 AUTHOR BIOGRAPHY

For a little girl named Humiko

AUTHOR'S NOTE

MUSIC, TO ME, can be intensely evocative and palpable, sometimes eliciting tears when I hear certain songs—taking me back in time, leaving me happy, sad, uneasy, or resolved, and awakening images I hadn't thought of in years. I was astounded while listening to a CD from my set of *BEETHOVEN The Complete Sonatas RICHARD GOODE*.[1] I found an uncanny likeness between what I heard in the three movements of Piano Sonata No. 8 in C minor, Opus 13 (Pathetique), and my own anxious and fitful struggles with burgeoning issues of time, purposefulness, life, and death.

A composer creates a transcription by taking an original score, for instance, a piece created for a violin, and adapts the score for a different musical instrument, say, a cello. Maestro Goode's masterful playing of Pathetique drew me into the substance of the music, inspiring me to transcribe Beethoven's work, not for a different musical instrument but rather, for the instrument of my voice. In the Appendix, I've summarized the organizing structural elements of this story and its alignment with the sonata.

PART I

Brilliant moon,
is it true that you too
must pass in a hurry
—Issa[1]

Leaning against the wall outside of the hospice room, waiting for my heart to slow down and sync with the still of the moment, I wondered how time could seemingly pass with such high speed—like a movie in fast-forward—then suddenly switch, just like that, to slow motion.

"She's ready. You can go in now," the nurse said. Her voice was kind, and she spoke with a slight Japanese accent.

I turned and saw Nurse Misayo greeting me with a soft smile. Tiny in stature, with an ever-so-shallow bow, she welcomed me into the room, her open palm guiding me toward the bed where her patient lay.

"The ride from the hospital was difficult, and she seemed a bit agitated," Nurse Misayo said in a lowered voice, "so I gave her something to settle her. I hope you don't mind."

I managed to nod in thanks. My feet were heavy and immobile.

Nurse Misayo smiled. "Go to her. Tell her you're here. She'll want to hear your voice."

I closed my eyes briefly and nodded again before the nurse left the room. Stepping toward the bed, toe-heel, toe-heel, I saw her lying there. Her breath was shallow but peaceful as if she were taking an afternoon nap under a crisp white sheet folded neatly over a loosely knit, white cotton blanket. Her arms, elbows slightly bent, rested gracefully at her side.

Her hands were relaxed and beautiful. Just a few days earlier, she had treated herself to a mani-pedi, choosing a rich, creamy, pinkish-salmon nail polish. The tips of her manicured hands contrasted with the whiteness that cradled her, reminding me of early blossoms of her beloved *sakura*² after a light spring snowfall. The fragrance of fresh linen filled me. Time, once moving so fast then slow, now seemed to suspend itself for her, floating above her—buoyant—weightless. My tears fell onto her crisp, white sheets.

I wrestled with thoughts in my head.

It's her time now. Your journey together will end soon, and she'll need to let go.

Must she?

She must.

*But I need more time.*³

{

At ten years old, my childhood bedroom was next to the kitchen. I'd never needed an alarm clock to get up for school because each day I awakened to the quiet, gentle voices of a percussion concerto, and my mother was the solo percussionist as she created the beautiful sounds of preparing dinner for that evening.

Shooshing running water whispered in the background sounded like a wire brush's soft, continuous, rhythmic circles on a snare.

The slow, steady beat of her chef's knife cutting through crisp vegetables on a wooden cutting board clacked like a temple block.

Her wooden chopsticks, answering the temple block, tapped staccato on a porcelain bowl while she whisked her sauces.

When the vegetables eased into her hot, lightly oiled wok, they sounded like pebbles falling through an upended rain stick, filling the air with a burst of luscious aroma.

In between her symphony, sounds like cowbells, each with a different *timbre*,⁴ ever so softly tinged, dinged, and clinked as she quietly handled her bowls, kitchen tools, pots, and pans. Lovely sounds and spellbinding fragrances drifted into my bedroom.

Will we have miso soup laced with silky egg strands, cubes of tofu, and strips of kombu for breakfast today? Or last night's fried rice topped with thinly sliced pork and slivers of egg crepes? I wondered.

My thoughts were interrupted by the smell of toast.

"Mom, what's for breakfast?" I asked from the bed, eyes still closed.

"Scrambled eggs and toast," she replied.

"Oh." My eyes opened.

That's it?

"Then what're we having for dinner?"

"I'm making nishime," she said. "And don't forget to wash and soak the rice after school. I'll finish making dinner when I get home from work."

Ah, yes, nishime.

My thoughts returned to comfort food fantasies.

Nishime, a Japanese village stew, prepared Hawaiian style, is filled with carrots chopped in triangular chunks; thick, diagonally cut slices of celery; thinly sliced bamboo shoots and lotus root; matchstick-cut gobo,[5] small strips of konnyaku[6] slit down the center and turned inside themselves; shiitake mushrooms, and chicken chunks. Kombu, once sheets of hard, dried seaweed, is soaked in water, reconstituting it into tender strips, then tied into knots. All are quickly stir-fried to seal in flavor, then simmered in a soothing dashi[7] broth, lightly flavored with shoyu.[8]

Just before serving, she'll sprinkle frozen peas in the stew giving it a shock of bright green polka dots. What a feast!

The sounds of my mother's percussion concerti were the gentlest way of waking up each morning. That was what love sounded like. And over the years, hearing those cherished remembrances always brought me solace and peace.

A "Depression Baby," my mother was waste-averse to a fault, in my childish opinion, although as an adult, I became enlightened by her thrifty ways. She was ahead of her time throughout the introduction of society's use of "throw-away" convenience packaging.

"Mom! The bags are attacking me! Why do you have to save these things anyway?" I'd complained in childish hyperbole. I'd wanted to go out with friends, but my mother insisted I first wash the dishes. Every time I bent down to scrub a bowl or pan, static-rich plastic bread bags hanging from clothespins on a makeshift line over the sink, slow-danced with my short black hair and straight-cut bangs. When I stood up, the bags clung to me as if an embrace.

"Hai![9] Oh, Susie, look at you!" My mother giggled as I dramatically wrestled with the bags, trying to get them off my head.

Jumping from her chair, my mother said, still laughing, "Okay, okay, I'll take them off!"

I don't think my mother ever met a plastic bag she didn't like and was compelled to wash each one after its first use. Inverted bags, in various stages of dripping and drying, were always ready for their next mission of usefulness.

She even discovered reuse, or extended use, of green onions.

"Why are there green onions in those glasses?" I once asked her, pointing to the windowsill.

"Oh, that's my green onion patch. After chopping up most of the stalk for meals, I stick the root-end in a glass of water, and in a few days, fresh green onions sprout up, just like that!"

Pretty crazy. Little did I know, I would follow my mother's lead in the future and find it quite useful, especially for that last minute, all-important garnish for my meals.

As a child, together with my brother, Dennis, three years older, we sometimes unwittingly presented a certain critical mass of frustration for my mother. We knew what her house rules were, but due to our youthful convenient short-term memories, we seemed to forget. One of those rules was that we were to turn off lights when we left a room—simple enough to uphold, but impossible for us to remember.

"Electricity is expensive! Do you think money grows on trees?" she would holler.

Coming home exhausted after work and seeing our rumpled jackets, shoes, and socks strewn around the house, items she and my father spent their hard-earned money to buy, she would bark, "Clothes are expensive—do you think clothes grow on trees?"

Dennis and I would scurry to pick up our things.

Then one day, seeing half-eaten apples lying on the coffee table, my mother yelled her mantra.

"Look at all this waste! Do you think apples grow on trees?"

Rushing to get rid of the evidence, Dennis and I stopped in our tracks and looked at each other as we processed what she had just asked. We started laughing.

"Yes!" we called out. My mother's furrowed eyebrows softened as she'd realized the context of our laughter and couldn't help but laugh along with us, even with her weariness and exhaustion from a full day of work.

She was a clerk at the Eugene Dietzgen Company, a company that manufactured German-designed precision drawing instruments and supplies. Always loving a good bargain, my mother bought rolls of linen drafting cloth "seconds" at the company's end-of-year employee sale. Architects and engineers coveted this bluish-colored, starch-coated fabric for its strength, durability, and its translucency for blueprinting, and used it as their "paper" upon which they drafted delineations. But my mother had other ideas altogether. She soaked long lengths of the drafting cloth in our bathtub full of hot water, and during her many hours of peeling and scrubbing away the starched surface, a clean, minty fragrance wafted throughout the house. What emerged from her labor were yards of beautiful, lightweight, pure white linen that she sewed into fancy slips and dresses for me, and functional bed linens for the family.

She also took advantage of the company's sale of overstock precision drafting instruments and various types of technical papers.

"For Dennis," she said proudly when she brought them home. "In case he becomes an engineer."

The black, leather-bound case for drafting instruments had two slightly domed, copper snaps incised with the Eugene Dietzgen Company logo. I disengaged the snaps and opened both leather flaps, finding a thin sheet of felt protecting instruments in the green, velvet-lined case. When I removed the felt, I gasped.

Stainless steel tools, like surgical instruments, some polished to a high mirror finish, some with a satin finish, were nestled in depressed, custom-shaped spaces for each device: compasses of various sizes, along with a stainless steel extender for drawing oversized circles; a small circular stainless steel and leather compass point protector; cartographer's ruling pen; pattern divider; and small individual stainless steel capped cylinders holding replacement lead points, metal points, and screws.

I took out the ruling pen. Unlike the other instruments, it had a rosewood shaft with two, delicately pointed opposing stainless-steel spring blades—one flat and the other convex, between which ink, added one drop at a time, would fill the space between them. Line thickness, determined by the flow of ink, was adjusted by tightening or loosening the small knurled compression screw that determined the distance between the points of the blades. Holding the instrument, I felt the warmth and smoothness of the rosewood, its precision, and perfectly weighted body.

"But Mom! Dennis never draws anything, and I draw all the time. I want this—now!" I demanded with hands on my hips.

"Susie, you're only eleven. You're too young to use those instruments," she said, "and besides, if Dennis becomes an engineer, he'll need them."

The only engineers I knew about were the ones who drove trains, and in my young, little mind, didn't know why or how they'd find time to draw.

"Dennis will never be an engineer; he's not the type! Maybe I'll be an engineer!" I said. I somehow knew in my heart that one day, my mother would give me those instruments and papers. Maybe when I went off to college to become an engineer, I would create beautiful drawings—one day.

"He's not going to be an engineer!" I yelled one more time. My mother smiled, and I stomped off.

☙

Preparing for a party one day, I heard my mother call, "Susie, it's time to fold your wontons." I was fully absorbed in playing my first, official classical piano piece for beginners, Beethoven's bagatelle, "Für Elise." I enjoyed banging out the slow, opening theme, DA da–DA da–DA da da da–DAAA, of what was meant to be the delicate, melancholy, flowing measures of the first movement.

"Susie?" my mother called again.

"Okay, okay, I'm coming." I wondered if my mother really needed me to fold wontons that very minute, or if she'd just had enough of my heavy-handed rendition of Beethoven's piece, but she would never admit it if that were true. After all, it was she who convinced my father to buy a pre-owned, Lyon and Healy baby grand piano when my teacher assured her, I had "promise."

Unbeknownst to me, my wonton training had begun earlier that year, when my mother decided she and I would together learn origami, the Japanese art of paper folding. She bought an instruction book and several packets of six-inch square, colored paper. The origami book demanded patience and acute analytical skills to decipher its arcane diagrams and haphazard, part-English, part-Japanese instructions. But we persevered. After we struggled with a few projects, my mother left me to my own devices and encouraged me to continue.

Origami paper, very thin and perfectly square, was unlike any paper I had ever seen. Each sheet was saturated with pure, intense color on one side, the "right side," and on the "wrong side," color was absent but for mottling, where the color had soaked through. Its tactile eggshell finish and weightlessness felt as if I was not holding the paper at all but rather, holding color itself, and I was drawn to make something beautiful with it.

One day, my father was in the kitchen fixing a clock, while I was at the dining room table working on an origami project.

He joined me and asked, "What's all the huffing and muttering about?"

"This box looks more like a stupid ball—it's nothing like the picture in the book!" I threw it down on the table, folded my arms, and flung my back into the chair.

He picked up the box and examined it.

"What did you expect? Look how sloppy you made it," my father said.

"It's not sloppy!" I blurted. "I followed the instructions, and that's how it turned out. The instructions are too hard to read—why can't they write them all in English?"

"The words don't have to be in English. Look and *see* what the diagrams are telling you," my father said. "Aren't all the corners lined up in the picture? Yours are cockeyed. Do you see the wrong side of the paper showing in the picture? I see a lot with yours. And what about the folds? Yours are hardly even creased. Do you see?"

"I made my folds and corners good enough, and it still turned out looking like a ball!" I said.

"Achhh!" He scoffed. "If you think your folds and corners are good enough, then that's what the project will be—good enough. And if you think good enough is fine, then why are you complaining about your ball?"

"It's not a ball. It's a box!"

"Okay, your box," he said.

I remained silent, my eyes growing hot and full, and turned my head away from my father. I couldn't look at him or my box.

"Susie, if you're not going to do something right, then why bother to do it at all?" He sighed. Not waiting for an answer, he walked back to the kitchen.

I'll show him.

Over the next few weeks, I practiced and practiced, slowing down as I made my objects, all the while realizing, good enough was not good enough for me. My father's question seared itself into my mind and followed me throughout my life.

In origami, I learned that folded creases must be sharp and confident, and edges and corners must be perfectly aligned, so the "wrong side" of the paper would not be exposed in the completed object.

Before long, I was folding small, colorful paper hats, boxes, frogs, boats, elephants, giraffes, birds, and the iconic Japanese crane. I folded cranes with anything I could get my hands on—origami paper, of course, as well as gum wrappers, paper napkins, cloth napkins, handkerchiefs, newspaper, recycled Christmas wrappings, anything. My friends marveled at my talent, and as for my mother, well, she was delighted.

Months later, figuring I was ready, my mother taught me how to fold wontons for one of her parties. Wontons are small, delicious, deep-fried dumplings, and no matter how many we made, there were never enough for the crowd. She set up a bowl of ground pork mixed with finely minced ginger root, garlic, green onions, finely chopped water chestnuts, a little shoyu and miso, and a touch of sesame and vegetable oils. Her workspace also included a large wooden cutting board dusted with flour, a small bowl of water near-by, and stacks of wonton wrappers that were paper-thin, three-and-a-half-inch-square sheets of dough. She laid out as many wrappers as would fit on the cutting board, corners facing upward, so the wrappers looked like diamonds, not squares.

"Okay, scoop a little bit of the pork mixture in the center of each diamond," my mother instructed me.

"Like this?" I asked.

"No, that's too much. By the time that big lump of pork is cooked through, the wrapper will burn, so use only about a teaspoon scoop of pork." She continued, "Dip your index fingers in the water, and from the bottom corner of the wrapper, slide your wet fingers along the edges to the side corners. Okay, wipe your hands on the towel and bring the top corner down to meet the bottom one, covering the pork filling."

The square was then a triangle.

"Is this right?" I asked.

"Yes," she said. "Press the edges down. Careful, don't press too hard! All right, that looks good. Now stretch the two long ends of the triangle, so they cross one over the other, just above the pork filling. Good! Dip a finger in the water bowl and wet the wrapper where they cross against each other near the pork. The water acts like a 'glue' to keep the wrapper together."

The finished wonton assembly always reminded me of how cowboys wore their triangular kerchiefs around their neck with the point facing downward under their chin and the long ends tied behind their necks.

I challenged myself to work quickly and with little wasted motion for reasons of efficiency and timeliness. In my young mind, I believed there were more important things I needed to do than spend hours making wontons all day. After I finished folding many wrappers (thousands, it seemed) and thought I could make my getaway from the kitchen, my mother brought out more stacks of wonton wrappers to fold.

Was it a coincidence that when I harnessed my newfound talent for origami, I became my mother's best (and only) wonton maker in the house, or was it a clever plan she'd hatched all along?

Only she would know.

My mother taught me how to use a small paring knife to transform radishes into roses, celery, and carrots into pretty bouquets, cauliflower into fluffy white clouds, broccoli, blanched and shocked, turned into bright green miniature trees, and sliced cucumber and zucchini spears. She artfully arranged them on a platter, delighting even the most hard-core meat-eaters.

When I got a little older, I graduated to using a chef's knife, and she looked over my shoulder as I cut green onions for sukiyaki.

"No, not that way—your strips are too wide. Cut them in slivers on a narrow angle, so they're long and graceful."

Holding my knife almost parallel to the green onion stalk, I cut them, indeed, into beautiful slivers.

※

Although I'd been advancing my skills in the kitchen, I was still behind in physical size. I was a small, skinny kid—all arms and legs. My overall health was fine, but with such tiny little muscles, I was a real weakling to be sure, caught colds easily, and needed glasses at a young age. As such, my family treated me like a dainty flower and, surprise, surprise, I always thought of myself as physically weak, fragile, and lacking stamina.

"Oh, Susie, rest, don't overdo it or you'll get sick," my mother would say.

"That's too far to walk, I'll drive you," my father would insist.

Attempting to open a jar, Dennis would come to my rescue. "Here, I'll get that."

Dennis was my opposite—strong, athletic, popular, good-looking, healthy, and even got an award for never missing a day of high school. I think he felt sorry for me and decided to take me on as his project to "improve" me, a makeover of sorts.

When he made the high school track team, he decided I needed to learn how to run fast and far. One day, we stood on the sidewalk, and he challenged me to run.

"Susie, keep your chest and head up, elbows bent, look forward when you run, and don't look down. Okay, GO!" he ordered me.

I ran and ran, arms flailing.

"Elbows bent and keep your head up!" I heard him yell.

"Okay, but I'm running out of breath," I yelled back.

"Don't talk, run!"

Looking straight ahead as he instructed, I missed an uneven part of the sidewalk, and down I went. Breathless, I howled, "I don't wanna run anymore! Leave me alone!"

When Dennis took judo lessons, he tried to teach me how to get out from under some thug who might, one day, hold me down. He pinned me.

"Okay, turn your hips and slide to your knees."

"What? You're too fat. I can't!" I grunted.

"Turn your hips and slide your knees under you. Turn! Turn your hips!"

I found this lesson ridiculously futile, got a case of the giggles, and couldn't stop. Dennis finally gave up. With his busy high school life, to my relief, he no longer bothered trying to help me avert what he probably thought was my impending doom of being a totally nerdy weakling.

And then I turned sixteen.

"You have to first step on the clutch with your left foot, shift into first gear, and then ease up on the clutch as you press down on the gas pedal with your right foot. Okay?"

He was teaching me how to drive his beloved 1950 VW Beetle. Beloved, because he'd spent months rebuilding its engine by following directions from his well-worn, spiral-bound copy of *How to Keep Your Volkswagen Alive, A Manual of Step by Step Procedures for the Compleat* [sic] *Idiot*.

I loved how the smooth, round, ivory-white gearshift knob, with a black incised diagram delineating the direction of the gears, fit so perfectly in my hand.

"Hey. Are you paying attention? Go!" he barked from the passenger seat.

"Oh yeah, okay."

I followed his instructions, but we suddenly lunged back and forth while a loud, high-pitched, metal-on-metal grinding sound screeched, and the car sputtered into silence.

Dennis took a deep breath. "All right try again. Don't forget, release the clutch *after* you shift gear and slowly press the gas pedal down at the same time."

Again, whiplash, and that annoying grinding sound. I tried it another time.

"Press down the clutch. Press it. Press it down. Keep pressing it!" His voice got louder as he kept repeating himself. The grinding sound screamed louder.

I tried it again.

"SUSIE! ALL THE WAY DOWN! PRESS THE CLUTCH ALL THE WAY DOWN BEFORE YOU SHIFT INTO GEA—"

That awful sound. His otherwise friendly face was now red, tightly contorted, and through the morning sun coming into the car, I saw the spit spraying out of his mouth as he shouted at me mercilessly. The windows were rolled up, creating a vacuum-like environment in the Beetle, and his loudness made my ears feel as if they had gotten boxed.

"STOP YELLING AT ME!" I started to cry.

"Okay," He said softly. "Try it again."

I repeated the process of the clutch, shift, gas in a variety of sequences until I eventually got the hang of the arcane art of driving Dennis's stick-shift Bug. At the time, I didn't appreciate his efforts to help me avert the certain impending doom of becoming a nerd, but retrospectively, he was just a good kid trying to help his little sister.

※

Christmas in our house was all about Dennis and me when we were children. Train sets and footballs for him, hula-hoops and dresses for me, and all my aunties in Hawai'i sent us gifts, creating a mountain of presents under and around our Christmas tree.

New Year's, however, was all about the adults. My family's Japanese heritage called for a New Year's Eve party as well as an open house the following day. Throughout the year, but especially during the Christmas and New Year's holidays, music filled the house. My father's favorite Hawaiian Christmas songs were those sung by Bing Crosby, including

"Mele Kalikimaka," playing from his eight-track tape player. My parents spent days preparing for their big New Year's Eve party hosting at least thirty guests, and another thirty for their New Year's Day open house.

"Balloons, party hats, toot horns, noisemakers, confetti, and a Happy New Year sign. Is there anything else we need?" my father asked.

"Don't forget paper plates, napkins, plastic forks, knives, spoons, and champagne glasses," my mother replied.

"Okay, after I pick up all of that, I'll go to the liquor store and get drinks and pop."

"And what about vacuuming and dusting?" she asked

"Don't worry, I will," he replied cheerfully.

These yearly parties were about the only times my father expressed himself "cheerfully," and for sure, ever pitched in with house duties. I thought it quite odd seeing a vacuum cleaner hose in his hand. But it was his party, and he happily helped my mother prepare for it. My mother spent days and nights preparing and cooking. Beautiful, delicious food was of utmost importance to her.

"Haoles won't try new foods that aren't pretty," she always said.

By haoles, she meant their Caucasian friends. Haole, a word used in Hawai`i that had neither negative nor positive implications, indicated Anglo ethnicity. She loved introducing her friends to elegantly presented Asian foods of new flavors and beauty. Although she felt her meals were simple, to her haole friends, they were an exotic leap from their typical palate. I believe my mother felt her guests' enjoyment of her cooking, a fusion of Japanese and Chinese foods with a flair of Hawai`i, was a small sign of their acceptance of her family and of our culture, which seemed so very important to her.

Served in the dining room, buffet-style, her feast presented a riot of colors, textures, and glorious fragrances. The breadth of my mother's New Year's Eve party menu was staggering:[10]

> Fried wontons
> Fancy cut fresh vegetables
> Sumi Salad
> Namasu Salad
> Cold soba noodle salad

Gobo salad
Purple Okinawan sweet potatoes
Seaweed salad
Chow Mein with pan-fried noodles
Fried rice with vegetables
Charcoal-grilled teriyaki chicken and vegetable kabobs
Tonkatsu
Oven-roasted Char siu short ribs finished on the grill
Tabletop-cooked Sukiyaki
Vegetable and Shrimp tempura
Nishime
Inari sushi
Chirashizushi

And for dessert, mochi, haupia, andagi, and fruit salad.

When my mother finished putting her food on the table, my father dinged a spoon against his cocktail glass. "Hey, everybody, dinner is served. Dig in!"

The guests queued in the dining room, merrily continuing their living room conversations and eager to eat.

"What's this?" asked my mother's neighbor, Patsy.

"We call it Tonkatsu. It's breaded, deep-fried pork. Don't forget to use the dipping sauce," my mother replied.

"Delicious—so delicious! I'd ask for your recipe, but it's easier to come over here and have it!" Patsy laughed.

"And what about that?" Eileen, my mother's co-worker, asked, pointing.

"Oh, Eileen, it's Inari-sushi. I brought some to work once, remember? You liked it, so have it again," my mother said.

"There's no raw fish wiggling around in it, is there? Ha-ha! I'm just kidding—I know they're not there," Eileen said. "Yes, I remember now, it's so good!"

"My favorite is her fried rice." Doug, Eileen's husband, chimed in.

My parents' guests tried all my mother's dishes, and no one went home hungry or thirsty. My father, the bartender for the night, kept everyone's cocktails fresh. At the stroke of midnight, everyone sang a robust "Auld Lang Syne" and a high-spirited rendition of "Mele Kalikimaka" with Bing Crosby singing in the background. My parents celebrated their New Year holidays like this well into their senior years.

{

"Susie, what do you think?" Bob asked, smiling as he joined me in bed. We curled into cozy spoons. He, at six feet tall, and I, at five feet four inches, fit together perfectly.

We read the small job advertisement that Bob had cut out from the Chicago Tribune posted by Rex-Hanna Corporation. If he went for it, this would be Bob's first "real" job application in his area of college studies, industrial management.

"Wow! $4.85 an hour?" I asked. "That's so cool! Are you going to apply?" It was a big salary for the early 1970s.

He thought for a minute. "Yes, I think I will!"

I giggled. "What would we do with all that money?"

We were starting our post-college lives together in our little two-bedroom, third-floor walk-up in Evanston, Illinois, a suburb north of Chicago.

"With my Japanese and your Nordic genes, our baby's gonna be beautiful, don't you think?" I asked, stroking my belly.

"Definitely." Bob laughed. "As long as he or she doesn't get my big nose!"

"Oh, you, I like your nose. It's very—you know—chiseled, like your jaw, and so Scandinavian!"

Bob got the job, and a few months later, our baby girl, Kristin, was born.

{

Bob and I started a tradition of celebrating a quiet New Year's Eve with our friends, Marcia and John. We'd known each other since Marcia and I were college roommates back in the day, and the four of us double-dated. My friendship with Marcia grew over the years—we knew each other inside and out, and our parents had become each other's parents. The fact our mothers, both with their kind and gentle natures, were alike in so many ways, and that Marcia's middle name was the same as my mother's first name, sealed our bond.

Bob and John, about the same height at six feet tall with similar colored hair, resembled each other, likely due to both having Scandinavian ethnic roots, Bob as Norwegian and John as Swedish. Although Marcia and I were both about five feet four inches tall, our appearances were worlds apart—she, a curly red-haired Irish/Dutch and I, a black-haired Japanese. Yet Marcia, an only child, and I were as close to being "sisters" as could be.

One New Year's celebration, not long after Marcia's father died, we invited her mother, Marcella, to join us for our usual calm New Year's Eve celebration. Marcia's daughter, Jennifer, like her mother, had curly red hair, and Kristin had straight dark brown hair, not black like mine—Bob's Caucasian genes had managed to squeak out some say in that regard! Only a month apart, our two babies played together, crawled around, and "talked" to each other as Marcia and I got dinner ready.

Marcella, with sweet delight, watched the children's every move.

"Look at those girls—they're so beautiful. And they look so much alike, don't they?" she exclaimed.

"Ummm," I said.

Marcia laughed. "Mom, you think they look alike?"

"Oh, Marcia, you know what I mean. Both of them crawling, putting everything in their mouths, talking to each other in their secret language. Babies are so much alike!"

Marcella was right. There is a universal beauty about babies that make people laugh and cry with joy. And our baby girls were no exception.

꙳

Fifteen months after Kristin was born, Bob and I had our second child, Jonathan. We'd come home from the hospital a few days after his birth when my parents, who lived a couple of miles away on the north side of Chicago, came by to meet their new grandbaby.

My mother, full of smiles, clapped her hands together. "It's lunchtime! I made *jook*,[11] so let's heat it up and eat."

"Thanks, Mom," I said, "but maybe later, okay? I'm not very hungry right now."

She turned to Bob. "Susie's nursing, so she needs to eat. Heat it, *wiki wiki!*"[12]

Bob dutifully took the shopping bag, filled with containers of food she'd brought, into the kitchen to prepare.

I lifted baby Jonathan and put him into my mother's outstretched arms.

"He's so big!" my father said. "He'll be as tall as Bob. How much does he weigh?" my father asked, leaning forward to get a better look, his bushy eyebrows raised high.

"Eight pounds five ounces," I said. "Yeah, our baby's a big guy! It was funny—when they wheeled me into the delivery room, the resident doctor predicted I would have a girl, and she would be very petite. Surprise!"

"*Kawaii, neh?*"[13] my mother said, stroking Jonathan's headful of black hair. "Look at his tiny fingers and that little nose, just like Kristin's! *Hapa haole*[14] children are always so beautiful!"

My mother spoke primarily English, interspersing Japanese and Hawaiian words and phrases now and then. I only spoke English but understood what she meant. Hapa haole is a term used in Hawai`i where my parents, my brother, Dennis, and I were born. After living there all their young-adult lives, my parents had moved to Chicago when I was three years old. While I was born in Hawai`i, I grew up in Chicago and considered the city my hometown. But my roots remained firmly in Hawai`i.

In spite of my parents' small frames, my father at five feet seven inches tall and my mother at five feet three inches, they had bigger-than-life spirits and hearts. In their mid-fifties, they were healthy, active, and over the moon, their family had expanded to two grandchildren.

As my mother and I continued to fawn over Jonathan, my father knelt by the window with Kristin.

"Ish meshy, meshy oba deh," she told my father, pointing to something outside.

"Meshy, meshy?" my father asked. He scratched his head.

Overhearing their "conversation," I smiled. *Oh boy. My father wasn't the most experienced or patient person when it came to figuring out what a toddler was trying to say.*

Kristin repeated, pointing upward. "Meshy oba dey. Meshy!"

"The sky?" he asked.

Frowning, she said, "Uh, uh. Oba dey! Oba dey!" She pointed upward.

My father looked outside again. "The clouds?"

"Uh, huh. Da cow."

"The clouds are meshy meshy?"

"Uh, huh. Da cow meshy! An den com dow!"

"Meshy," my father pondered, stroking his chin with his finger and thumb. "Messy? Do you mean messy? The clouds are messy?"

Kristin smiled broadly and said, "An den com dow!" She raised her arms over her head, and then let them fall.

"The clouds are messy, and then come down?"

"Uh, huh!" Kristin squealed, her eyes wide as she nodded up and down.

My father thought for a moment. "Yes, yes!" He laughed. "The clouds are messy, and then will come down. You're right; it does look like it's gonna rain today, Kristin!" My father and Kristin hugged with joy discovering their new common language.

He turned to us. "Did you hear that? She's a smart kid!"

I laughed. "I think you're the one who's pretty smart, figuring out that one!"

"Mom, what should I do with these eggs?" Bob called from the kitchen. "Are they cooked?"

My mother settled Jonathan in my arms as I sat in the rocking chair, and she scurried off to the kitchen.

"Hai, they're hard-boiled," she said. "Peel and slice them, okay? I'll heat the jook."

"How thick should I slice them?" Bob asked.

"Oh, I don't know—about like this." She held up her thumb and index finger about a quarter of an inch apart. "Do you have small bowls for the garnishes?"

"Will this work?" he asked, showing her some porcelain *chawans*.[15]

"Hai. When you finish with the eggs, you can cut the chicken—it's cooked."

"Sure!" Bob took care of the eggs, but when it came to the chicken, he hesitated.

"Umm, do I cut this way or that way?" Bob asked, holding his knife parallel to the long side of the chicken breast.

"Wait." My mother took his knife and swiped the blade several times against the bottom, unglazed part of the chawan's foot. "There. The knife's sharp now," she said, wiping off the knife. "Cut the chicken against the grain so the slices won't be stringy and chewy—here like this." She made a few cuts, her knife at a slight angle and perpendicular to the grain, creating thin, smoothly textured slices.

"Okay, everybody, lunch is ready," my mother announced.

I laid Jonathan in his bassinet while my father seated Kristin in her highchair.

My mother brought the pot of jook to the dining room table, and Bob followed her carrying a tray of nicely arranged garnishes, dishes, and bowls. He placed the tray on the table and ladled soup into each of our bowls, dropping small pieces of cubed chicken he'd cut for Kristin's bowl and an ice cube to cool it down for her.

I thought I wasn't hungry but smelling the rich aroma of my mother's jook wafting in the air aroused my appetite, and my stomach suddenly growled with emptiness.

Traditionally made with a seasonal turkey carcass, but not available this time of year, my mother improvised her jook by making it chicken-based, its broth lightly flavored with a bit of dashi and a delicate hint of ginger and shoyu. The tiny, shimmering droplets of oil dancing on top of the broth were mesmerizing. Alternate slices of tender white and dark meat lay splayed like a fan on an abundance of gently cooked celery in the rice soup. We took our bowls and topped the mixture with freshly blanched bean sprouts, cilantro leaves, and slices of hard-boiled eggs. A side dish of cubed tofu over mixed greens with a salad dressing of miso, sweetened rice vinegar, shoyu, sugar, and sesame oil, completed the meal.

"Oh, Mom, this is so good," I said. I turned to Kristin. "Do you like jook?"

She was too busy to answer. We were all silent watching her. Holding her baby spoon like a shovel, we saw her struggle trying to keep the soup from spilling out before getting it into her mouth. She tried again.

My hand flinched.

My mother put her hand on mine and in a lowered voice, said, "Give her a minute—let her use her *atama*."[16]

Kristin persevered. She finally ditched her spoon altogether, and took matters into her own hands, literally. Using her thumb and index finger, she delicately picked out the chicken pieces, bean sprouts, celery, and all the rest, one-by-one, relishing each of her treasures, and then put the bowl to her mouth and drank the soup.

"See, I knew she'd figure it out!" my mother said.

Kristin's broad smile showed off her sweet little baby teeth.

"Why?" Kristin asked. Just over two, I'm pretty sure she wasn't trying to torture me with her constant questions, but that was the net effect.

"Because when toys are on the floor, Jonathan can fall over them and hurt himself."

"Why?"

"Because he's not as steady on his feet as you are."

"Why?"

Upon hearing his name, Jonathan looked over at us.

Exasperated, I tried a different strategy. Switching my "voice of reason" to a higher-pitched, energetic tone, I said, "Okay, kids, it's time for a 'let's-clean-up-the-house' contest! Who can put the most toys in the toy box?"

"I can!" On a mission, Kristin scurried around the living room and dining room with reckless abandon, loading up her arms with toys.

"Good job, Kristin!"

Jonathan's primary mode of travel was crawling, but in an attempt to imitate his sister, he used the coffee table to hoist himself up to his feet and, walking like a drunken sailor, inadvertently got tangled up in Kristin's legs, bringing both kids tumbling to the floor. Toys flew everywhere, and Kristin and Jonathan howled with alligator tears as I scooped them up in my arms to console their bruised egos.

I sighed.

Well, that didn't go so well.

My attention was instantly piqued when I heard the sound of the front door latch turn.

Bob's home!

By the end of each day, having a conversation with anyone over two feet high brought me much needed "Mommy relief," and Bob's unfailing cheerfulness always perked me up. Handsome, lean, and tall with ash-brown hair, and eyes that, depending on what he wore and the hue of light around him, varied from sky-blue to deep-green, Bob was a welcome sight for my weary eyes.

"Hi! How was your day?" he asked, joining us on the floor in the mire of toys.

"Great. Just great. How was work?"

"My carpool didn't turn out so well this morning." He laughed. "I stood outside waiting for Gary to pick me up, and it turned out he was outside of his house waiting for Denny to pick him up, and Denny was waiting for anyone to show. When no one came, we drove ourselves, and we were all late for work. Other than that, I had a good day," he said as he went to the bedroom to change clothes.

"So why didn't you talk to each other and coordinate beforehand?" I asked, but he didn't hear me. "Dinner will be ready in a few minutes," I called out. "And don't forget, I'm spending the night at the Art Center."

After dinner just before dusk, I drove north on Sheridan Road under the lush canopies of grand elms and oaks, through one of Evanston's most prestigious neighborhoods. I turned east, onto a long driveway that led me to the Harley Clarke House. In the 1920s, Mr. Clarke, president of several utility companies, commissioned Chicago architect Richard Powers to design this nearly 20,000-square-foot, ivy-covered, rough-faced limestone Tudor Revival mansion. The home stood near the edge of a wooded bluff on idyllic grounds exquisitely designed in the Prairie Style by the landscape architect, Jens Jensen.

Over subsequent years, the property had changed hands several times until the City of Evanston had acquired and leased it to the Evanston Art Center—this was where I made art.

I parked, got out of my car, and walked a few feet east to the edge of the bluff, being careful not to step too far. I paused. Before me was the big sky above, and looking down the shallow but long, descent of stairs leading to the water, I saw the wave crests of Lake Michigan unfurling themselves along the beach shore in a slow, gentle tempo. I felt lightheaded, and my heartbeat quickened fearing I'd fall from the bluff. I stepped back and steadied myself. A gust of wind grabbed my hair, lifting it high to dance, like a waltz, twirling it in all directions, cooling my face, and tickling my scalp. I closed my eyes, intoxicated by the rhythmic sounds of water below and the scent of native plantings behind me.

Turning, I followed the aromas of the prairie, their country-like essence growing stronger as I approached the Art Center. Using my assigned key, I entered the mansion, stopping to admire, as if in reverence to its grand, elegantly curved staircase and wood-paneled surround, that led to the second and third floors.

An independent study student, it was my turn to oversee the pottery firing that evening. A high-fire gas kiln requires a preheat, firing, and cool-down, taking about eighteen hours, so no matter what time the firing process began, a late night of "kiln sitting" was usually required.

Arriving downstairs in the pottery studio, I found it empty of students and welcomed the silence. I took a deep breath and reveled in the fragrances of clay, glazes, and pots. The pots were in various stages of creation—wet, recently thrown pots waiting to dry to a leather-hard state for trimming, greenware ready for a bisque firing, and bisque ware waiting for glazing.

I walked through the central open space filled with counter height, canvas-covered tables for hand-building projects, electric and kick wheels, and open shelves along the walls. Passing the glaze room where buckets of ingredients such as silica, oxides, colorants, and salts were stored, and the clay room for mixing different types of clay bodies, I arrived at the kiln room. I went directly to the log of temperatures and notes my teacher had left me for the current firing. He'd had to leave the studio minutes before I'd arrived, so his log offered good coordination and information. I looked inside the kiln through its peephole and saw that one of four *pyrometric cones*[17] had bent.

Good progress—but we've got a ways to go.

I wedged an eight-pound ball of clay and threw it onto the wheel plate of my electric potter's wheel, aiming as close to its center as I could. Sitting down, I respectfully gazed at my honorable opponent—a malleable, greenish-gray beastly lump of stoneware clay with whom I would do battle. I sprinkled water on it to diminish friction between my hands and the clay. The whirring vibrato voice of the wheel's motor sang higher and higher in pitch as I pressed the foot pedal to accelerate the wheel plate's rpm, creating a powerful centrifugal force on the clay with which I would reckon. If I didn't maintain full command while getting my opponent centered on the wheel plate, it would vigorously catapult itself off the wheel airborne, across the room, or perhaps, into my chest.

Centering clay requires certain ambidexterity. Like the ebb and flow of an eddy, each hand takes on dominant and submissive roles, guiding the clay's defiant energy to its harmonious center. With my left elbow anchored firmly against the front of my hip, I leaned forward, and my left palm pushed against the beast empowered with the laws of physics, and with an equal and opposing force, my right palm pulled it toward me while the thick base of my thumbs pressed downward to compress it. I released my hands ever so slowly to briefly drizzle on a thin coating of water and continued my push-pull combat with the wobbling lump.

Following a good fight, my opponent finally acquiesced to my hands and settled into a symmetrical mound, dutifully centered on the wheel. The motor lowered its voice to a rhythmic hum as I reduced pressure on the foot pedal. I felt the clay body slowly rotating under my hands—wet, slippery, and submissive yet at the same time, noble and firm. The beast was tamed and beckoned me to transform it into a tall, beautiful vessel. I turned off my potter's wheel and rested. In the quiet of the studio, hearing only the low rumble of the gas kiln and feeling its warmth on my back, together with the heady, earthy scent of clay, I was at peace.

After several hours of intermittent inspections through the peephole and making necessary adjustments to the kiln's gas and oxygen control valves, the moment I'd been waiting for had finally arrived.

In a high-fire, about 2300+ degrees F, glazes go through a dramatic and violent chemical change from the consistency of a thin, pancake-like batter poured or brushed onto bisque ware, to a final hard finish when the firing is complete.

As the kiln approached its target temperature for clay body and glaze maturation, I watched the glazes go through its spellbinding metamorphosis. *"The glint of the sun on the ice,"* said Dr. Strawn, my undergraduate pottery professor years ago. It was a magical time when the glaze was neither solid nor liquid but rather, fluxing, shivering, and shimmering just before it bathed the pots with its final glass-like coating in the white-hot kiln. Carrying the euphoric image of the *"glint of the sun on the ice"* in my mind throughout my life, I searched to see and feel that extraordinary moment again not in the heat of a kiln, but as I later discovered, on certain cold winter days.

While monitoring the kiln, unwelcome thoughts burrowed into my head, filling me with anxiety.

What if something happened to Bob? I'm not talented enough to rely on my pottery sales to support the children. And what about college? There's no way!

"Nothing is going to happen to me, Susie," I imagined Bob saying. "I'm healthy, and I'll always be here for you and the kids. Now stop worrying; everything will be fine."

I wasn't convinced. Life happens. Death happens. I had to find a career that would allow me to contribute to our little family, and if necessary, support it. I had spent four years earning an undergraduate degree in art education with a minor in ceramics, and here I was, at age twenty-seven, realizing I had no clue about who I wanted to be, or what I wanted to do now that I was "grown-up."

Days later, hoping for inspiration, I requested curriculum catalogs from Northwestern University, whose campus was just a few blocks away, and from the University of Illinois at Chicago (UIC), located west of Chicago's downtown *Loop area*.[18] Northwestern's catalog arrived in the mail first, and with great anticipation, I skimmed their program offerings envisioning myself in various fields of work: Education, Law, Psychology, Healthcare, Social Services.

Nothing resonated.

Now what?

When UIC's catalog arrived weeks later, my enthusiasm had waned, and I put the package, unopened, on the coffee table where it lay for days.

Our living room's decor was stereotypical for the times: two faux-Parsons tables, one lemon yellow and the other bright chartreuse, and an overstuffed, light-brown, faux-leather couch on our faux Oriental rug. Flanking the sofa was a tall Dracaena Marginata on one side and a rubber tree plant on the other, with many philodendron vines in small pots balancing on the sash of windows that had been painted shut. A six-feet wide by five-feet tall macramé wall hanging I'd made while in college hung on one of the walls, and on another wall, a Peter Max-inspired Environmental Graphics wallpaper dominated the room. Groovy, it was.

Sitting in the sunny living room one morning, Bob sipped his cup of coffee while reading the newspaper, and the children quietly played with their toys as Vivaldi's music filled the air. Bob was a bit of an audiophile and had been an aficionado of classical music since he was in high school. When drafted into the army and sent to Vietnam in 1969, Bob spent some of his military stipends on a Sansui 5000A receiver and Teac reel-to-reel tape deck purchased from the PX. Bob and I married a few months after he fulfilled his military duty. With his brand-new prized acquisitions, along with his existing AR-XA turntable and Knight speakers, we always had excellent, quality music playing in our apartment. A member of the Musical Heritage Society and Columbia Record Club, he received a monthly vinyl album or cassette tape of symphonies, concerti, cantatas, piano solos, or chamber music by composers, like Bach, Beethoven, Chopin, Mozart, and Vivaldi. Classically trained in piano when I was a kid, but as an adult, I preferred listening to the music of Stevie Wonder, Roberta Flack, the Beatles (all of them), Eric Clapton, Harry Chapin, John Denver, and Rod Stewart.

On this day, however, I found the sound of Vivaldi's Concerto for Two Mandolins and Strings, II, Andante, GM RV 532, very soothing. Every time I heard this movement of the concerto, I'd remembered my early stages of labor with Jonathan as I lay on the living room couch in the middle of the night, waiting and listening to this very piece. The slow, dreamy pizzicato strings, like a heartbeat behind the sound of the mandolins, counted the seconds of Jonathan's journey. I wondered if that was why he was such a calm baby.

I glanced at UIC's packet of information lying on the coffee table. Opening it, I implored the envelope to include *hope*. Starting with 'A,' I began to review UIC's alphabetical list of program offerings. Suddenly, a program leaped off the page. "Architecture."

"Bob, this is it! I want to be an architect!"

He looked up from his newspaper and smiled. "Oh?"

"Yes, it's a perfect blend of my art background anchored by the technology I wanted. It found me!"

Hope emerged.

"I remember I wanted to be an architect when I was in high school," he said.

"Really? Why didn't you go for it?" I asked.

"I told my father, and he suggested I go into industrial management instead. So, I did!" Bob said with a shrug. "But I think you should go for architecture. How long is the program?" He paused. "And what about the kids?"

"I think it's a three-year master's program. Don't worry, I'll check into childcare. It shouldn't be a problem."

It was a problem. We were in an era when most mothers stayed at home with their kids, so there was little need for childcare centers, and those that did exist only accepted children who were potty trained, which Jonathan was not. But I discovered a little-known organization on the UIC campus called the Parent Co-op, located in the Student Center. There was a small fee, and its protocol was that for every three hours of class time, parents were asked to volunteer one hour of their time to help the teacher. It was a perfect arrangement for the children and me to transition from being together twenty-four-seven to being separated just a few hours at a time. I was one step closer to becoming a student again.

Bob was fully on-board with my plan as I went through the paces for acceptance into the architecture program. Some of my friends, however, were skeptical.

My downstairs neighbor, Karen, came up to visit one afternoon. She was pregnant with her first child, and between sips of our tea, we played with Kristin and Jonathan.

"An architect—huh." Karen's voice was measured. "That's interesting. When will you find out if you're accepted?"

"I don't know. It's been a month since I sent in my application and slides of my art portfolio. I want to know one way or another so that I can get on with my life."

"Well, listen, don't worry, if it doesn't work out, you can always be an interior decorator—that's what my mom is, and she loves it! And anyway, architecture is for guys!" Karen's eyes were bright, and her smile broad.

"Oh, I guess so." A fake smile pasted itself on my face.

What was she thinking? I'm going to get in, and that's that!

Coming home after a walk with the children a couple of weeks later, I found a packet from the University of Illinois, too large to fit in our tiny mailbox, laying on the mosaic tile floor in our building's little vestibule.

Okay. This is it.

Rather than waiting until we made the trek up to the third floor, I decided to open it then and there. I twisted and turned, taking Jonathan out of his baby backpack and held him on my lap as I slowly sunk myself onto the carpeted stairs.

"Kristin, why don't you sit down next to me, okay?" I grabbed her pink blanket from my big bag and gave it to her.

"Okay!" she said.

I opened the packet. Tingling in my scalp then rushed into my chest and down my arms. My hands trembled, and tears flowed as I read the cover letter.

"I'm in."

Turning to Kristin, I said, "I'm IN! I got into architecture school! Mommy's gonna be an architect!"

"Mommy, don't cry!" she said, near tears herself.

Standing Jonathan up on my lap, Kristin crawled into my outstretched arms, and I hugged both kids, bouncing them up and down.

"I'm happy, not sad!" I said.

I laughed and cried, hearing my joy echoing throughout our apartment building hallway.

It's all real now. It's gonna happen!

༚

The summer before my graduate studies began, Bob and I actively searched for our first home. We couldn't afford housing prices in Evanston, and I'd remembered when my undergraduate class was getting ready for student teaching, many of my classmates wanted an assignment in Oak Park, a suburb west of Chicago, because of the community's excellent school system. Bob and I looked in Oak Park and found an affordable home for our growing family. It would be a long, financial leap for us—after all, the purchase price was a whopping $32,000! But in our youthful spirit, we were filled with hope and confidence in our future.

༚

Susie Uehara, Suzie Uehara, Suzi Uehara. As a kid, I'd tried on each name for size. Because they were homophones, no one was aware of this name transition, but my young mind thought there were differences, visual mostly. In my simple, light-hearted experiment of looking for an identity, I'd written my name three different ways, but always, with hearts over the 'i.' In the end, though, I felt like the same person.

My second name transition occurred when I'd married Bob. Back in those days, society had little patience with a woman who kept her birth name, forsaking her husband's surname. Actresses did it all the time, but they seemed exempt from the long arm of the societal rule.

"What about the children's last name?" *they* would ask.

"There will be children, correct?" *they* would ask.

"How will people know if you're married or single?" *they* would ask.

I had the choice of keeping my name, for sure, but given the state of society at that time, I'd followed the path of least resistance and took Bob's name, Rakstang. I was surprised how difficult it was to change my name, not so much the administration of official documents but rather, with my identity. By acquiescing to societal tradition and changing my name to one thrust upon me, I broke the tether of my own family, in-name-only, of course. Still, it separated me from my mother, father, and brother, and I felt different.

What's in a name? Suck it up and deal with it.

It took a few years to grow into my new persona of Susie Rakstang, but eventually, I got used to it.

My third name transition happened when I began my graduate studies. I thought "Susie" was too cute for the serious architect I'd imagined and hoped to become.

"I changed my name," I announced to Bob one evening.

"What're you talking about?" he asked.

"Susie is too childish. When I start school, I don't want my professors resisting their paternal urge to pat me on the head. I'll introduce myself as 'Susan.' That's what I want." I gave a head nod to seal the deal.

"By me too? But I've always known you as, you know, Susie. You want me to call you 'Susan' now?"

He frowned.

I smiled.

"Okay, if that's what you want. I can tell you right now—it won't be easy, Susan. But I'll try."

Poor Bob—throughout all the years we'd known each other, I'd pushed his envelope asking him to support all my crazy ideas, projects, and aspirations, and he tried very hard to go with the flow. And he was always a good egg about it.

Some of my long-time friends found it pretty weird to make the name switch, and some avoided calling me by name altogether, which was okay with me but eventually, following Bob's lead, most managed. To my family and old friends, however, I am and will always be Susie—and I find that endearing.

On the first day of school, I was far from having a rhythm in getting the kids and myself up, dressed, fed, packing Jonathan's big baby bag with all things needed, finding Kristin's crucial pink blanket, making snacks for them, and getting together all my books.

I was lucky to get an assigned parking space on campus, halfway between the Art and Architecture (A&A) Building and the Student

Center, where the kids would be. Arriving in the campus parking lot, I retrieved Kristin's *Umbroller* stroller from the back of our old, preowned, school-bus-yellow Volvo station wagon, took her out of her car seat, and settled her in the stroller. After taking Jonathan out of his car seat, I wrestled him into his baby backpack, then gathered all our things for the day, and headed for the childcare center.

Wearing Jonathan on my back and walking up the stairs backward, I pulled Kristin in her stroller until we arrived on the second floor, where we wove our way through a crowd of students until we arrived at the Parent Co-Op. The facility was lovely, with its floor-to-ceiling windows bringing excellent daylight into the central learning room. Walls lined with lightly stained wood cubbies, each holding games, puzzles, and books, made the space look and feel organized and uncluttered. Separate bathrooms for boys and girls, as well as a crib room with a diaper changing station, accommodated all the needs of the pre-school kids.

Having met Miss Tamara, the children's teacher, only once during orientation, I re-introduced myself. A soft-spoken woman, compact and sturdy, about thirty-five years old with warm brown eyes and short black hair, Miss Tamara was trained in Montessori pre-school education.

"So good to see you again!" I said.

"And good seeing you," she said. "Let me get Jonathan out of his backpack."

I turned, bent my knees so she could reach him, and Miss Tamara lifted him out. Holding him in her arms, she bent down and welcomed Kristin.

"Why don't you go now," she told me. "The other parents and I will take good care of them while you're gone." Miss Tamara smiled and nodded.

Do I have to leave so soon?

I left my children on their first day of school, feeling a knot in my stomach as I walked to the A&A building for my first day of class.

The architectural curriculum at the university was robust and well planned. Presuming I would learn how the merging of art and technology would give me skills to design beautiful buildings and spaces, I'd found it was much more. A confluence of structure, means and methods of materials, context, technology, sociology, anthropology, psychology, history, art, mindfulness of all one's senses—that was architecture.

My day was a blur of activity. I enjoyed meeting my new classmates and professors and exploring the A&A building and other parts of the campus but was eager to get back to the co-op and see my kids. Shortly after I arrived, a hand tapped me on the shoulder, and I spun around.

"Susan, may I have a word with you?" Miss Tamara asked.

My eyes widened. *Uh oh.*

"Kristin refused to take her nap on a cot in the learning room with the other children," Miss Tamara said. "She's so sweet but headstrong! I just wanted you to know that Kristin insisted on napping on the floor next to her brother's crib. She said she wanted to make sure he didn't get lonely without her. She'd been firm about that, and there was no use arguing with her, so I made sure she slept on a blanket and had a cover and her pink blanket. Is that okay with you?"

Miss Tamara's words melted my heart as I heard how concerned Kristin was about her brother.

As she spoke, I remembered what had happened the previous day when I'd told the children, "All right, kids. Sesame Street is over. Time to stop watching TV."

"Awww. We wanna watch some more," Kristin whined.

Jonathan, eyes wide, nodded.

"Here's the deal, Kristin. You and Jonathan can watch fifteen more minutes, but after that, *you* have to turn off the TV. Okay?" I asked.

"Yes!" Her eyes lit up.

When the time was up, I reminded her to turn off the TV.

"NO! I want to watch some more," Kristin implored.

"Do you remember our deal?" I asked.

She nodded.

"So, you'll turn off the TV?"

"No!"

"Do you want to go to the corner?" I asked.

"NO! No corner! No corner!" she wailed.

I never understood why "going in the corner" was considered such a horrific threat, but I must admit, it was a pretty useful tool for action—although on this day, not so much.

"So, you'll turn off the TV?"

"NO!"

I guided her to the corner, and she cried with vigor.

In my periphery, I saw something moving on the floor. It was Jonathan. He'd quietly crawled up the stairs, found Kristin's pink blanket, somehow managed to safely crawl back down the stairs and dropped it at his sister's feet while she stood in the corner, facing the wall, crying her heart out. In his little young mind, he'd figured that this would bring Kristin comfort.

After a few minutes of hugging her blanket, Kristin stopped crying and quietly walked over to the TV and turned it off.

Wow. These kids are the best. I was filled up with love thinking about that moment.

Bringing me back to our conversation, Miss Tamara reiterated, "Ms. Rakstang? If you're not all right with Kristin napping on the floor, I could work with her and see if she would join the other children. What do you think?"

I shook my head. "Oh, no, that won't be necessary. Thank you for telling me. Kristin and Jonathan are best buddies, so I'm not surprised she wants to be with him, and he, with her. Thanks for understanding."

I packed up the kids and their things. Leaving the Parent Co-op, I looked back and saw Ms. Tamara kneeling next to a little boy. She was smiling and speaking softly to him as he returned a game, albeit a bit reluctantly, back in the cubby from where he had gotten it.

So that's how she keeps the co-op so tidy! I love this place.

In the 1970s, architectural students didn't key-in data into a computer for delineations but rather, drew presentations and details by hand. Drawings were an essential means of communicating our ideas and intentions to fellow students, professors, and eventually, to clients and contractors.

The ritual of architectural drawing aroused my disposition and internal inclination, giving me a heightened sense of fulfillment and satisfaction. I worked on mastering the precision of Rapidiograph technical ink pens with its interchangeable points measured in millimeters and handling the geometric forms of architectural and engineering scales, triangles, compasses, and circle templates. I loved drawing on smooth, milky-white translucent mylar sheets under which lay a flat, vinyl Borco desk cover. The Borco yielded to my pen pressure, allowing a continuous, uninterrupted flow of ink that connected lines to meet each other—exactly. Many of my drawing instruments were given to me by my mother when I'd majored in Art Education in undergraduate school—yes, she'd finally given up on Dennis becoming and engineer. I used those instruments so often that they became an extension of my hand, mind, and spirit. The further I delved into my graduate studies, the more I claimed architecture as mine, and knew it would become my passion and life's work.

One of the most horrible, exhilarating, frightening, yet instructive events of the architecture design studio was the end-of-quarter *crit*.[19] After preparing for weeks and pulling many "all-nighters," students presented and defended their drawings and models to jurors, who were visiting architects or architecture faculty, as well as an audience of our professors, fellow students, and anyone else who cared to attend. Our first project was to design an architect's office. Between classes, studying, and tending to my family's needs, I eked out as much time as I could to work on this project, but most of my progress happened after Bob and the kids were in bed. I was *en charette*,[20] preparing for my first crit the next day, and I was running out of time.

During these late-night hours, I rediscovered the magic of classical music. I played records by Mozart, Chopin, and Bach for background music when I needed to concentrate on my concept and design, and Beethoven when I needed a boost of energy and stamina while drawing and model making. On breaks, I listened intently to inspiring works by the great Ashkenazy, Rubenstein, Arrau, Gould, and Goode. It wasn't until the wee hours of the morning when I put the final touches on my project. I was ready.

Before going to bed, I decided to dress professionally for the crit, just in case that mattered, and would wear my hair pinned up in a bun.

But what, in my wardrobe of T-shirts and jeans, could work? And what the heck do professional women wear, anyway?

I rifled through old issues of Cosmopolitan magazines. The only photos I saw were of models in either a dress with low-cut necklines for a fun night out or a casual blouse with puffy sleeves and skin-tight, silky bell-bottom pants for a fun day out, with few options in between.

There's gotta be something in my closet.

Hearing Bob's usual thunderous snores, I knew he was fast asleep, but I tiptoed around him anyway and slid into our closet. Closing the door behind me, I turned on the light.

What a mess.

Seeing nothing viable for the crit hanging on the clothes rod, I resorted to looting the hamper. I found the navy skirt and white blouse I'd worn to a baby shower a week earlier. I inspected the garments, brought them to my face, and took a whiff.

Okay, this should work.

The only problem I saw was a pair of cute, red, and purple handprints on the back of the blouse.

Jonathan.

I remembered when it had happened. At the shower, after eating a bunch of blueberries and strawberries, Jonathan had come to me wanting me to carry him. When I picked him up, he wrapped his little arms around me, resting his sticky, gooey, red, and purple hands on my back.

It'll have to do. I'll hand-wash the blouse.

But the next morning, I found that through washing, the bright, colorful handprints had turned to murky, pukey, grayish-orangish, brownish amorphous stains when the blouse had dried.

Great.

I put on a sweater to cover it up and got the kids dressed, fed, and packed-up, but they were both moving in slow motion.

"C'mon, kids, we gotta get going!"

"Can we stay at home today?" Kristin asked in her sweet voice.

"No, not today. We have to go to school. C'mon, let's go!"

I nestled them into their car seats, then went back to the house to retrieve my project. My drawings, mounted on large sheets of foam-core board, barely fit flat in the back of our station wagon. I ran back to the house, got my model, and laid it on top of my drawings. Checking my watch, I saw we were running late. Our chilly autumn of 50 degrees the past few days had turned unseasonably warm that morning, so I took off my coat and threw it on the passenger seat.

Before putting the car in gear, I looked back to check the kids. I got out, went to the backseat and unbuttoned their jackets so they wouldn't overheat, as I seemed to be doing.

Arriving on campus, I parked the car, packed up the kids and their stuff, and took them to the Parent Co-op then ran back to my car to get my model. Carrying it like a precious wedding cake, I delivered it to the A&A studio. Returning to the car once again, I gathered my drawings and supplies for last-minute touch-ups and rushed back to the studio. I'd become hot and sweaty and couldn't wait to get settled in the studio where I knew I'd cool off.

The large, windowless, open-plan studio had concrete floors, walls, and high ceilings. With many classes held at the same time, it's no wonder there was always a frenzy of conversations, lectures, laughter, and sporadic outbursts of frustration, each utterance ricocheting from one concrete plane to another. Students consistently milled around, and seldom was there a quiet moment—except on crit days.

Were people quiet out of respect for the formal occasion, or in solemn sympathy for the poor students whose heads would soon be on the block?

Murmurs of about twenty people in the audience, sitting on drafting stools strewn around the studio, fell silent, as our professor, Mr. Dick Whitaker, and the three jurors, one-by-one navigated a circuitous path around audience members to the presentation area. Mr. Whitaker introduced, thanked, and welcomed the jurors, faculty, and students, and announced the order of presentations. I was scheduled to be the fourth of thirteen classmates to present. Instead of cooling off, my body temperature continued to rise. The crit commenced.

What the hell? Why hasn't the HVAC[21] kicked-in?

I learned later that mechanical systems for extensive facilities such as universities are not able to switch back and forth quickly from heating to cooling and back again to heating during temperature-fluctuating transitional seasons like fall and spring. It would be like trying to turn an ocean liner one hundred eighty degrees on a dime—it can't happen, and people just had to deal with it.

But I didn't know that at the time. All I knew was I was hot, and the sweater I wore, meant to hide the stains on the back of my blouse, was making me more so. I didn't want to take it off before I finished presenting my project, but when a bead of sweat rolled down the side of my face, and then another, and another, I knew I had to take it off.

When I did, I felt the grotesque stains on my blouse, in my mind's eye, inexplicably sear into my back like a branding iron.

The jurors were discussing the third project. The air around me was so thick with tension I kept forgetting to exhale before finally letting out a burst of a breath. I listened intently to the discussion, but the pesky image of that branded stain on my back kept muscling into my mind.

Mr. Whitaker called my name, and all eyes were on me. My heartbeat quickened, and feeling lightheaded, steadied myself as I got up from my stool. My nerves were on edge, but I somehow managed to present my work, then waited for the jurors to comment.

Silence.

I could practically hear the tick-tock of my watch.

Finally, a juror, a young man of medium height with blond hair and round, wire-rimmed glasses, spoke.

"Susan, your drawings are nice—very precise, clean, crisp. Your design concept is okay, but could have been stronger," he said.

Hmmm. Pretty lukewarm, but I'll take it!

Then another juror, a middle-aged, tall, dark-haired faculty professor, his thumb under his chin and his index finger stroking his mustache, stood up and inspected my model.

"Why did you use so many curvy walls? What's the point?" he asked.

"Well, I thought the curved walls made the workspace flow nicely and—"

"I hate curvy walls," he said. "Straight walls are so much more efficient. Your curvy walls are arbitrary and irrelevant. This plan is ridiculous. My seven-year-old son could have designed a better space than this!"

I was horrified, wounded, and embarrassed.

How can he be so uncivil?

My crit was a disaster.

Over the next few days, my mind replayed the crit like a needle stuck in a loop on a scratched record groove—my plans, the model, design concept, the jurors' comments. I was exhausted. I wanted to quit school and run away. Eventually, though, I managed to stop the cycle of my mind's torturous and constant rewinds and replays when I admitted to myself that maybe the professor had made essential points. I did not have a good defense for my concept, and in the end, I understood there was no room for arbitrariness in practical design. Every line on a drawing had to have a purpose, and I tried never to make that mistake again.

A week after the crit, I stopped by Mr. Whitaker's office and asked if he had a moment to talk.

"Of course, come in! How are you?" He smiled.

Tall and lean with bright blue eyes and a bushy, salt-and-pepper mustache, Mr. Whitaker, my first of many professors over the following three years of studies, would introduce and mold my thoughts and sensibilities on the art of architecture. Now a practicing architect in Chicago, he was one of the principal designers and founders of *MLTW*,[22] the architectural firm that designed the iconic Sea Ranch along the northern coast of California in the 1960s. It was he who sensitized me and opened my imagination to the notion of contextual design and experiencing architecture with all my senses. It was he who inspired me.

"Oh, fine, I guess," I said. "I'm pretty much over the crit, but it did a number on me."

"How so?" He wrinkled his brow.

"You know, the part about the juror's seven-year-old son could design a better space than me. It was pretty humiliating."

"Oh, *that!*" Mr. Whitaker waved his hand. "Don't worry about it. It wasn't an appropriate thing for him to say—jurors aren't usually as animated as he was. You handled yourself well, so just put it behind you."

Really? Hallelujah!

"I'll try. Thanks so much."

"Say, as long as you're here," Mr. Whitaker said, "I've meant to ask you—I'm working on a project and could use some help with the drawings. Would you be interested in doing some part-time work?"

Wait. Did I hear him right? He wants me to work for him?

"Yes! I would be very interested!" I said.

"Very well. We can discuss the details later. Is there anything else you'd like to talk about?"

"Uh, no, not at all. Thanks for your time and understanding. Thank you."

I turned and left Mr. Whitaker's office, floating on cloud nine.

Yes!

At the end of my first year of studies, I received a letter of congratulations indicating that, based on my design portfolio and professors' letters of support, I'd been awarded a coveted scholarship from the Women's Architectural League (WAL), Chicago Chapter. The organization's membership was comprised primarily of wives of architects. The award would be a tremendous help to Bob's and my desperately challenged finances, given the costs of tuition, books, and supplies. I was happy, honored, and grateful to receive the scholarship and couldn't wait to tell my family and friends. But a few weeks later, I received a phone call from the organization's president who, in an officious tone of voice, indicated that WAL must renege on the award.

"I'm sorry, but the scholarship terms specify the award shall go to the most qualified *boy*," she emphasized, "in the UIC architecture program."

"But—but I'm not sure I understand," I said.

She rephrased her position, but the message was clear: WAL wouldn't give me the scholarship they'd promised.

I could barely hear myself say, "Yes, I see. Okay, thank you."

Numb, I returned the phone, in slow motion, to its cradle. While trying to process what had happened, self-doubt, lack of confidence, and paranoia suddenly blasted into my head with the power and speed of a runaway freight train.

Did my professors change their minds and retract their letters of support for me? Did WAL have second thoughts about my worthiness?

A wave of shame enveloped me.

Then dark, conspiratorial thoughts jumped into my fast-moving mind.

It seemed so ironic that a league named after women would give scholarships only to boys. Was WAL's real goal to discourage women from the field of architecture to preserve their husbands' brotherhood of architects?

I was angry—I shook my head.

Gender-specific discrimination was never a part of my world of family, friends, pottery, or even in my new academic environment that I was aware of—or was it?

My mind was in a muddle. I found Bob in the dining room. Pushing out a sigh, I swallowed deeply.

"That was the president of the Women's Architectural League," I said, barely over a whisper.

"What?" he asked.

I repeated myself.

"What's that?"

Feeling my cheeks and the back of my eyes heat, my impatience with Bob spiked.

"You *know*, the group who awarded me the scholarship. The president said I couldn't have it because only boys qualified." My voice cracked.

"What are you talking about?" Bob asked.

He's making me spell it out!

Taking a deep breath, I spoke slowly. "They're reneging my scholarship. The president said they'd only award it to the most qualified *boy*."

"They can't do that—what did you say?"

By then, I was in pure and complete frustration mode, my voice loud, rising about two octaves higher, and tears flowing.

"I told her, 'Okay, thank you.' What else could I say? She's the president of WAL, and I'm just a first-year grad student!" I spat out. "I didn't want to make any trouble. I was lucky even to get accepted into the program!"

"You deserved that scholarship, Susan. They can't get away with this. You need to stand up for yourself."

Right. I should have asked, "Why don't you change your damn outdated, gender-biased rules!"

But I felt weak. I didn't have the courage or chutzpah to stand up for myself and for other women who followed in the program—all I could say was, "Okay, thank you." I regretted that. I also regretted that I would continue to financially burden my family for two more years with all the expenses of my studies. By this time, I was sobbing.

"We have so many bills, Bob! Pediatrician. Charge-accounts. Companies keep calling, asking for payments. How can we keep this up for two more years? This scholarship would have at least covered my school expenses."

Bob reached out and wrapped his arms around me.

"Don't worry about the bills, Susan. I've had people shooting at me in Vietnam aiming to kill. Nothing can be scarier than that, at least not bills. We'll get through it," he promised.

Later that night, I looked at the calendar and saw I had just enough time to apply for a merit-based tuition waiver from the university for the following academic year. A couple of months afterward, I was informed that I got it. The award helped to assuage the sting of the WAL scholarship debacle but did not help me forget.

༄

The Parent Co-op was a perfect childcare solution for us. Still, as the children got older, Bob and I thought a local Montessori International pre-school and daycare would provide a good foundation for learning before they entered grammar school. With Miss Tamara's early childhood training in the Montessori method, we thought the children's experience with her would offer an ideal transition to a full Montessori school.

Bob, the children, and I visited the school for the first time. Sharing space in a building owned by Calvary Memorial Church in Oak Park, this grand Romanesque style of warm, rough-hewn granite, limestone arches, and a large bell-tower was a beautiful setting for the creative and supportive Montessori learning method.

We made our way inside and found the classrooms. Like the Parent Co-op, many windows in the space naturally lit up the room. Cubbies lined the walls, and some rows extended into the room, creating peninsulas holding beautiful learning materials. The cubbies weren't jammed-packed with toys and books like ours at home but rather, in each cubby, sat a single attractive, tactile, colorful, or natural wood learning material.

"Good morning! You must be Mr. and Mrs. Rakstang?" asked Mrs. Gupta, the head-teacher. She was a mature woman with large, warm brown eyes, a single, long black braid cascading down her back, and a lovely soft, gentle voice that seemed to have a blended accent of part British, part Indian.

"Good morning, thank you for letting us visit your school," Bob replied.

"You're very welcome. Let me call Estelle so she can join us," Mrs. Gupta said.

Estelle had short, dark hair with soft curls and appeared to be Mrs. Gupta's junior. Bending down on one knee and looking directly at Jonathan, Estelle said, "Good morning, Jonathan. I'll be your teacher. Would you like to see the classroom?" She shared Mrs. Gupta's lovely accent. Estelle extended her hand to Jonathan. He nodded, letting go of my hand, taking hers, and off they went.

See you, Jonathan——how easily he took her hand!

Mrs. Gupta also bent down to Kristin's level. "And I'll be your new teacher. How are you today?"

"I'm fine." Kristin looked down at her shoes.

"How old are you?" Mrs. Gupta asked.

"I'm four years old," Kristin said, her face brightening. "And that's my brother." She pointed to Jonathan across the room. "He's three years old." She then glanced at me. "That's my mommy, she's thirty years old, but I don't know how old my daddy is!"

Mrs. Gupta's eyes became full, and her mouth opened with surprised delight. She, Bob, and I laughed. Mrs. Gupta and Kristin turned and explored the classroom.

"I love their teachers!" I whispered to Bob.

"Yeah, and the kids seem to as well," he said.

Children of varying ages, between about three to six years old, were either sitting on the carpeted floor or at tables "working" with the learning materials in groups or singularly. I could hear a rhythmic murmuring of conversations, but it was not noisy.

After seeing the children so engaged with the other children and teachers, I looked up at Bob, smiled, and nodded. He responded with a grin and gently squeezed my hand.

"I wish we could let this visit last longer, but I have to take them to the co-op and go to class—I'm gonna be late if we don't leave right now," I told Bob.

"Yeah, and I have to get to work. Let's let the kids know we have to leave."

Driving to campus, I asked the children what they thought about the school they'd be attending.

"I like it!" Jonathan said, "They gave us cookies!"

"I do too. Is it going to be our new school from now on?" Kristin asked.

"Uh, huh. Dad and I need to get some paperwork to them, and then you can start going there instead of the co-op, okay?"

"Okay!" they said in unison.

On the children's first day of their new school, I was confident they would settle nicely into the excellent Montessori environment. Walking into the classroom with the children, I said, "Okay, here we are! Oh, Jonathan look, there's Estelle. And I see Mrs. Gupta too!"

Estelle walked over with a huge smile. "Hi, Jonathan. Let's go with Kristin and take her to Mrs. Gupta, okay?" Smiling and nodding, Estelle and I made eye contact, and she mouthed the words, "You can go now."

As I turned to leave, Jonathan looked up at me with a confused expression and called out,

"Mommy?" Suddenly, he wrapped his little arms and legs tightly around one of my legs.

"Mommy, don't go! Don't go, Mommy! Let's go home! I wanna go home! Don't leave me!"

Kristin's eyes widened, and she began to sob.

Oh my god! I'm a horrible mother!

Estelle quickly began to whisper to Jonathan as she peeled him away from my leg. "Go ahead, Mrs. Rakstang. They'll be fine." Mrs. Gupta hurried to comfort Kristin.

I took a deep breath and walked away. When I got inside my car, the tears flowed.

At the end of my day of classes and work, I hurried to the children's school and looking through a small window in their classroom door, I spotted Kristin and Jonathan. Kristin was with a teacher's helper working with cards of colorful geometric shapes, and Jonathan was on the floor, working on a three-dimensional puzzle.

My heart leaped when I saw their content faces.

Maybe I'm not so horrible a mother, after all.

My brother, Dennis, and his wife, Jane, stayed with us for a few weeks before leaving for their road trip to California. He had just finished med school at the University of Illinois, the same place where Jane was a medical researcher.

Helping me put Kristin and Jonathan to bed for a nap one Saturday afternoon, Jane whispered, "I can't believe they go down for their naps so easily!" Soft-spoken, of slight stature, and with long, straight black hair, Jane was a kind, caring person.

I smiled. "The children still love to sleep, thank goodness—I need the break!"

Jane and I kissed the kids, and off they went into dreamland. Leaving their rooms, she said, "Boy, when I have kids, I sure hope they love to sleep, too!"

We went downstairs and joined Dennis and Bob in our living room. The room ran the width of our house, a little over twenty feet, and about fifteen feet deep. Four pairs of floor-to-ceiling arched doors, each with French-style divided panes of glass, spanned the entire front, south-facing wall letting in glorious daylight. During the autumn, when nearby trees changed colors, the sun bounced from the trees to our living room, lighting it up with a riot of fall colors.

"Are you excited to go to California?" I asked Jane.

"Yes, I'm looking forward to it! I have relatives there, so it'll be great spending time with them."

"How long did you say you'd be there?" I asked Dennis. At five feet ten inches tall, with a compact build and shock of thick black hair, he always seemed bigger-than-life to me when we were growing up—but then again, I was such a small kid everyone seemed bigger-than-life to me.

"Well, I'll be at the University of California, Irvine for a year so I can do my internship in general surgery," he said. "After that, we'll come back to Chicago for my two-year residency in emergency medicine at the University of Chicago Hospitals and Clinics."

"Wait, I didn't know there was a specialty for emergency work. I thought any doctor—dermatologist, ear-nose-throat doctor, or whatever, did moonlighting in emergency rooms. Last time I went to the ER for stomach pain, my doc was an ENT."

"Yeah, that's how it is now, but it's changing. More and more hospitals are slowly but surely offering emergency medicine residency programs. Hopefully, when I finish at U of C, I'll get a job here in the city. At least that's the plan."

We were all young, in our early thirties, and high-spirited with big ideas for a prosperous future. But in the meantime, with little pocket money to spare, Bob and Dennis resorted to their own creative devices for entertainment.

"It's gonna be nice tomorrow," Bob said to Dennis. "Wanna golf?"

"Sure, same time, same place?" Dennis asked.

"What golf course?" I asked.

"Canal Shores," Bob said, "in Evanston."

Bob and Dennis looked at each other with mischievous smiles.

The next morning, they left our house before Jane, the kids, and I woke up. But oddly, the pair returned as we were fixing breakfast.

"Wow, that was a fast game!" Jane remarked.

"Yeah, well, we ran into a little interference. We saw the guy in the hut, so we left," Dennis said, chuckling.

"A guy in a hut stopped you from playing?" she asked.

By now, Bob and Dennis were laughing and 'fessed up.

"We got to the course by 4:30, before daybreak," Dennis said, "like we always do, and no one was at the pay booth hut—they're never there that early, so we just started to play."

"And you didn't pay anyone to golf?" Jane asked Dennis.

"Well, no. There was no one in the hut!"

I laughed. "Hooligans! So, you played golf in the dark for free? All this to save a four-dollar green fee?"

"No, it was dark for only a few holes, and besides, four dollars is a lot of money!" Dennis said.

"And then around the sixth hole," said Bob, "another golfer asked if he could partner up with us. He was pretty good."

"He was too good. I was getting depressed," Dennis chimed in. "We can usually play all eighteen holes for free because the guy at the ninth-hole hut, who's supposed to check for paid receipts from golfers, never showed up. But this morning, he checked everyone. So, we left."

"You left in the middle of the game?" I asked with a laugh. "What about your golf partner?"

"Oh, he had a receipt, so he kept playing. And besides, he was too good for us," Bob said, nodding.

"You just left him alone?"

"Yeah. What's wrong with that?" Bob asked.

"I can't believe you," I said, giggling. "You're like a couple of high school guys—talk about youthful indiscretion!"

I think that may have been the last time they played for free at the Canal Shores Golf Course. Years later, we learned that actor Bill Murray and his brother were caddies and concession workers at that very golf course in the late 1970s, and some of their experiences inspired scenes for the movie "Caddyshack." Who knows? Maybe one of them was the guy in the ninth-hole hut.

※

Working for Mr. Whitaker was magical—there I was, a second-year student working for an architect of highly acclaimed projects.

Crazy.

His loft office was unlike any workspace I had ever seen. There were high ceilings with few wall partitions. The open floor plan, interrupted only by structural columns and drafting tables, was surrounded by perimeter brick walls with large spans of industrial windows bringing in diagonal swaths of sunlight, dynamically accentuating the breadth of open space. To me, the loft environment expressed an honesty in architecture with its exposed infrastructure of columns, beams, HVAC ductwork, plumbing pipes, neatly spaced electrical conduit, all of which would forever mold my thoughts about the architectural language of open, interior spaces. It was a joyous discovery.

That night, I thought out loud to Bob. "Let's see—first, I'll drive the kids to Montessori, and then head to UIC to sit for my exam. After that, I'll catch a bus to Mr. Whitaker's office to work for a few hours, take the bus back to campus to pick up the car, drive to Oak Park to pick up groceries for dinner, pick up the kids from school, and then come home." I sighed. "So, that's my plan for tomorrow."

"What about lunch?" Bob asked.

"No time for lunch. I'll have to grab something from the vending machines."

"I'll be in meetings all day tomorrow. What time do you think you'll be home?" he asked.

"Probably around six."

After bundling up the children in their snowsuits, boots, hats, scarves, and gloves the next morning, I situated them into their car seats, their arms and legs sticking out like little penguins, and ran back to the house to grab my books and supplies. When I returned to the car, I discovered Kristin had thrown up all over the place.

"Oh my god, Kristin! Are you okay?" She started crying, and Jonathan followed in sympathy. I unpacked them from their car seats, and we went back to the house.

She had a fever. After cleaning her up, I called the pediatrician and made an appointment for later that morning.

Time, time, time. What do I do now?

My experience of being denied a scholarship due to my gender was still lingering in my mind—I thought it was behind me but apparently not. That incident had transformed me. It was a bell that couldn't be un-rung.

Do I tell Mr. Whitaker and my teacher the truth, that I won't be showing up today because my kid was sick? If I do that, will it remind them that I was a mother, consequently reinforcing stereotypical notions that calling-off because of kid issues, is why hiring women would be a hassle?

Or do I lie?

These were the kinds of issues with which I grappled. I was a woman in a male-dominated industry, many of whom had wives at home, like the women of WAL, to take care of such familial situations. Running out of time, I had to make the calls soon. I made my decision.

"Hello, Mr. Whitaker? It's Susan. I'm afraid I've come down with the flu and won't be able to come in today . . ."

"Hello, Mr. Gerstner? I'm afraid I've come down with the flu and won't be able to take the exam . . ."

I had no mentor, nor seasoned females to reach out to because women in architecture were far and few between—I felt very alone. Some time ago, I'd decided to set rules for myself so that I wouldn't stand out. I didn't wear frilly, ruffled, laced clothing or jewelry except for my wedding ring and occasionally, the strand of pearls my mother had given me. I kept a pair of jeans, a shirt, and Red Wing steel-toe boots in my desk drawer, so I'd be prepared for any emergency job site visits. I didn't keep family pictures on my desk or talk proudly about my children—and for sure, I wouldn't call-off because of a sick kid. "Be prepared, keep my nose to the grindstone, don't look up, and maybe they won't notice I'm not a guy." That was my mantra.

Negotiating this steep, jagged terrain of work outside the home was a daunting venture. Seldom feeling I had a solid foothold on these kinds of familial situations that faced me, I had little upon which to rely, except my instincts, few tools, and little experience to handle the climb. I sometimes thought of myself as a circus clown, trying to keep all the bowling pins in the air, and each time I was distracted, the pins would come crashing down. Nevertheless, I persevered.

A few hours after we got home from the pediatrician's office, Jonathan threw up.

Yep. Sure, why not?

I called my mother for some sympathy I'd desperately needed.

"I took Kristin to the doctor today. She has the flu. And now, Jonathan has it!"

"Oh no—*kawaiso, neh?*"[23] How are they?" my mother asked.

"Kristin has a fever, but not Jonathan. But they can't keep food down without throwing up."

"Did you give them *okai?*"[24] she asked. My mother made that for me when I was a sick kid, and it was always so comforting.

"Oh, yeah, I forgot about okai. How do I make it?"

"It's easy. Just cook rice with a lot of water and let it cool down," she said.

"Like, how much water?"

"Oh, I don't know—a lot. Four or five cups of water for one cup of rice, maybe. Keep checking while it's cooking and add more water if you need to. The rice should be nice and soft."

"Do I need to do anything else?"

"You can add a little dashi, just a bit for flavor. And add some miso, *chotto*[25] so that the children will get a little protein. Do you have chicken?"

"Uh, hang on." I checked my freezer. "Yes, I have some."

"Okay, cook it and cut it up in tiny pieces and put it on top of the okai. And maybe a little bit of well-cooked celery—just a little bit, so they get some vegetables."

"I'll make it right now. Thanks, Mom!"

The kids ate the okai after their nap and seemed to feel much better.

When Bob got home, I told him all about the kids.

"Why didn't you call me?" asked Bob.

"I didn't want to bother you. You said you had meetings all day. What could you have done if I called you, anyway?"

"Well, nothing, but at least I would've known."

"Whatever," I said.

It didn't matter. The thought of calling Bob never occurred to me. Short of a real emergency, I knew these kinds of issues were mine, and mine alone. That's just how it was.

The children recovered from the flu and continued to do very well at the Montessori school. One night, as Bob and I were putting dinner on the table, Kristin and Jonathan happily chattered away.

Kristin began to sing. "Goslaf is everywhere. Goslaf is over me, goslaf is under me, goslaf is around me, goslaf is everywhere."

Bob and I had no idea what she was singing about until we started eating.

"Mommy, can I have more goslaf?" she asked.

"What is goslaf, Kristin?"

She pointed to the coleslaw.

"Oh my god, Bob. She's been singing about coleslaw! I wonder if her class had been singing about God's love is everywhere, but Kristin thinks it's about coleslaw!"

Bob and I started laughing hysterically.

"Okay, that's it!" I said in between laughs. "We need to introduce religious education to our children's lives. Don't you think it's about time, now?" I turned to Bob.

He was laughing too hard to answer.

And that was how we went from worshipping coleslaw to God.

※

"You're sure you want to go ahead with this?" Bob asked.

His knees were bent, torso slightly forward, hands firmly wrapped around a crowbar as he would a baseball bat, mouth still, but his eyes, looking blue/green that day, were full and sparkling. Looking like a batter in the box, he held his breath, waiting for me to pitch the answer so he could take a swing and start demolishing walls.

"Yes, I think so," I answered. "No, wait!"

Checking his swing and standing up tall, Bob pushed out his breath with an audible sigh.

"Wait for what? We've talked about this for months!"

Our home was a real fixer-upper. I was still an architecture student, not yet ready to change the world, but ready to experiment on our house, a two-story, fifty-plus-year-old, traditional 1920s American Foursquare. Its first floor had a kitchen, breakfast nook, dining room, and living room, and four boxy-shaped bedrooms tucked in each corner of the second floor, all pleading to me for change, or so I was convinced. Like a mad scientist, I wanted to use our house as my laboratory to deconstruct, reconstruct, replace, alter, and re-alter architectural elements to learn how our living environment could more meaningfully affect our senses as we moved through space.

"Susan, did you hear me? Wait for what?" Bob's question brought me back to the present.

"Uh, well," I said, "we need dust masks, more tarps to protect the floor, a fan set in reverse so it can suck the dust out of the house, and the smoke detectors need to be covered."

I was stalling. Like the loft where I worked, I wanted to release our home's traditional, spatially constricted rooms and deconstruct its walls so space could flow without bumping into partitions. But the minute Bob asked me what I was waiting for, the thought of actually demolishing walls suddenly confounded my sensibilities of how high the toll in time and money this project would cost. My mind was stuck. Then I thought, "A journey of a thousand miles . . ."

"Okay, yes, let's do it!" I said.

Bob smiled. He landed his first blow to the wall with the curved part of the crowbar, but the solid plaster wouldn't budge. Again, he swung.

"This isn't working, can you hand me the sledgehammer?"

I did.

And with the will of a mighty batter, he swung, penetrating the wall, then shoved the curved end of the crowbar behind the lath and plaster and pried chunks of it away from the wood studs. Ubiquitous plaster dust left its veil everywhere, including on Bob. When he took off his safety glasses, his ghostly face turned to me, and his smiling eyes looked ever greener.

That was the start of rehabilitating our living spaces for the next two decades, not just the first home we would eventually outgrow, but our next home as well.

※

My third and final year of architecture studies brought almost unbearable curricula requirements when the pace ramped up in speed and intensity with daunting demands of tight deadlines for design projects, exams, presentations, structural engineering, environmental controls, and means and methods of technology. Those subjects paled in comparison to my head spinning, hair-splitting scheduling demands at home.

I was grateful for Hephzibah Children's Association. Hebrew for comforting mother, Hephzibah began as an orphanage in Oak Park in the late 1800s, but as time passed and society changed, it evolved from an orphanage to a before-and-after school daycare center. True to its long and honorable history, Hephzibah continued its safe, nurturing environment, allowing children to flourish socially, culturally, and academically. Bob and I took turns, depending on our schedules, dropping off and picking up Kristin, who was in first grade, and Jonathan, in kindergarten, from Hephzibah.

Under normal conditions, our daily routine ran like a well-oiled, albeit fragile, machine. All it took, however, was a mere pebble to bring down that machine to fits and sputters. The flu, a cold, a tummy ache, not to mention Bob's last-minute business travel, were enough to throw my schedule into a tailspin.

"I'm flying to New Jersey Thursday morning for a meeting, and I'll be home Friday, in time to pick up the kids from Hephzibah," Bob said.

"What?" I asked. "You told me you were going out of town *next* week. I have a study group Thursday night that I can't miss—my final is Friday!"

"I *am* going out of town next week, but I told you I'm going *this* week too."

"Fine! I'll figure out something," I groused.

I didn't make it to the study group. After picking up the kids from Hephzibah, fixing dinner, making lunch for their next day, and getting them settled in bed with a story, I was finally ready to study. Hunkered down at the dining room table with my calculator, books, notes, plenty of scratch paper for figuring out formulas, number two sharpened pencils neatly lined up before me, I braced myself for a long night of number crunching. I was preparing for my final exam in Statics, the analysis of loads and forces on a system, and developing calculations to bring those forces to static equilibrium.

Suddenly, I gasped. My Texas Instrument calculator, inexplicably, had gone dark. I changed the battery that reaped nothing. Not a simple four-function calculator, this was a fully loaded scientific calculator with functions of sin, cosine, logarithmic, trigonometric, and exponential functions, all of which I needed for my exam.

My heart rate quickened—I could hear it and feel it.

This can't be. No! No! Breathe.

I called some friends to ask if they had an extra one. Of course, they didn't—these calculators, well before personal computers were available, were expensive and no way could any of us afford to have an extra one.

I looked at my watch. It was late, but I still had time. In my last-ditch effort, I called Sears Roebuck to see if their electronics department had the calculator I desperately needed.

"Please, please, please answer," I begged the phone.

"Oh, hi. Do you have a Texas Instrument TI-30 calculator?" I waited for the salesperson to check. He returned and gave me the answer I needed. "Thank you! I'll be right there! Oh, wait, what time do you close? Okay, thanks!"

YES!

I had enough time to get there. I called my neighbor and asked if she would come over while the kids slept.

Arriving at Sears at such a late hour was a little eerie as I was seemingly the only customer left in the store, but I caught up with the salesperson with whom I spoke on the phone.

"Thank god, you have the calculator, thank you so much!"

"Yes, here's a new box. It's the last one! Oh, it's heavy—must be a pretty fancy calculator," he remarked.

I paid for my life-saving purchase, turned, waited for the security attendant to unlock the door to let me out, and dashed home. I made a fresh pot of coffee and looking at my watch, saw I'd already lost a lot of time. I sat down and took the calculator box out of the bag.

Lucky, lucky, lucky. How lucky was this? I smiled.

I opened the box. In it was a thick, substantial owner's manual. I removed it, and my heart stopped. I could feel my scalp tingle, and my hair stand up. Other than the manual, the box was empty. The calculator was absent. Gone. Incredulous, I rummaged through the box, again and again, trying to make sense of this disaster.

Damn! You've GOT to be kidding me.

"The calculator must've been in Sears's display case, and this was the box for it," I whispered to myself.

I checked my watch and saw that Sears had closed. I'd run out of options. I'd run out of time.

I shut my eyes. My head hurt, my body ached, and hot tears flowed as I went into full-throated, inconsolable, irrational, self-pity mode. I felt as doomed as *Sisyphus*,[26] who spent time pushing a boulder up a hill, only to have it repeatedly roll back down. My mind started its downward spiral into a dark abyss as I realized what an enemy Time was. It stepped in front of me, getting in my way, stealing minutes from me, and then hours, and then days. Time was my thief, and my wristwatch was its accomplice. The timepiece, inextricably integral to my wrist right down to the skin, muscles, and bones, dictated its commands to me, checked on me, reminded me of the children's schedules, Bob's work travels, house cleaning, laundry, meal planning, food shopping, and cooking. Time taunted me. I was always behind schedule, never ahead of it, and trying to steal back time I believed was rightfully mine was like trying to grab a thread of water. I surrendered to Time and its accomplice as if I was their humble servant, and wondered if pursuing an architectural career was a deal made with the devil.

My watch confirmed how late it was, and I dreaded the thought of how using my little four-function calculator would extend my study time exponentially. But I had no other choice. I marched through formulas exhaustively until I no longer could.

Bleary-eyed the next day, I arrived at the test site and borrowed a scientific calculator from the graduate assistant. I did fine on the final exam, my last hurdle in my three-year journey in architecture school. But I did not feel like celebrating. Thoughts about my place in my family and work continued to haunt me.

How long can I keep pushing the boulder up the hill over and over again?

Fresh out of school, I'd landed my first full-time job at the respected architectural firm of Metz, Train, & Youngren, located in the forty-storied Kemper Building in downtown Chicago.

On my first day, I met with Mr. Montgomery, the principal hiring and office manager with whom I'd initially interviewed, and we went over the usual personnel orientation. I had admiration and respect for this mild-mannered, soft-spoken man with salt-and-pepper hair, and whose kind spoken words and smiles came easily.

Fantastic views of the city surrounded us as Mr. Montgomery took me around the open-plan studio, introducing me to my supervisor and co-workers. Each of the two-person workstations had a low height cubicle, its exterior wrapped in gray flannel fabric with a navy-blue electrostatic powder-coated metal trim. The same gray material appeared on the inside walls, serving as a tack-board in front of navy, plastic laminate work surfaces, matching navy task chairs, and two-drawer file cabinets. I found everyone friendly, cheerful and welcoming.

Shortly before I accepted the offer from Metz, Train, & Youngren, I wondered with uneasiness, about whether women would or wouldn't be regarded professionally in the office environment. But upon meeting my colleagues, both male, and female, my concerns upgraded to cautious optimism. A one-hundred-person firm, people of all levels in the organization were approachable and personable in spite of the demands the high-powered business of architecture brings. Finding a lovely camaraderie with my peers, albeit most of them single and several years younger than me, we all jumped in with both feet, committing ourselves to our work during the day, as well as at night while en charrette, to meet pressing deadlines. I had lunch with the group many times, but respectfully declined invitations to their usual Friday-after-work drinks—I wanted to get home to my family.

I attributed the fellowship of my peers to Mr. Montgomery, who seemed to have keen intuitiveness for hiring people who fit well within the team.

My assigned project was a high-rise building in Denver. Figuring out details for handrails and balcony railings, taking notes that my supervisor, Jorge, had given me, and transferring his *red lines*[27] to the construction documents were a far cry from my student days of creating grand, theoretical "masterpieces" of architecture. But my work, menial as it appeared, taught me how construction documents were put together from the ground up. I loved it.

Eight months after I started working at the firm, I had my first performance review with Jorge, who was a young, small-statured man around thirty-five years old. Thoughtful and gracious, Jorge often expressed his appreciation for the work I did for him. Although I was nervous about my performance review, I felt confident Jorge's assessment of my work would align with mine. I later met with Mr. Montgomery for a follow-up meeting.

"I'm looking at your performance review and it's quite impressive!" Mr. Montgomery continued, "And you've demonstrated that you're a valued member of our team." He then informed me that as a result of such a positive review, I had earned a salary increase, effective immediately.

A few weeks later, still buoyant from my review and raise, I decided to open a checking account at the bank on the ground floor of our office building. As I stepped into the elevator, Mr. Montgomery slipped in just before the doors closed. Always friendly, I was surprised when he averted his eyes from me and I'd sensed weird vibes.

My radar immediately went up, and for some reason, I was tempted to tell him my intentions: "I'm about to open a checking account downstairs. Do you have any thoughts on that?"

But I didn't ask the question. We shared awkward silence as the elevator took us to the ground floor. When I approached the bank teller, I paused.

Just open the stupid account and stop being such a worrywart.

Before I received my box of new checks from the bank, Mr. Montgomery called, saying he wanted to speak with me. His voice sounded strained.

The air in his office was still, and his expression was solemn.

"We're having a slow-down of work, and I'm sorry to tell you that I need to lay you off," he said.

"Really? My review was so positive, I don't understand," I said.

"I'm sorry, it's decided."

"Am I the only person being laid off?"

"No, there are a couple of others who we'll lay off later."

"May I ask you a question?" My eyes fixed on his.

"Yes, of course," Mr. Montgomery said.

I don't know what came over me to feel so bold, but I had to know.

"Did the decision to lay me off right now," I asked, "have anything to do with the fact that I'm married, and you all figured I could manage more easily without a job than a single person?" I took a deep breath.

Silence.

Mr. Montgomery looked downward, blinked slowly, and nodded up and down.

I let out my breath and left his office.

After picking up the kids from Hephzibah, I settled them at home and began to mindlessly prepare dinner. The sound of my footsteps, in constant motion, moving from the sink to the fridge, to the kitchen counter, back to the sink, and the clattering of dishes, pots, and pans, echoed the negative energy I released. I was certain if I'd stopped moving, I'd surely explode.

"I can't believe it!" Bob said after I told him the news. "You were laid off because you were married? I think that's illegal."

"No, he told me they lost their biggest client, and the studio was running out of work. I was on their short-list because, I guess, they figured a lay off would be easier for a married female than an unmarried person. What can I do, sue them? Don't wanna go there." I sighed. "I'll start looking for another job."

Within a month, I had two job offers. One was from Skidmore, Owings & Merrill (SOM), the iconic, world-renowned, highly coveted architectural office located in Chicago, with thousands of employees worldwide. SOM's portfolio included high-profile projects in Chicago, such as the Inland Steel Building, the University of Illinois at Chicago, John Hancock Building, Sears Tower, and countless other noteworthy commercial buildings across the globe, winning hundreds of awards.

The other offer was from Raymond J. Green & Associates (RJG), the antithesis of SOM. A three-person firm located in Evanston, Illinois, RJG's main focus was providing architectural services to school districts throughout the northern suburbs of Chicago.

Our national economy, in these days of the 1980s, was tanking from a severe recession and Chicago was not immune to its effects—inflation was up, prime rates were up, unemployment was up, and gas rates were over the top.

I wanted to work for SOM so badly, but the economy was a mess, and I knew large, new projects relied heavily on low prime rates. Although SOM was a large firm with a long-standing history, I was afraid of going through another lay-off. I had school loans—tons of them.

I accepted the offer from RJG. Their offices were located in Evanston but had plans to move in a few months to River North, a trendy section of Chicago north of the Loop. The commute on the '*L*'[28] from Oak Park to Evanston was about one and a half hours each way, and I'd thought this would be an ideal time to study for my architect's licensing exam. The test included five sections: mechanical and electrical systems, architectural history, structures, building systems, and a separately scheduled, twelve-hour lengthy examination requiring a design, plans, and details for a specified building type. I needed three years of documented hours working under a licensed architect before qualifying to take the design portion of the exam and working at RJG would help me bank those needed hours.

The economy continued its downward trajectory, and the big guns fell hard. Three months after I took the job at RJG, SOM had a Saturday night massacre of sorts, laying off massive numbers of architects in their Chicago office. Metz, Train, & Youngren continued to lay off architects, and as history would later have it, the firm was all but defunct within five years.

But I was safely employed at RJG. The firm made its move to a classic, timber loft space in the city, with hardwood floors and fourteen-feet-high ceilings on Hubbard Street, just a few steps from the Merchandise Mart. It was also a stone's throw from the Hubbard Street Dance Studio, where I often took ballet classes at lunchtime. I was happy and settled at RJG.

Unlike the flurry of activity of so many people at Metz, Train, & Youngren, this office included my boss, principal architect Ray Green, his administrative assistant, and two architects, including me.

Ray Green was a very tall guy, needing to duck slightly before passing through most doorways—standard doors are typically six-feet-eight inches high. His ash-brown hair had a cast of red, and his full beard, along with his booming bass-baritone voice, would be intimidating for sure, but not so with Ray. A knowledgeable, seasoned architect, he was friendly and courteous. What I most appreciated was that he had confidence in my abilities and potential, giving me responsibilities I would never have experienced in a large architectural firm so soon after graduating.

RJG had ongoing contracts with various suburban school districts, and I had been working on these institutional projects for nearly a year, assisting the other architect. Then one day, Ray called me to his office.

"We got a new project for School District 65." He smiled. "It's a middle school addition, and I'd like you to be the project manager.

Here's the *program*.²⁹ Draft a contract, and we'll go over it."

Whoa! Are you kidding me? Does he think I'm ready for this?

"Thank you, Ray," I said. "I look forward to working on it!" My eyes were wide with disbelief.

I worked directly with our client, and after completing the design and construction documents, the project commenced. On my first day on the job site, I heard one of the workers behind me say with surprise, "The architect's a girl!" I smiled.

I was quite satisfied with my position in my office but discovered women in architecture were not altogether embraced or understood within the industry and assimilation, to be sure, would take time.

One morning, I was first to arrive at the studio, and as I settled at my workstation, a man called from the intercom phone at the building entry. He was a sales representative from a company that made plumbing fixtures and wanted to talk to an architect about his new products.

I buzzed him up.

Meeting him at our reception entry, I said, "Hello, good morning! I'm Susan. C'mon in."

"Uh, yes, thank you." His eyes darted around the room, and when they landed on Ray's office with its lights turned off, I sensed his disappointment. "I'm Mr. Jefferson," he said.

Oh, MISTER Jefferson, so we want to be formal, do we?

Medium height with a pleasant face, his old tweed fedora gave away his age as being in his fifties, maybe sixties.

"Good to meet you, Mr. Jefferson. I'm Ms. Rakstang."

I extended my hand and was startled to find, instead of a handshake, he'd shoved his hat into my hand.

You've got to be kidding!

I stood there, staring at his hat hanging from my hand when he asked, "Are you his secretary?"

Okay, you really shouldn't have asked that.

"Pardon me?" I stayed calm.

That was truly a dumb thing to ask. Don't ask again. No, really— don't ask.

"Are you the architect's secretary?" He asked, smiling with delight, holding his arms up, fingers wiggling in the air as he mimicked typing.

Achhh! He asked.

I laughed. "No, Mr. Jefferson, I *am* the architect."

I saw his expression change from a cheerful smile to an expression of sheer befuddlement.

"Mr. Jefferson, why don't we go into the studio and you can tell me all about your new products. I'm working on a pretty large project, and your information may be useful."

I gave him ample time to unload his suitcase full of samples and brochures and give his spiel about his products.

"Thank you—you've been helpful. I'll call you if I have any questions. Let me walk you to the door."

We walked to the reception area together and before he left the office, we said our good-byes, and he was gone. Leaning my back against the door inside the reception area, I took a deep breath, shook my head, and let out a chuckle.

Being an architect at RJG, with all its stresses, long hours, and ever-changing priorities, also brought me great satisfaction of professional and personal growth, and one particular benefit—a paycheck. With a little extra cash in our pockets, Bob and I were able to enjoy activities we were unable to do while I was in graduate school. We could finally afford to buy tickets to piano concerti at the internationally renowned Chicago Symphony Orchestra. We also attended intimate piano recitals in venues around the city, all of which helped me develop a keen sense of appreciation and a discerning ear for world-class music.

My parents had given me my old Lyon and Healy baby grand piano, but I did not have the talent to simply sit down and play. I'd have to fight for every key and knew it would take years of practice before I could make music again.

"Boy, if only I had time to take lessons," I lamented after each concert.

"You have to make the time! I would love to hear you play," Bob said.

"Achhh! With all I have going on, I have no time for lessons."

Although I used the excuse of lack of time for not going back to the piano, I knew it was more than that. It took courage to play, as it tested one's mental acuity, memory, and intellect, and I did not have the appetite for testing myself in that way, nor did I have the courage.

There was a treasure trove of tools and equipment in the basement of my parents' apartment building. Any project could be accommodated from woodworking, stripping and rehabbing furniture, to starting seeds for spring planting and anything in between. My father had space, equipment, and knowledge to do the job. A table saw, radial saw, drill press, and lathe sat in the middle of the basement, while boxes, buckets, and glass jars with labels neatly identifying its contents, lined the shelves along one of the walls. He knew exactly where every tool, nut, bolt, screw, drill bit, and chuck were stored. Stacked high along another wall were televisions, radios, stereo equipment, and his prized audio and television vacuum tube collection. He was a television and radio repairman, and over the years, had amassed collectibles like an Edison antique cylinder player phonograph, Bakelite radios, retro televisions, and stereo components.

One day, I had an idea for a project and called my father.

"Hi, Dad, how're you doing?" I asked.

"I'm okay. What's wrong?"

"Nothing's wrong. Can you help me make a flag case?"

The US government gives survivors of veterans a flag, and the three-cornered wood case I wanted to make would hold the flag of Bob's deceased father, Kenneth Rakstang, a WWII veteran, who had died five years earlier. Bob's mother had given Ken's flag to Bob.

Before my father would answer, he proceeded, as I expected, to volley a plethora of questions to which I was prepared. And I knew his answer would eventually be yes.

"Why do you want to make a flag case?" he asked.

"For Bob's father's flag, in time to give it to Bob on Memorial Day."

"What kind of wood will it be?" he asked.

"Cherry. And I'll use a dark stain."

"What about hardware?"

"Brass hinges and clasp."

"I've got brass hinges you can use." He asked, "How're you gonna make it?"

"I'll work up drawings, but I'll need to use your table saw. Is that okay?"

"When do you want to do it?"

"Soon. Memorial Day is in a month."

"Okay, I'll help you."

"Thanks, Dad, I'll call you when the wood I ordered comes in."

Whew! Interrogation, done.

I folded the flag in its traditional triangle form such that when settled in the case, one star would be perfectly centered in the top, ninety-degree corner, and aligned above a row of three stars. I measured the flag bundle and developed working drawings. We'll need to miter all three corners of the case, and I have a feeling the bottom two corners will be easier to draw than to build.

When the 2x2 cherry wood and ¼ inch flat trim stock arrived, I headed for my father's workshop. I laid the wood and my drawings on his workbench, and he and I planned our strategy.

"The top corner has to be ninety degrees, and each bottom corner has to be forty-five degrees," my father said, "so the two pieces that make up the bottom corners have to be twenty-two and a half degrees, each. But I think it'll be dangerous using my table saw. I better set up some jigs."

They were, indeed, tricky cuts, but my father set up a sophisticated series of blocking to allow me to cut the wood safely, and all the corners came together perfectly. In the end, after sanding, staining, adding protective glass, and brass hardware, the flag case turned out beautifully.

Bob was moved to tears, knowing my father and I had made a case for his father's flag.

His parents, Ken and Shirley, and my parents had become close friends from the time they'd met when Bob and I started dating—so much so that they got together without us. Ken had been tall, good-natured, and was the Norwegian half of Bob and his sisters, Kathy and

Sharon. Shirley was sturdy in stature, more serious by nature, and the German half of their kids. Our four parents, all in their forties when they met, vibrant, healthy, and high spirited, had each other over for dinner and traveled together. When Ken passed away after a long illness, my parents were deeply saddened to lose their good friend.

I think it was as meaningful to my father, as it was to me, to make this symbol of remembrance of Ken.

⸘

Nearing the end of the children's school year was always a busy time. Rushing from work to retrieve the kids from Hephzibah, driving Jonathan to his baseball game and Kristin to her ballet recital rehearsal, I could practically feel the minute hand of my watch hurrying me along.

"Mom, did you bring my ballet slippers?" Kristin asked from the backseat.

"Aren't they in your bag?" I asked.

"Nope."

"And my mitt's not in my bag either," Jonathan said.

"Achhh! Okay, we'll go home and get them. Do you know where everything is?"

"YES!" they called out in unison.

Arriving home, I let them in the house, and they scurried around and got what they needed. After dropping off the kids, I made a quick trip to the grocery store, headed home to put things in the fridge, picked up Kristin as she finished her rehearsal, and we arrived at the park in time for Jonathan's game. Sitting in the bleachers with my eyes closed, warmed by the sun, hearing laughter and murmurs of children in the background, I began to calm down after all that running around.

"Mom?"

"Hmmm?"

"After the recital, I want to quit ballet, okay?"

My heart jumped, and my eyes opened.

No way! I forbid it! End of conversation!

"Kristin, why would you want to quit?" I looked at her, "You've worked so hard these past four years, and your teacher told me you're doing so well."

"Since I've been taking ballet twice a week, I never get to see my friends anymore. And I miss all their birthday parties. That makes me sad," she said, her expression compelling, and voice, indeed, sounding sad.

"You're only eight years old, and there'll be plenty of parties in your life. How about cutting back on lessons to once a week, like before?" I asked.

"No, I need a break from ballet. Maybe I can do it again later."

Now how am I supposed to argue that logic of hers?

I remembered when I wanted to quit piano lessons and my mother had none of it. I ended up taking lessons for another couple of years, complaining all along, practicing seldom, and being a real pill. Continuing lessons was counterproductive, expensive, and a waste of time—or so I thought when I was a kid. I promised myself, if I ever had kids, I would never, ever force them to take piano lessons, and here I was now, wanting to push Kristin to continue her ballet.

"Kristin, I want you to keep dancing, but if it's not right for you, then you should quit. Give it a little more thought before you do, okay?"

"Okay!" Her mood immediately brightened.

Bob, Jonathan, and I attended Kristin's recital a few weeks later, and she and her classmates did a great job. I was still baffled as to why she'd wanted to quit ballet—she got along well with the other girls and seemed so happy performing. Maybe after the recital, she'd change her mind.

"Okay, can I quit now?" she asked the next morning.

NO!

"All right, if you're certain about this. I'll let your teacher know."

I was going to miss watching her dance—and that made me sad.

What had I done? Was she old enough to know what was best for her?

I had to admit, yes, she did. I knew that ballet was very rigorous and challenging, and only she knew what was happening inside her own body.

She's growing up too fast!

My mother was busy cooking a feast in our kitchen, as my father helped Bob with a construction project. They were deep in conversation about their electrical project in our dining room when I walked past them and tossed the metal tape measure I had borrowed into one of several tool buckets my father had brought to our house.

"Hey, not in there, that's the plumbing bucket." He frowned. "The tape measure goes in the carpentry bucket."

"Oh, sorry, Dad, the buckets all look the same to me," I said with a sigh. I was annoyed that he would correct me for such a small mistake. Then, seeing my father's tools cleaned, segregated by trade in their toolbox or bucket, lined up looking like an army ready for battle, I remembered how efficient, organized, and resourceful he was.

He commanded our respect and attention. A practical thinker, he shared his no-nonsense approach to the art of construction, which sometimes to my chagrin, was less art and more just-get-it-finished. But the job was always completed neatly and precisely.

"That pipe is in our way. Get out the *Sawzall* and cut it," my father told Bob.

Bob got on the ladder and asked, "Shall I cut over here?"

"No, not there, over there," my father barked, pointing to another location.

Bob sawed the pipe. ZZZZZT! Sparks flew, and Bob yelled, "Shit!"

"What happened? Are you okay?" I called out of our kitchen. "The lights went out!"

My father chuckled. "I guess your previous owners used that old pipe as a conduit."

Back in the day when contractors modernized old houses, converting gas-fueled light fixtures to electric lighting, they used the abandoned black gas pipes as a conduit for their new wires.

Bob was not amused. But he gained respect for any pipes he ventured upon in the future. Although Bob had high regard for my father's knowledge and experience, he nonetheless trod carefully taking orders from him.

They spent the rest of the day bending new conduits, pulling wires, and installing recessed downlights in our ceiling. Just before dusk, when Bob flipped the switch, we had lights in our dining room. We all cheered!

"Mom, when are we going to eat?" asked Jonathan.

"Susie, *gohan o mazeru*[30] before you put it on the table," my mother reminded me.

"Okay," I said. When the rice finished cooking, I slid the flat part of a rice paddle vertically against the side of the pot's interior and pushed the paddle handle downward, forcing a large scoop of rice upward that I gently flipped over. I repeated this along the rest of the pot's side as well as in the middle, being careful not to overwork or smash the grains. This process introduced air to the cooked rice, *gohan o mazeru*, fluffing it up, cooling it down a bit, and keeping it from getting overcooked and soggy.

"Mom, when are we going to eat?" Jonathan asked again.

"Soon. I'll let you know when dinner is ready. Go to your room and play."

"I already played in my room—I'm hungry!" he persisted.

"Jonathan, GO!" `

My mother said softly, but loud enough for Jonathan to hear, "Oh, Susie, kawaiso, neh? Give him a little taste of the chicken—he's hungry!"

Jonathan and I made eye contact, and he grinned broadly, exposing a missing front tooth.

How could I resist that cute seven-year-old smile?

I gave him a chicken wing, and he gnawed into it. Still looking at me, he said, "Grandma, this is so good!" He giggled and ran off.

"Mom?" I called.

"Hai," she answered.

"Are we about ready?"

My mother was laser-focused while preparing a meal and had little inclination to chitchat unless it was instructional.

"Almost," she said while finishing up the pork fried rice. "Shred some lettuce for the platter, arrange the teriyaki chicken on it, and use the pineapple slices and some parsley for garnish. Don't forget to clean up any drip marks around the edges of the platter."

I wasn't sure why she told me to tidy up the platter edges—I figured she was just thinking out loud. I'd been her assistant cook since I was a kid, after all, and knew that nothing went on the table unless it was perfectly presentable.

"Okay, I finished arranging the chicken—shall I cut the cucumber and carrots for the namasu salad?" I asked.

"Hai. I made a sweet vinegar sauce—it's in your fridge. Pour it over the salad, grind some sesame seeds on top, and put it back in the fridge until we're ready to eat. Also, the vegetables are ready, so cut them up and arrange them nicely on a plate."

Fragrances from my mother's cooking throughout the day ravaged us with hunger. Her feast was gorgeous, as always.

Bob and my father finished cleaning up after their project, and before we all settled down to eat, Bob threaded a tape of Mozart piano sonatas in his reel-to-reel tape deck. Dinner and music were ready.

My mother's pairing of sweet and salty in the teriyaki glaze of the roasted chicken lit up my *umami*[31] taste receptors, bringing perfect, savory satisfaction. Her fried rice had all the flavors and textures we were so fond of: tender, sliced char siu pork complemented the quickly cooked vegetables against the slight crunchiness of the fried rice. The crisp sliced cucumbers and carrots offset the delicate, tangy yet cleansing mild sweetened rice vinegar, the nuttiness of sesame seeds, and a touch of grated ginger of the namasu salad. The smoked fish, accompanied by her dipping sauce—a bold combination of shoyu, rice vinegar, hot chili pepper, a whisper of sugar, and a few drops of sesame oil—stood up to the husky smokiness of the fish, creating a riot of flavors in every bite.

Both my parents were masterful with chopsticks, especially when eating fish. They could meticulously pick up even the tiniest morsel, evading all bones, to relish their small treasures.

Like the hot rice, the macaroni salad, and simply prepared roasted vegetables, gave our palate a welcomed contrast in between the more robust dishes.

"Mom, everything is so oishi!" Bob said.

My parents looked at each other and broke out in laughter.

"You know what that means, Bob, oishi? How do you know what that is?" Mom asked.

"Yes! It means delicious! I hear you say it all the time!" Bob beamed.

"That's because she eats so much of her cooking and says how oishi it is!" My father laughed.

"Ahhhh! Don't listen to him. He doesn't know what he's talking about, that man," my mother said, holding back evidence of a smile. We all laughed.

Aside from her family and friends, my mother's passion was food. She loved reading about it, handling it, smelling it, preparing it, sharing it, and she loved eating it. It's no wonder she was so, well, so full-figured! She was always jolly about her weight and often poked fun at herself about her pudginess.

But I thought she was beautiful. She was healthy, happy, and although she was compelled to go on one diet after another, I believed she was ultimately at ease in her own skin. A portly five feet three inches tall, she always wore her salt and pepper hair short and curled. Her soft brown eyes twinkled as she smiled, and her high cheekbones added even more beauty to her warm, friendly face. And her infectious laugh brought a smile to all those around her.

She'd once decided to tackle a low/no carb diet, which of course, eliminated rice. She was on that diet only a few days when Bob, the children, and I visited my parents. My father waved us in.

"Hey! Good to see you!" He turned to Jonathan. "Look at you—you're almost as tall as your sister!" And to Kristin, "Better be nice to him, Kristin, he's going to be bigger than you pretty soon!"

"Hi, Grandpa! Hi, Grandma!" Kristin and Jonathan called out.

My mother, walking out of her kitchen, dabbing her mouth with a napkin, greeted us with her outstretched arms and a bright smile.

"Hi! How're you folks?" she asked, hugging us.

"Good!" I replied.

Then Bob and I started giggling. We couldn't stop. My mom, who always welcomed good fun, joined in the merriment.

"Why are we laughing?" she asked.

"What's that on your nose, Mom?" Bob asked.

"What?" She swiped it. "Ahhhhh!" she squealed.

We all, including my mother, laughed a big, deep belly laugh. On the tip of her nose was a single grain of white rice!

"Busted, Mom! So, how's that low/no carb diet going for you?" I managed to ask between spasms of laughter. The elimination of rice from my mother's diet was a diet doomed.

I loved visiting my parents. On the north side of Chicago, their apartment building, circa 1920, was a lovely, sturdy structure typical of the city's neighborhoods. Typical, because after the Great Fire in 1871, the city developed building codes requiring fire-resistant building materials for its structures; hence, my parents' three-flat was constructed of solid, three-wythe-thick brick walls. My father proudly maintained his property, treating it as if it was a member of our family. The three-bedroom apartment with oak hardwood floors throughout and high ceilings consisted of a large living room with an adjacent sun parlor, a spacious dining room, and of course, a well-stocked kitchen.

Although their apartment was large, it was warm, cozy, and welcoming. A place of respite for me, the familiar furnishings, knick-knacks, and family photographs unchanged since my childhood, calmed me.

※

Mary Walter and I became friends while working at a women's clothing store, The Limited, in Skokie, Illinois. Right out of undergraduate school, it was our first job. Mary was a salesgirl, and I was a display girl. Our sense of aesthetics quickly coalesced as we picked out blouses, jackets, skirts, pants, belts, and scarves from the store's inventory, and merged those parts into the sum of well-presented outfits. As a result of our wardrobe coordination, customers rarely purchased just the blouse or just the belt, but rather, they bought the whole outfit—quite the innovative and lucrative business model, to be sure.

Mary grew up on the family farm. While her father and brothers farmed soybeans and corn and her mother provided all the meals for them and their helpers, Mary spent her youth sewing, learning about fibers and clothing construction, and then majored in Textiles and Design in college. Mary moved to Chicago for her job and maintained her salt-of-the-earth, authentic, thoughtful sensibilities, and unassuming presence. Medium height with brown hair, and a bright, porcelain complexion, Mary's great smile showed off her beautiful white teeth—she'd never had a cavity in her life!

She had a vision for women and a goal for herself. Now that women, armed with professional degrees and entering the world of banking, business, law, and such, she knew they would need a source for "dressing for success," and Mary was determined to provide that source by opening a store of her own. Working women's clothing was either rigid, stuffy suits imitating men's, or flouncy, ruffled, décolletage-exposing dresses. But Mary changed all that.

"Instead of stiff, highly structured navy, black, and pinstripe suits like the men, I'm going to sell women's suits that are subtle colors and made of natural, supple fibers. My shirts aren't going to be heavily starched cotton, but instead, are going to be soft, Egyptian pinpoint cotton that I'll special order, or fluid silk blouses. And instead of neckties, I'm going to sell hand-painted silk scarves.

"What about accessories? We used a lot of them in displays at the Limited, remember?"

"Yes, I remember. I'll have plenty of accessories. They'll be low-key, not distracting, and will be a great finish to the outfit—my customers will look sharp, confident."

"Thank god, Mary. I'm not a shopper, and you know that. I don't have the time or patience to go through racks of dumb suits meant to make me look like a little man. Your store will be fantastic!"

In the late-1970s, after working several years in retail, Mary opened her first, eleven hundred square foot store in the newly built American Hospital Supply Corporation Tower in Evanston. She forged her path of providing the wardrobe women needed to assimilate into their new, mostly male, work environment. She had asked me to design her store, but I was only a grad student at the time, and not yet licensed to practice architecture.

The early eighties brought an economic recession, but Mary basked in the triumph of her successful store. And she was poised and ready to expand her business.

"I need more inventory! Clothes are flying out of the store, and I need more space," Mary told me over the phone. "There's a twenty-five hundred square foot place that's available across the corridor from where

I'm at now. What do you think?"

"Mary, we're still deep in the recession, and I don't see an end anytime soon. Are you sure you want to expand right now?" I asked.

"Recession be damned!" she said. "I'm not kidding, my customer base is expanding, and I have little room right now to meet their demands. Susan, you'll be my architect, right?"

"Yes, I'd love to! I'll have to ask Ray if he wants to take it on—I'm sure he will, but the project will need to go through his office."

In spite of the recession, the RJG office remained stable and busy, I believed, because Ray maintained a public, institutional client base. It wasn't elegant work, but we always had a backlog of projects waiting for us to tend. I brought the idea of the Mary Walter, Inc. project to Ray, and he was delighted to take on the job. I would be the project designer and architect.

I loved the construction phase, but sometimes, not all things went as planned. One day, a cacophony of hammering, drilling, sawing, and men's voices filled the air at the Mary Walter construction site. Workers, about ten of them, moved in all directions, climbing, kneeling, pulling, pushing, and smoothly by-passing one another as if in rehearsed choreography. I watched the carpenter make fresh cuts in two-by-four wood studs for wall blocking—it was he who was responsible for dispersing the evocative scent of pine throughout the space. With my drawings and metal tape measure in hand, I called out to the contractor superintendent.

"Sam! The dressing rooms aren't right!"

He turned. Cupping his hand behind his ear, he yelled something back. I saw his mouth moving but couldn't hear anything coming out.

"The dressing rooms—they're not the right size," I repeated, poking the air with my finger in the direction of the dressing rooms.

Sam held up his palm to me, turned, and let out a piercing whistle. Silence immediately fell. Tall, young, and personable, he walked toward me.

"What's up?" he asked.

"The end dressing room is too small," I said.

"Nah. I followed your drawings."

"I'm afraid not," I said, nodding 'no.'

He put the drawings on a makeshift desk of plywood over wood sawhorses, and turned the twenty-four inch, by thirty-six-inch pages of the construction documents, until he reached the layout page. We both bent over the drawings.

"There! You called out the dimensions for six dressing rooms. But when we laid out the rooms, there wasn't enough space for all six." Bending lower and reading the drawings more closely, his eyebrows furrowed. "And so. And—so, the last dressing room ended up pretty small."

"Only one dressing room is called out with dimensions to hold, right?" I asked. "And the rest is pretty clearly marked to be divided into five equal spaces. See? Look, equal, equal, equal, eq...."

"Okay, I get it, I get it. Can't we leave the small dressing room as is?"

"Sorry, we can't," I said.

"Why not? It's not that much smaller than the others."

"It's not serviceable. You've gotta bring down the walls and rebuild."

"Oh, c'mon, Susan! I scheduled my electricians for tomorrow. If I reschedule them, it'll delay the job. You don't want that, do you?"

I shrugged. "Delaying the job is not an option."

"How 'bout I give Mary a credit to the contract amount and keep the small room?" he asked.

"Nah, they've gotta go. Your electricians haven't run their lines yet. The drywall isn't up—the walls are just metal studs that'll come down fast, so what's the big deal? Just rebuild it, right."

His shoulders and chest sunken, he turned and walked away, muttering, "Gahdamnsonofabitch, where's the carpenter who laid out these walls?"

Sam was not a stupid guy. He knew he'd screwed up, tried his best to offer a deal, and was smart enough to know this was not the hill to die on.

The walls came down and rebuilt correctly.

One evening, well after the workers had left for the day, I met Mary at the job site, and we sat in the middle of all the construction with a bottle of Cab we'd opened to celebrate the project.

"What're those pipes for?"

"Let me show you on the drawings." I unrolled the documents. "See here? That's the symbol for your sink and coffee bar—and there it is." I pointed to the pipes on the job site. "Just where we told them to put it!"

"Wait, I need to get my bearings." She took the drawings and oriented them to where she stood. "Oh, I see! And this is the reception area where men can relax and wait? And this is the cash-wrap?"

"Yep. And there's the dressing room area and over here is where the tailor will pin your customers' clothes for alterations. The mauve carpet with gray pin dots will be here, and solid gray carpet will be over there." I pointed.

"What do all these dollar signs mean?"

"Where? Oh! They *do* look like dollar signs—that's to remind you how many dollars this project is costing you," I laughed. "Just kidding—the letter 'S' with a line down the center delineates the locations of your light switches."

"Wow. Now I can read your drawings!" Mary said. I can't wait until my store's finished!"

Upon completion, Mary and her customers loved the store. The Mary Walter Project was among a handful of other projects by young architects selected to appear in an exhibit. Sponsored by the Chicago Bar Association Young Lawyers Section in cooperation with the Chicago Architecture Foundation and Chicago Chapter, American Institute of Architects, the show was an exciting event. I even got a tip-of-the-hat from Paul Gapp, then the architecture critic for the Chicago Tribune.

After all the attention and fanfare from Mary's project, I settled back into my quiet life in the office and continued my sprint in life at home.

⸘

When I was a kid, my father worked long hours, often making evening house calls fixing customers' televisions, and when he came home, a hot dinner always waited for him. Aside from their New Years' celebrations, domestic chores were beyond the realm of his world, and he received no complaints from my mother about the unevenness of the division of familial labor. My mother's only resources for help were her strength of conviction, sense of duty to her husband and children, and her work ethic. She was a wife, mother, tutor, cook, laundress, house cleaner, and personal shopper for her family. She was a selfless "Supermom." It only made sense that I tried to take on all aspects of domestic duties early in Bob's and my marriage, with full intentions to also become a "Supermom."

But I felt off-balance and hopelessly in over my head. I needed counsel from my mother. After taking her shopping at the Asian grocery store, we went to her house to make lunch.

"I thought we could make something simple like egg foo yung," she said.

"Sounds good, I'll start cutting the veggies." I sliced the carrots julienne style, peeled off the tough strings of the celery and cut them in small diagonal pieces, then cut thin slices of green onions, and put all the veggies in a bowl. After chopping up the shrimp, I placed them in a separate bowl.

"Mom, shall we use some of the bean sprouts you bought?" I asked.

"Oh, I almost forgot!" she said. "Start boiling water for them and get a bowl of ice water ready."

"Okay." Waiting for the water to boil, I turned to her. "How did you do it, Mom?" I asked, searching for the pearls of wisdom I needed to help me earn my Supermom-ness.

"Do what?"

"You cooked every day, took care of everything in the house with little help from Dad, Dennis, or me, and on top of that, you worked full-time. How did you do it all? I'm trying, but doing a miserable job!"

"I did what I did because I was stupid," she said. "Check your water."

"Huh? Wait, what did you say?"

"Your water, it's boiling."

"No, not that, about being stupid. What did you mean? You never told me that. You never complained!"

"What would complaining do?" she asked. "When I was growing up in Hawai`i, our family lived the Japanese way. My mother worked in the plantation fields with my father, and then came home and took care of everything else for the family."

While my mother spoke, I blanched and shocked the bean sprouts, putting handfuls in the boiling water, letting them sit for a few seconds, promptly drained them, then quickly submerged them in the ice water. I strained the cooled bean sprouts again and added them to the veggie mixture.

"Susie, it's different today," my mother said. "Bob wants to be helpful, so let him help, even if he doesn't do things exactly as you would do. Let him help, and don't complain!"

I was silent watching my mother finish making the egg foo yung. She tossed the chopped shrimp in a little cornstarch and shook off the excess. In a hot, lightly oiled wok, she stir-fried the shrimp and set them aside to cool, followed by stir-frying the veggies. She cracked six eggs in a bowl and, holding four chopsticks in one hand, whisked them until well-mixed. After the veggies and shrimp were thoroughly cooled down, she added them to the bowl of eggs and stirred. In a hot, oiled, cast-iron pan, she ladled pancake-sized rounds of the mixture and fried them until done.

Lining up the egg foo yung patties on a platter, looking like fallen dominoes, she garnished the feast with chopped green onions and served it with hot rice. Beautiful!

So, she thinks Bob should help around the house and with the kids? Hmmm.

I felt liberated from my pesky aspiration to become a Supermom. I felt empowered.

A few weeks later, on a typical quiet evening, the children were sleeping, Bob was watching TV, and I was in the kitchen deciding what to make for the children's school lunch the next day. I looked in the refrigerator for deli meat and saw nothing. Cheese, nada. Carrots, celery, none, none. I looked in the pantry for canned tuna, gone. I had forgotten to go food shopping, and the cupboards were bare. Exasperated, I had no choice but to make peanut butter and jelly sandwiches. I stopped.

I realized I'd made that for two days in a row. Frustration mounted, then anxiety, then anger.

You have no one to be angry at but yourself. If you had made the time to go to the grocery store, you wouldn't be in this situation right now. It's your own fault.

And then I turned and saw Bob sitting in the living room laughing at a sitcom. I always thought it was funny and cute when he laughed out loud while watching TV—but not on this night. There he was, father of our children, the man who had no worries other than his work and picking up the kids when convenient to his schedule, the man who got his clothes washed, ironed, and meals cooked, by me, every day. I seethed.

"I can't do it all anymore!" I yelled.

"Did you say something?" Bob called out.

"Yes, we need to talk." That always caught his attention. He joined me in the kitchen.

"Listen, I know you're tired from work." I continued, "I'm tired from work. I'd worked overtime every night this week, and I'm exhausted. How come I had to cook dinner, clean up the kitchen, figure out what to make for tomorrow's lunch for the kids, and—" I looked at my watch. "It's 9:30, and I've got a load of laundry waiting for me right now, so everyone can have clean underwear tomorrow, and you get to sit back and enjoy TV? Huh? How come?"

"Well, you always do that stuff." Bob paused. "But if you want me to do the laundry or make their lunches, I will!"

"Oh," I paused. "Okay, fine. Make their lunch."

He looked in the fridge, and the pantry then began making peanut butter and jelly sandwiches.

"But they've had peanut butter and—never mind," I said with a sigh.

Letting go. That was going to be difficult for me. My mother didn't let go of any of her duties. She did it all. But then again, she was kicking herself for it now.

Bob was intrigued by his newfound domestic responsibilities. One step at a time, he ventured into a little cooking finding it satisfying, especially when the kids and I raved about his meals. He fiddled with a little bit of Italian cuisine, and some American comfort foods, but settled his interest in Asian meals and picked up a few tips from my mother.

One evening, Bob, the kids, and I visited my mother and father. Bob and my mother were in the kitchen, and the rest of us watched the evening news in the dining room.

"I usually make a jug of this and keep it in the fridge so I can add it to stir-fry or even something as common as sliced, fried, hot dogs," my mother told Bob. She showed Bob how to make the basic but essential ingredient in so many of her dishes—her much-coveted teriyaki sauce. She recited the list of ingredients, as Bob scribbled it down on his notepad.

- 1 cup of shoyu
- ¾ cup of water
- ¾ cup of brown sugar, more or less if you want
- ¼ cup of mirin
- ¼ cup of honey, more or less
- 1 teaspoon of grated ginger, or more
- 1 teaspoon of grated garlic, or more

"Got it," Bob said. He measured and combined all the ingredients in a pot and stirred it over a medium-low flame. Once the mixture blended, she gave Bob a spoon to taste it.

"Do you want it a little sweeter?" she asked.

"Mmmm, no, it's delicious the way it is," he said.

"With anything you cook, make sure to taste it and make adjustments if you want. Okay, turn up the flame a little bit and bring the sauce to a boil. But don't leave the stove for even a minute. It'll eventually come to a boil all of a sudden, and even if you turn off the fire, it'll continue to boil and bubble up and go all over the stove," my mother cautioned.

Bob diligently watched the pot and continued to stir.

My mother, in the meantime, thinly sliced some rib-eye steak, chunky-chopped red and green bell peppers, round onions, and wedge-cut some firm tomatoes.

"Bob?" I called from the dining room. "Look—on TV, the 'Where's the Beef' commercial is on!"

Bob rushed into the dining room to take a peek, and we all laughed together.

A few minutes later, my mother squealed from the kitchen, "Ahhhh!" She moved the pot of teriyaki sauce to a cool burner. "Oh, my goodness!" She laughed.

The sauce had boiled over onto the stove. Bob rushed in to clean up the hot, thick teriyaki mess with paper towels.

"I'm so sorry!" he said.

"Oh no, everything's all right! Well, now you know—don't take your eyes off the pot, even for a minute!" she said with a big smile. "Okay, start heating the wok with a medium flame and let's make Beef Tomato," she told Bob.

He did.

After a few minutes, my mother hovered her palm over the wok. Then she wet her hand under running water and flicked her fingers to sprinkle the water onto the pan. It danced on the pan's hot surface. "It's ready. Pour a little oil in the pan, let it heat up, and swirl the oil to cover the bottom of the wok," she told Bob.

He did.

"Here, put the onion slices in the pan and stir fry for a few minutes," she said. It sizzled in the hot oil. "When it's softened, push them off to the side around the wok, and then add the bell peppers."

"Okay." Bob gently turned the peppers.

"And when they're softened, you can push them over with the onions." My mother instructed.

She brought the beef slices to him. "I marinated the beef in your teriyaki sauce, drained it, and then shook it in a plastic bag with cornstarch," she said.

"Uh, is there enough oil in the pan to cook the beef?"

"Mmmm, why don't you add just a little more, but let it heat up before you cook the beef."

Bob added the beef. It sizzled in the pan, releasing a fantastic aroma, beckoning the kids, my father, and me to come in the kitchen.

Jonathan's eyes lit up. "Look at Dad—he's a chef!"

Seeing Bob at the stove diligently tending to his creation was a sight to behold. He looked so calm, yet focused. After the beef was cooked rare, my mother continued her instructions.

"Mix the beef with the vegetables and push everything around the side of the wok," she said. "Now sear the tomatoes—work quickly, wiki wiki!" She laughed.

"Like this?" Bob asked as he started flipping the tomato wedges back and forth.

"Oh, leave it cooking and flip it once. You don't want to fiddle too much, or you'll smash them."

He did.

"Now, add some teriyaki sauce, blend everything, and let it simmer for a few minutes. The cornstarch on the beef will thicken up the gravy so you can add some water if it's too thick, then turn off the flame."

Bob's meal was colorful and beautiful. The tomatoes were firm but not raw, the peppers and onions had an ever-so-slight crunch, and the beef teriyaki, as it simmered in the gravy, was very tender.

"Oishi!" We called out.

{

After three years of working at RJG and passing my licensing exams, I flirted with the idea of starting my own architectural firm. But I was so exhausted by day's end I could hardly think about where even to start.

"We should give it a go, Susan. Let's do it together!" said Heather, a classmate from graduate school.

"I dunno. It would be impossible for us to get anything going while still working full-time. I'm so busy with my projects, and besides, RJG is such a small firm, I'd have to sneak around making and taking calls. No way, I can't picture myself doing that—it just wouldn't be right."

"Yeah, but there's gotta be a way," Heather said.

Later that night, I told Bob about Heather's and my conversation.

"Why don't you take some vacation time and think about it? I just saw an article in the *Oak Leaves*[32] that said Village Hall is looking for an architect to head-up their facade improvement program. Maybe you could check it out," he said.

"Great idea," I said. "I can look into incorporation, insurance, and all that administrative stuff too. Okay, I'll tell Heather!"

I had a blast spending my two-week vacation exploring Heather's and my new architectural firm. It was great, albeit short-lived. Heather, who worked full-time at Standard Oil, thought once we got our new company going, she would leave her job and join our practice. Due to personal reasons, however, she was unable to follow through with that plan. But I'd been bitten by the bug of entrepreneurship and was enjoying it, so I continued to plow forward and gave my notice to Ray. Thus, my company, Rakstang Associates, Architects and Planners, Inc., was born.

Bob and the kids were excited and supportive of my new business. As a mother of young children trying to work on architectural projects at home, throwing in loads of laundry, and cooking meals in between, I discovered my start-up venture was not particularly "exciting." Keeping all the balls in the air and my late-night hours of working was stressful to be sure, but at least I was at home and felt more a part of Bob's and our kids' lives.

One afternoon, the kids ran circles around the dining room as I tried to work.

"All right, you guys, you're too wild, hold it down!" I growled.

Kristin and her friend, Mandy, laughed heartily as Jonathan and his friend, Louie, playfully shoved each other around.

Then—the red phone rang.

"It's the RED PHONE!" Jonathan yelled. Suddenly the air was quiet and still. I had installed a red phone that had a different ring tone from our home line. When it rang, the children knew it was a business call, and they needed to cease all noise. I answered the phone, my voice turning on a dime from grumpy mom to a cheerful architect.

"Good morning, Rakstang Associates, can I help you?" I asked, most pleasantly. "Hello! So good to hear from you! How was your vacation? Uh-huh. Uh-huh. Oh, wonderful! Yes, of course, when would you like to meet?"

As I spoke, the children began silently mimicking me, lip-syncing my conversation, nodding their heads back and forth, up and down, gesturing with bent elbows and limp wrists, eyebrows raised, giggling, and were hardly able to contain themselves. I raised my index finger to my lips and mouthed the words "QUIET!" That settled them down for a few seconds until their imitations and giggling started again. I stood up, hand on hip, and gave them the "mother's stink-eye," which worked long enough for me to put my client on hold.

"Okay, everybody, out to the backyard, NOW!" I roared. Off they scurried, and I finished my phone conversation, once again, in my pleasant voice.

So, this is what "exciting" looks like. I sighed.

※

After dinner one night, Jonathan set up his homework on the dining room table, and I joined him as I sifted through the day's mail.

"Oh look, here's a flyer about a meeting at the Methodist church for anyone interested in joining the Cub Scouts," I said. "Let's see, Tigers are seven years old, Wolfs are eight, Bears are nine, and Webelos are ten—so you'd be a Webelos, Jonathan. You interested?"

He shrugged.

"Well, are you, or aren't you? We can go to the meeting if you'd like."

"Is Louie going?" he asked.

"I don't know. Ask him."

The following week Jonathan and I arrived at the church's social hall filled with men and women happily mingling with each other as their sons ran around like little boys do. Being a full-time worker, I was not part of a "mom clique," and as usual, I knew few people in the room.

"I see Louie. I'm going over there, okay?" Jonathan asked.

"Sure, go ahead."

I headed for my "go-to" hangout place in situations like these: the punchbowl and cookie table. After a few minutes of awkward fidgeting with my watch band and sneaking peeks at the time, a woman about my age and height with short, dark brown hair in soft curls greeted me. She had a warm, welcoming smile.

"Hello, I'm Margaret Lastick. Thank you for coming!"

I introduced myself and pointing across the room, "And there's my son Jonathan."

"So glad to meet you!" Margaret said.

"Are you the pack leader?" I asked.

"Well, sort of—oh, I better go, the meeting needs to start soon."

Margaret led the meeting and talked about projects, the pack schedule, events, and badges they would work on, along with the paperwork necessary to join the Cub Scouts.

I caught up with her after the meeting.

"Margaret, thank you for being the pack leader."

"Well," Margaret said, "I'm not technically the pack leader, but I'll serve as one." She pulled me aside and whispered, "The Scout organization frowns on women serving in this leadership position. Men Only practice, if you know what I mean." She said with a wink.

"If women aren't allowed, then how—?"

"Shhhhh!" Margaret's eyes widened.

"How did you become one?" I whispered back.

"It was easy." Margaret beamed. "When I filled out the Scout forms, instead of writing my name as pack leader, I wrote down my husband's name instead!"

"Doesn't it make you mad that the Scouts discouraged you from being a pack leader just because you're a woman?" I was all too familiar with that rodeo.

"Nah, it's a win-win for all of us," she said. "My son, yours, and other boys have a den, and the Scout organization thinks they have their pack leader-man. By the way, do you think your husband would be interested in being a co-den mother with my husband?"

The thought of Margaret fulfilling her responsibilities as pack leader using her husband as a front, and both our husbands assisting her as den mothers made me giggle, which got Margaret started. If we didn't laugh so hard, we would cry at the irony.

"Mom, can we go home now?" Jonathan asked.

"Okay, one more minute."

"Margaret, we should get together sometime. I work from home now, so would you like to come over for coffee one morning?" I asked.

"Oh, I'd love to—how 'bout tomorrow?"

"Sure, after Kristin and Jonathan go to school, say 9:00?"

"Okay, see you then."

Nice—I'll have a coffee-klatch buddy!

Between my family, grad school, and working, I had little time to connect with parents of my kids' friends. Now, working from home, I looked forward to getting to know Margaret and other Oak Parkers.

The next morning, after getting the kids off to school, I put on a pot of coffee and brought out a bowl of fresh fruit.

The doorbell rang.

"Hi, Susan!" Margaret was carrying a covered plate.

"Good morning! Oh my, what do you have there? C'mon in!"

"They're petit fours. I made them!" said Margaret.

Sliding my drawings, pens, and pencils off to the side of the dining room table, I made space for the fruit, coffee, and treats she had brought.

"Please excuse the mess! I've set up this dining room as my home office."

Margaret stepped up to the architectural sketches taped to the wall. "Wow. What is all this?" she asked.

"I'm working on a facade rehabilitation project for the Village of Oak Park—my first project since starting up my firm."

"You're an architect? How long have you been doing it?"

"I practiced at a couple of offices downtown for about four years, and then started my firm a few months ago. Hey, what about these gorgeous petit fours—you made them?"

"I did! They're sponge cake squares with raspberry filling, covered with chocolate ganache, and topped with a little candied violet. I bake cakes and desserts for my family and friends and just started my own company. It's called Le Royale Icing."

I put a scoop of the fruit, a salad of strawberries, blueberries, and chunky cut kiwi, onto each of our plates, then added a couple of petit fours.

"Mmmm, they're delicious—I taste almonds!" I said. "Where did the almonds come from?"

Margaret laughed. "That's a marzipan layer under the chocolate ganache—do you like it?"

"Oh, my goodness, this is fantastic!" I took another bite.

"So, is your company incorporated?" Margaret asked.

I swallowed and said, "Oh sure, in fact, my attorney got that taken care of before I even took on my first client. And I also have an accountant and an insurance agent. Wow, this is delicious!"

"Do you think I should be incorporated? And will I need insurance policies too?" she asked.

"Yes, I think so, but I don't know, Margaret. Maybe you should speak to an attorney. Soon. I mean, very soon. You're dealing with food, so don't wait!"

"Okay, I will. I'm so happy we met last night," Margaret said. "You're the only person I can talk to who knows what it's like to run a business. Such hard work!"

"It is a lot of work, for sure, but it's been fun for me working from home. Although one of these days, I hope to lease a space. It's a pain to clear off this table every time we have dinner—or have you over for petit fours!"

Both Margaret and I wanted it all and had the will to raise our families while growing our small businesses. Having supportive husbands, great kids, our youth, and good health, we never gave thought that we would fail. Consumed by our work and family with little time for anything else, Margaret's husband and Bob, as co-den mothers, kept us connected.

Later one day, Margaret called me. "Will you participate in the Cub Scout Holiday Cookie Exchange? We'll need about two dozen per family by next Saturday."

"Oh. I'm not much of a baker," I confessed. "But Bob, for sure, will bake the cookies."

When I got off the phone, I turned to Bob.

"That was Margaret. You have to make two dozen cookies for the Cub Scout Holiday Cookie Exchange."

"What are you talking about? Baking is for, for—"

"For whom?" I asked, my eyes narrowing.

"Well, you know, for the moms to do."

I laughed. "You're the den mother, so that makes you a mom now, and you have to make two dozen cookies!"

"Okay, fine," he groused.

"By next Saturday," I added.

}

Within three years of starting my practice at home, I believed my company was stable enough with ongoing clients and projects to sustain the overhead of a leased office space.

Bob was out of town, Jonathan was with friends, and Kristin had just walked home from school when I asked her if she wanted to look at a possible office space with me.

"Yeah! Where is it?" she asked.

"It's in the mall on Lake Street, let's go!"

The Village of Oak Park, in a herculean effort to boost economic development, in-filled one of its main arterial streets, Lake Street, to create a pedestrian mall. The shopping district had outdoor seating, quaint lighting, and berms that were landscaped with lush turf, seasonal flowers, shrubbery, and grand pin oaks.

The space Kristin and I visited was in a building with a Tudor-style facade of white plaster and dark-stained timber. The office, on the second floor, was a five hundred square foot space with a view of the mall and its many pin oaks.

"I love it!" Kristin said.

"I do, too, but it needs a lot of work. The carpet is pretty disgusting, walls have to be patched and painted, and I'll need a short wall to separate the entry from the workspace." I sighed.

"That's not a big deal, is it? I can help you—I can paint! You should take it, Mom. Next year I'll be twelve, and Jonathan and I can walk here after school!"

I laughed. "Hmmm. You can bring your friends over when you want to roam the mall if you'd like. Well, the price is fair, that's for sure."

"Mom, do it, it'll be fun!"

"Okay, I'll talk to the landlord. You're right. It will be fun!"

"Yay!" Kristin pumped her fist in the air.

I signed the lease the next day, and when Bob was back in town, I showed him the space.

"It's small, not much to show," I said, as we climbed up the stairs to my office. I unlocked the door.

"Here it is! The conference table and drafting board will fit here," I pointed, "the printing, files, and workroom will go in that little room, and my office will be over there— that's it. I love it!"

"Congratulations!" Bob said. "It's nice, and I like the view. So, what kind of rehab do you want to do here?"

"The electrical is fine, so we just have to patch the walls, paint, lay new vinyl floor tiles, and do some minor carpentry in the entry area," I said.

"When it's all done, does it mean no more banker's boxes full of files, or drafting table in our dining room? No more sketches on the walls? Wow, it'll be a real dining room again!"

I gave Bob's arm a swat, and we laughed.

Bob and I worked on the office rehab, and it was a walk in the park compared to the kind of work we'd done in our house. As for the kids helping, their enthusiasm waned when they discovered the mall held treasures of candy and toy stores, a magic shop, and places they could hang out with their friends. Not a problem, they were happy, as were we. When we finally moved my things to the office, life at home became infinitely more organized and comfortable for all of us.

After pacing back and forth in my office one afternoon, I finally made the dreaded phone call.

"Hello, Steve, Susan, how're you doing? Yeah, hey, listen, I have to tell you, I'm disappointed and pissed off. You promised me your drawings would be delivered to my office early this week—it's Thursday, and I've received nothing. You know I can't go much farther on my documents until I have yours, and we're on a tight deadline. What's going on?"

Steve was the principal of the mechanical engineering firm I'd hired to work on one of my projects.

"Uh, can I put you on hold for a minute?" he asked.

Coming back on the line, he said, "Susan, I checked with my project manager, and we dropped the ball. I apologize—give me the weekend, and I'll have the drawings to you first thing Monday morning. Will that be okay?"

After exchanging a few more words, we said our good-byes, and I slowly returned the phone to its cradle, pondering what had just happened.

Huh. So that's how guys do it.

Unbeknownst to Steve, his response to my displeasure with his office taught me a valuable lesson. If I were him, and one of my clients told me I'd screwed up, I would have been devastated, shocked, embarrassed, and definitely would have blabbered a plethora of, "I'm so sorry, I'm so sorry!" But no—Steve was calm, direct, owned the screw-up, made no excuses, and offered his apology—once.

Being only one of a handful of female architects in the area and fully immersed in my practice and family, I had no time to seek out camaraderie with the few women I knew in the field. As a result, I had no female mentors. But I did have the company of male architects, engineers, contractors, and clients with whom I worked, and I paid attention to their actions to give me insight on what my model would be for handling conflicts. Lesson learned.

Early Monday morning, Steve's drawings arrived.

A few months later, I called Bob at work. "You're not gonna believe this." I was ecstatic.

"Hi! What's happening?" Bob asked. Even though we were on the phone, I could tell he was smiling.

"Remember the proposal I submitted to the State of Illinois?"

"Yes!"

"I got the job!"

"Wow! I knew you would get it—congratulations! What kind of project is it?"

"I'll be rehabbing the National Guard Armory in Joliet. I'll find out more about the scope during our meeting next week." I could hardly believe this had happened.

At RJG, I'd typically worked on larger institutional projects, so I was eager to get back into that kind of work in my practice. I'd started my company with a small municipal contract with the Village of Oak Park, and while I did some residential projects to pay the bills, I wasn't interested in growing that area of work. This Armory project was my breakthrough opportunity, and I couldn't be happier.

Now, this was exciting!

The armory was the first of many projects I did for the State of Illinois over the years. Those rehabilitation projects led to other state, local, federal, and private commissions. It's funny—when I met people for the first time, and our conversation got around to what we did for a living, I told them I was an architect and founder of my firm. The same curious three questions seemed to pop up:

"Do you do interior decorating?"

"Do you do residential?"

"Is your husband an architect, too?"

I knew they were simple questions with no offense intended, but thoughts of what kind of projects a woman was presumed capable of handling made me bristle. It was satisfying to answer those questions with "no, no, and no." My target client and the kinds of projects I liked doing were those in roadwork, masonry and concrete reconstruction, roofing, and general rehabilitation projects for universities, post offices, mental health facilities, and armories. My firm also focused on the very satisfying work of retrofitting buildings to comply with the Americans with Disabilities Act (ADA). I learned from working at RJG that this kind of work, with this type of client, although not glamorous, would be recession resistant.

I did, however, design another store for Mary Walter in the River North area. It was fun working with her again and was a great way to exercise my creative, aesthetic side. But I continued to focus my core projects on inelegant work—the dirtier, the better—not as an interior decorator, not in residences, and certainly not with my husband, but rather, as an independent, licensed architect. And we always had a backlog of work.

{

Margaret blossomed from honing her little cottage baking industry, Le Royale Icing, in her home, to a renowned pastry chef working in her leased commercial kitchen/studio in Oak Park. Margaret and her staff created exquisite upscale sculptural cakes and pastries for weddings, corporate parties, event planners, hoteliers, high profile celebrities, and the general public across the country. She also continued making birthday cakes for Kristin with beautiful fresh or handmade fondant flowers, or sculptural cakes in the form of skateboards or baseball bats and mitts for Jonathan.

As my mother cut chicken for grilling one morning, she asked, "How many people are coming to the party?" We were preparing for Kristin's twelfth birthday party, and the whole family was coming to our house that afternoon.

"Let's see: Dennis, Jane and their kids, Julie, Lisa, and Kevin; Bob's mom, Shirley; his sister Kathy and husband, Roland, their daughters, Becky, Missy, and Kimberly; his other sister Sharon and husband, Jimmy, and their daughters, Meghann and Katie; Marcia, John, and their two kids, Jennifer and John Voll; and our next-door neighbors, Diane and Russ. So that's twenty-one guests, plus you and Dad, and my family," I said. "Oh, I forgot to tell you, Margaret will be bringing Kristin's cake, and said she'd stay for dinner."

"Wow, you're going to have a full house—it's a good thing we're making plenty of food!

"I haven't seen Margaret in a long time—how is she?" my mother asked.

"Very well. She can't wait to see you. I think she thinks of you as her mother in some ways. I told you about her mother, didn't I?"

"Yes, she died a long time ago?"

"Yes," I said, "a drunk driver hit and killed her mother when Margaret was just a toddler. She once told me she knew her mother loved her very much and remembered her mother's hugs. But Margaret wished she could remember her mother's voice and what she thought when she hugged Margaret."

"Kawaiso, neh?" My mother sighed. "The thought of little Margaret not having her mother makes me so sad."

"I know. But Margaret's a strong woman—she's doing fine. You know, after she told me about her mother, I decided to write letters to Kristin and Jonathan. Did I tell you?"

"What kind of letters? You send letters to the kids?" my mother asked.

"No, I bought a journal for each of them, and over the years, I wrote to them in their book, about what they were into, silly things they said or did, what their favorite color was at the time, and just everyday stuff happening in their lives. Tonight, I'll write to Kristin and tell her about today's party!"

"Oh, Susie, that's so nice."

"If anything ever happens to me, I want them to know how much I loved them and how proud I am of them. The children might forget what I looked like, or the sound of my voice, but they'll always have their letters from me. I'm grateful Margaret told me about her mom, or

I never would've thought to do this for the kids—and myself."

"Don't worry, nothing will happen to you! Will you give the books to them someday?" my mother asked.

"Someday, I guess. But I love going back to read the letters, reliving their young days. I might have trouble letting go of the books!" I chuckled.

Later that afternoon, Kristin came bouncing in the kitchen. "Mom, Margaret's here!" she announced.

"Got any room in the fridge for this?" Margaret carried a box holding Kristin's birthday cake. I carefully took it from her.

"Oh, Margaret, hi!" My mother hugged her.

"Hi!" Margaret's smile was broad. "It's been such a long time since I last saw you!"

After Kristin left the kitchen, I whispered, "Can we have a peek?"

"Oh, sure." Margaret carefully opened the box. A hush came over us.

"My gosh, it's beautiful," my mother said, putting her hands to her mouth.

"It's a chocolate devil's food layered cake," Margaret said, "and in between the layers, are fresh, whole raspberries laced with a white chocolate mousse filling. The frosting is buttercream, and those wide curly ribbons on the top and sides of the cake are paper-thin bands of white chocolate that I gathered into ruffles." She smiled.

"And Mom, look at the card between the ruffles, it says, 'Happy Twelfth Birthday, Kristin,' oh my god, she'll love this! Is the card edible?" I asked Margaret.

"Uh, *huh*. It's white chocolate, with dark chocolate writing."

"Thank you so much, Margaret," I said, clapping my hands. "Yum!"

"Hey, Margaret, we're about to make vegetable fried rice. Wanna help?" I asked.

"Oh, your mother's fried rice is always so delicious. Yes, I'd love to learn how you do it!"

I pointed to my mother. "You can learn from the master cook herself."

"There's nothing to learn, Margaret. It's so easy, you'll see," my mother said as she brought out a tray filled with colorful veggies. "I washed and cut these at home yesterday to save time today."

On her tray were piles of wedge-cut round onions; matchstick-cut carrots; diagonally sliced celery; chopped roasted red bell pepper; blanched and shocked bean sprouts, pea pods, and broccoli florets; and thin, diagonally sliced green onions.

"First, heat the wok at medium flame," she told Margaret.

As they waited for the wok to heat, my mother asked, "How is your business?"

"Good, good. It's hard to keep up with the orders, which is great, but I'm tired all the time, and I can't seem to get enough sleep," said Margaret.

"Don't overdo it, you'll wear yourself out and get sick. It's not good to be too busy," my mother said with a frown. "Oh, it looks like your wok might be ready. Hold your palm a few inches above the bottom. Do you feel the heat coming from it?"

"Yes, I think it's hot enough."

"Hai. Let's test it. Wet your hand with water and flick a little in the wok," my mother said. Margaret did, and the droplets of water sat there.

"Not ready yet," my mother said.

"I know I should get more sleep," said Margaret, "but with a small business, I have to keep going. It's one cake after another, and sometimes I wonder if it's all worth it." Margaret flicked water in the wok again, and the water drops danced on the bottom surface. "Is it ready now?" she asked.

"Hai. Yes, it's ready!" said my mother.

"Oh my gosh, I never knew when a pan was ready for oil. Thanks for that trick!"

My mother smiled and said, "Now pour a few tablespoons of oil and swirl it around. When you see the oil ripple, it'll be ready for the garlic."

As they waited for the oil to heat, Margaret said, "I got some good news this week. Jim Belushi ordered a cake from me!"

My mother looked at Margaret with a "deer in the headlights" gaze. She giggled. "Is he famous?"

"Margaret, that's so cool, I love Jim Belushi," I called out from the other end of the kitchen. "He's a famous comedian, Mom and he's in movies and on TV."

"Ahhh! He's a movie star—congratulations!" she said. "That's wonderful, but remember, don't overwork yourself. You have to stay healthy, okay?"

"Okay," Margaret said, "I promise, I'll try to get more rest."

My mother handed her a couple of smashed garlic cloves. "Do you use chopsticks, Margaret?"

"Not very well."

"Here, use this." I handed her a pair of tongs. Margaret smiled with relief.

"Fry the garlic until it's brown, it'll flavor the oil, and then take it out and throw away," my mother told her. "We'll start with the vegetables that take the longest to cook and end with those that take the least amount of time. Let's start with the onions—quick fry them and when they're a little soft, push them around the sides of the wok then add the carrots.

"Like this?" Margaret pushed the veggies back and forth.

"Hai, but don't fiddle and flip the vegetables too much, chotto, just enough. Good! Much better. Push the carrots around to the side against the onions and add the celery."

"I'm not sure if the carrots are cooked." Margaret frowned.

"Don't worry—they'll continue to cook while we work on the rest of the vegetables. In the end, you want the vegetables to be firm, not too soft," my mother assured her.

After Margaret quickly stir-fried all the veggies, my mother shook several tablespoons of thick oyster flavored sauce from its bottle. She showed Margaret how to mix the vegetables by carefully sliding the spatula against the bottom of the wok, in sections, and flipping the ingredients over. My mother picked some veggies up with her chopstick and tasted them.

"Margaret, Susie, you want to taste?"

"Sure." I gave a fork to Margaret and got one for myself.

Margaret took a forkful. "Mmmm. This is delicious. You only used the oyster sauce for flavoring?" Margaret asked.

"Hai. That's it. You like it?" We both nodded. She transferred all the veggies into a large bowl.

"We'll fry the rice now," said my mother. "We don't have to wash the wok since the food will get all mixed together. Margaret, heat the wok, add some oil, and fry some smashed garlic as we did before, okay?"

"Wow, this is great," I said with a laugh. "Margaret, will you come over more often, so I don't have to cook?"

"Better wait and see how this all turns out first!" Margaret laughed.

My mother brought out a pan of room-temperature rice. "I made the rice early this morning and spread it on this coated pan to cool off and dry out a little. That way, it won't be soggy when we cook it. Is the oil in the wok ready, Margaret?" she asked.

"Hai." Margaret said with conviction. My mother and I stopped and looked at her. The three of us broke out in laughter.

"Margaret, you speak Japanese now!" my mother said with a smile. "Okay, let's get back to work, wiki, wiki!"

My mother scooped enough rice to fill the wok about half-way. She tossed it, like a salad, so the rice had a thin coating of oil.

"We'll let it sit and fry for a few minutes. Then we can peek under a section to see if it's fried, and when it is, I'll flip it over."

My mother flipped over the rice, in segments, and then broke up the sections by poking them, vertically, with her spatula. "Almost ready," she said.

"It looks fried, but it's not brown like when I eat fried rice at a Chinese restaurant," Margaret said.

"It'll get brown. Watch." My mother sprinkled shoyu over the rice. It sizzled. "We have to work quickly now, so the shoyu doesn't burn." She flipped the rice, scraping from the bottom of the pan, sprinkled a little more shoyu, flipped, and repeated. The color of the rice ranged from beautiful caramel to deep tan and had a slight crunch. She then added some of the vegetables and tossed it with the rice. "Done!" she said.

"Wow. It's beautiful and smells so good." Margaret's eyes were bright.

"Good job, Margaret! You folks take a break and rest," my mother said. "Eat some fried rice, and I'll make the next batch."

"This is so delicious," Margaret said.

Our family and friends had arrived. Bob and Dennis grilled the chicken, hot dogs, and hamburgers, and my father watched over the children as they ran around in the yard. The other adults chatted over crackers and liver pâte, chips and salsa, and croissant-wrapped sausages that Shirley and Sharon had brought. When dinner was ready, everyone helped put the food on the table: teriyaki chicken, fried rice, hamburgers, and hot dogs, condiments, potato salad, and green salad. Kathy laid her dish of cheesy, oniony baked hash browns on the table, Jane arranged her sushi on a platter, and Marcia brought her famous black-eyed peas dish.

Amid the frenzy that comes with birthday parties and the joy of eating, my mother and Margaret, plates of food in hands, found a few quiet minutes in the breakfast nook off the kitchen, a cozy little room, surrounded by windows.

As I loaded the dishwasher, I heard the two quietly talking and did not interrupt them.

Kristin loved the party, our family, her gifts, and the fantastic cake Margaret had made, and all had a good time.

The next morning, Margaret called me. "I had such a great time yesterday. It was so nice seeing your family again, and my god, your mother was just wonderful. She's so patient and generous with her time, teaching me to cook fried rice. And she seemed concerned about my health—so sweet."

"I'm glad you came and enjoyed the day with us. My mom enjoyed spending time with you too."

"Oh, Susan, I love your mother so much. You know, she told me how sewing brought her such happiness—nothing gave her more satisfaction than sewing a button on one of your father's shirts. She said finding the right button then sewing it on, was a project that she could start and finish."

I guess that's a nice thing to do. But a button?

Margaret continued, "With so many exhausting deadlines, it's hard for me to stop and think about what's satisfying. Your mother taught me that with each task, no matter how big or small, I have to slow down and appreciate what I've accomplished. I love her for that lesson."

My mother's words were wise. But I couldn't imagine pondering each day all I'd accomplished when there was always so much more to do. Maybe one day I'll understand.

Indeed, my mother found happiness in sewing. She had a workspace set up where she spent many hours altering, mending, and making clothes for herself, or sewing aprons, potholders, and other handy household items for her three sisters in Hawai`i, Nobuko, Se, and Aiko. She used to make things for all five of her sisters, and she missed sewing for Norma and Margie who had passed away.

When I visited my mother, I sometimes brought my different alteration projects and used her workspace. She would sit near me and we talked as I sewed.

"Mom, remember the first outfit you helped me sew?"

"Mmmm, which one was that?" she asked.

"It was a light-aqua colored skirt and matching vest. Boy, I was so proud of it even though you did a lot of the work."

"Yes, I remember now! You were so small, and we had to alter the pattern before you could even start sewing." She laughed.

As a teenager, I was so tiny that the only store-bought clothes that fit me were children's size eight, and those styles were too clunky and childish for me. My world opened up when my mother taught me to sew my clothes.

I didn't have a permanent sewing workspace set up as she did, and when I visited her with a sewing project, I knew it made her happy. And it made me happy too.

}

When Kristin and Jonathan were in their early teens, they stayed with my parents on New Year's Eve, and we picked them up the next day. Marcia and John came with us to my parents' New Year's Day open house. As we approached the landing of their second-floor apartment building, Marcia stopped.

"All those shoes—there're so many! What are they doing here?" she asked.

"Marcia, it's a Japanese household. We take off our shoes before going into the house. C'mon, take yours off and let's go in!"

"No, wait, I have to count them. I've never seen anything like this."

I laughed. Marcia worked for a company that did inventory for stores in the Chicago region. "You can count later. You're off the clock now, let's go!"

I opened the door, and we all stood there, taking in the sight of my parents' apartment. Strewn on the floor and furniture were streamers from party poppers, half-deflated balloons, toot horns, celebratory hats, and tiaras. To me, this was a pretty typical scene the day after my parents' New Year's Eve party, but to Marcia, whose parents were more sedate, it was a sight to behold.

Marcia giggled. "Your parents' New Year's Eve party last night rocked—much livelier than your party. I say from now on, we come over here to ring in the New Year!" She winked at me.

"Kristin, Jonathan, hi!" we all called out. Hugging them, I asked, "How was Grandma and Grandpa's party last night?"

"Pretty good," Jonathan said, "but it got boring later on. Everyone seemed to be laughing about nothing."

"Well, older people can be like that." Bob and I shared a glance and a smile.

"Marcia! John! So glad you came!" My mother squealed with joy coming to greet us. "Go make a plate—there's plenty of food!"

Marcia and I settled in the kitchen and began eating, and my mother came and sat with us.

"Everything is so delicious. I can't eat it fast enough!" Marcia said.

"Thanks! Get some more," my mother insisted.

"So, what crazy thing has your husband done lately?" Marcia playfully asked my mother.

"Oh, you know, the usual," my mother said. "I complained to him that it's hard to carry groceries up the stairs because my knees hurt, and I wanted one of those stair lifts." She laughed. "But instead, he built a contraption with a bucket and pulley so I could put the groceries in the bucket, and he would pull it up to our apartment. But my knees still hurt because I have to keep walking up the stairs—oh, that man!" They both giggled.

"My husband won't turn down anything someone wants to give him," Marcia said.

"Yes, my husband too!" my mother chimed in.

Marcia continued, "Our two-car garage has his workbench, tools, a table saw, a drafting table, file cabinets and a chest of drawers filled with I don't know what, an old car that doesn't run, an old water heater, and my freezer. Let's see what else—"

John was in the dining room, filling his plate with "seconds."

"John?" Marcia called out. "I'm talking about your garage—what's in it?"

"Did you tell her about the Buick?" John asked, joining us.

"Yes, I said it was an old car that doesn't run."

"NO! It's a 1966 Buick, very valuable!" he countered.

Marcia turned to my mother and in a lowered voice, said, "Yeah, as I said, it's an old car that doesn't run."

We all laughed.

"What about the extra sails for the boat, did you mention those? And strings and soundboard for a player piano, three outboard motors, and what else, oh yeah, a 1964 Honda motorcycle that works!" John said.

Marcia rolled her eyes. "See what I mean? By the way, there's no room in the garage for our cars. It's so crowded I can't even get into my freezer. I've been begging him to clean out the garage, but he won't, and I have no idea what's growing in that darn freezer!" My mother laughed as she left the kitchen to tend to her other guests.

"Hey, there's Dennis," I said as he came in the front door with Jane and their three kids.

"Hi, Susie!" Jane joined us in the kitchen, "Oh, Marcia, hi, so good to see you! Is your husband here too?"

"Yeah, he went over there," Marcia said, pointing to the living room. "How are you? Your children have gotten so big. Is this Lisa?"

"No, this is Julie. I think Lisa and Kevin are in the living room too."

"Jane, make a plate. I'll go with you," I said.

Her eyes grew big when she saw the spread of food on the dining table. "Your mom out-did herself again. Oh, all this food, it's beautiful—I don't know how she does it. I love her Okinawan dishes—oh my gosh, she even made andagi!"

"Okinawan dishes? Which ones?" I asked.

"What? Oh, let's see," Jane said, pointing, "Soba noodles, Okinawan purple sweet potatoes, seaweed salad, gobo salad, and andagi."

"I thought those were Japanese dishes," I said.

"No, they're Okinawan. I'll bet your mom learned how to make them from her mother. You know your grandparents were from Okinawa, right?"

"I have no idea what you're talking about, Jane. I thought we were Japanese—and you too!" I was bewildered.

"Uh, uh. You're not Japanese—you're Okinawan. And so am I!"

"Dennis?" I called out.

He sauntered over to Jane and me, picking at his overflowing plateful of food.

"Hi, Happy New Year," he said.

"Happy New Year to you. Hey, aren't we Japanese?" I asked Dennis.

"Negative, we're Okinawan, why?"

"What? Why didn't I know we weren't Japanese?"

"I don't know. Didn't anyone tell you?"

I waved Marcia in the dining room and said, "They're trying to tell me I'm not Japanese, can you believe it?"

"Oh yeah, I knew that," she said.

"Get. Out. What in the world are you talking about?" I asked.

"You always said you were Japanese, but I knew you weren't. You didn't look Japanese—Asian, yes, but not Japanese." Marcia chuckled, looking at Dennis and Jane.

She was in on this charade. It was crazy. Ridiculous! Unbelievable.

I flagged down Bob.

"Jane just told me I was—" I turned to her. "What am I again?"

She swallowed a forkful of food and answered, "Okinawan."

Bob smiled. "Oh, you mean Uchinanchu? Yeah, I knew that."

"Give me a break. What do you mean, Uchi-whatever? How would you know more about me than me?" I was sure everyone was having their little fun gaslighting me.

"Your mom gave you a big, thick book a long time ago called Uchinanchu," Bob said. "It's about Okinawans living in Hawaii. It's on our bookshelf—didn't you read it?" he asked.

Sheepishly, I shook my head.

Dennis laughed. "Well, there you go—we all read the book!"

Now was not a good time to question my parents, but holy moly, I felt like a family secret had just exploded open, at least for me.

My parents' New Year's Day open house gave us a much-needed respite from work, and what had happened a week earlier on Christmas night. My family and I had come home from a lovely dinner at Dennis and Jane's house in Rockford, Illinois, a city about eighty miles northwest of Oak Park. We discovered a burglar had rummaged through our home while we were gone, taking only what he could carry.

I called my mother.

"Mom, we got burglarized, and he took the pearls you gave me!" I blurted over the phone. It was an exquisitely beautiful, delicate strand of pearls with an ever-so-soft cast of pink—a medium-sized pearl was in the center, and the rest subtly diminished in size, to the tiniest ones at the clasp. They were given to my mother by her father, and she had given them to me. The theft devasted me, tears streaming as I told her.

"Oh, no, it's okay, Susie, don't worry. Thank goodness nobody was hurt, that's the important thing."

"But, the pearls were from your father!"

"Susan, listen to me, they're just pearls. All you folks are okay, so don't worry about them—they were just pearls!" she insisted.

That was my mother—her value of our safety over "things" never wavered. I knew she was right, but I was sickened that the strand of pearls from her father, in my possession, was lost forever.

Jonathan took the biggest hit, finding some of his beloved, boyish stuff missing from his bedroom: a guitar, baseball bat, and mitt. Oddly, a three-ring binder holding Jonathan's prized Batman card collection that he'd organized in clear plastic sleeves, lay open on his bed.

We all stood over the bed, staring at it.

"Are you sure you weren't looking at them before we left for Uncle Dennis's and Aunt Jane's house?" Bob had asked Jonathan.

"I'm sure. I closed the binder and put it on the table next to my bed."

"So weird. The burglar must have been a kid, maybe a teenager. I can't imagine an adult stopping to look at Batman cards in the middle of a heist," I'd said.

The police had come quickly but resolved nothing. After the initial shock and being creeped-out knowing a stranger was in our house, we went about with our lives. But it took me years to get over losing my mother's pearls.

Shortly after the burglary, I saw Jonathan in his bedroom fully engrossed with a ball of string, a Kleenex box, tennis balls, and wooden blocks, working on a contraption of sorts. On the floor near him was a drawing with lines and lots of arrows on it.

"Hi! Watcha workin' on?"

"My project."

"I can see that. What project?"

One of the Christmas presents we gave Jonathan was a gift certificate to his favorite store, Radio Shack, and it was burning a hole in his pocket, so Bob had taken him to the store. Jonathan bought a cheap, simple alarm for his bedroom that would buzz if the door opened.

"I'm figuring out how *I*," he said, turning to me, "*only* I can keep the buzzer from going off when I open the door. Anyone else who opens it will set off the buzzer."

He completed his project, and when he pulled a hidden string hanging outside his bedroom door, it set off a whole series of subsequent actions inside his room in true Rube Goldberg fashion, that eventually disengaged the buzzer. I think Jonathan was determined never again to have his room be a part of another heist. I was proud and intrigued by his patience and meticulousness.

※

After years of on-again-off-again rehabbing our house, drywall dust and sawdust were still part of our construction-centric lives.

"I'm going now," Kristin called as she walked through the kitchen. "Jenny and her Mom are here to pick me up."

I noticed her steps left white, fluffy footprints on the floor.

"When you get outside, don't forget to wipe your feet on the mat," I called out.

"MOM! My friends all wipe their feet *before* going in their house. Why do we always have to wipe our feet when we *leave* the house? And when is this project going to be done?" she asked.

"I don't want you to track drywall dust into anyone's home, and the project is almost finished," I said, smiling.

It was the same question Kristin and Jonathan always asked when they left the house, and the same answer I gave. One might think I would be embarrassed by the state of our home, but I wasn't. I loved the chaos of ladders, canvas tarps, construction lamps, stepping around and over drywall boards, crowbars, hammers, and drills—and smelling the nostalgic fragrance of pine from freshly cut 2 × 4 studs, and the clean scent of drywall compound. Watching, step-by-step, a new and different environment emerging energized me. The kids were good eggs about it, and but for a few outbursts now and then, did little complaining.

Standing with Jonathan in the middle of construction, this time in our front hallway, I asked in a cheery tone, "Do you think you might want to be an architect one day?"

"No."

"What? Why not?"

"Because I don't like construction," he answered. "It's stinky and messy."

"How can you not like construction? Don't you think this is exciting?" My arms were outstretched, embracing our construction environment.

He shrugged and went upstairs.

What have I done to our kids?

This moment was just one of many I asked myself that question.

When we had moved from Evanston to Oak Park nine years earlier, I was determined to find a female pediatrician for Kristin, then a toddler, and Jonathan, still a baby. I'd wanted both kids to learn and assume women could be in any professional field, including medicine. There were few female doctors in those days, but I eventually found Dr. Jo Zurbrug, a wonderful pediatrician who cared for the children for many years.

When Jonathan was just a wee lad entering grammar school, he whizzed past me, heading for the breakfast nook window in the back of the house, as he did every week. Perching himself on a chair with elbows propped on the chair back and hands folded under his chin, he waited for the men. Jonathan loved watching them pull up the alley in their big garbage truck and do what sanitation workers do.

"I want to do that when I grow up!" he exclaimed, pointing to the men.

"Great! That would be a fun job! You could drive that truck and make the back open and watch all the garbage pour in and get squished! You can be whatever you want when you grow up, Jonathan. Anything! You can even be a doctor if you want."

He turned to me looking puzzled and asked, "Can boys be doctors?"

I gasped.

Oh no, what have I done?

In spite of a brief recession in the early 1990s, Rakstang Associates remained busy with a full docket of projects in varying phases of design and construction. From starting as the sole practitioner, my company expanded modestly to a team of three architects, two intern architects, and an administrative assistant. My practice flourished, and I looked forward to an optimistic, albeit undefined, future for my firm.

Although I had no imminent intentions of selling the company, I questioned whether the firm name would be a hindrance if that opportunity ever presented itself.

What value would a company have with the name Rakstang in it, if Rakstang was no longer a part of the organization?

I decided to change my firm's name from Rakstang Associates, Architects and Planners Inc., to Urban Resource, Architects and Planners, Inc. It would remain the same company with the same clients but just have a new name. I liked the idea.

Time moved quickly. Fully engaged with all things high school kids do, Kristin, a senior in Oak Park-River Forest High School Orchesis Dance Company, and Jonathan, a junior, was involved in his garage band. Bob was now president and owner of the same manufacturing company at which he'd applied for his first job nearly twenty years earlier.

Along with my architectural practice, I became an elected member of the Board of Trustees for the Village of Oak Park—another seemingly full-time job.

I enjoyed my Trustee work but was astounded at how time-consuming it was. Oak Park was an activist town, leaving few issues unaddressed. I found the many committee meetings, sub-committee meetings, community meetings, community organization receptions, meetings with the public and concerned citizens all very exhausting and yet, satisfying at the same time. I felt my involvement was an opportunity to give back to the Village I loved. Bob sometimes accompanied me at various receptions and dinners, but for the most part, my time with him and the kids reduced significantly.

A few days before each formal board meeting, several three-inch-thick binders filled with background information on ordinances, resolutions, and motions for approval were hand-delivered to each trustee to study, analyze, and evaluate. The board meetings, convening on the first and third Monday evenings each month, ran live on local cable TV for public viewing and often lasted well into the night.

Margaret came over to our house and watched the board meeting with Bob.

"I forgot your board meetings were televised," Margaret told me over the phone the next day.

"Bob mentioned you stopped by. Pretty boring, huh?" I asked.

"No, it was cool to see you in action. Your meeting was so complicated, how do you even know which way to vote?"

"Well, Oak Park's not divided into wards like the City, with aldermen who serve only their areas," I told her. "We're at-large trustees and represent all citizens in the Village, so that means a lot of one-on-one and group meetings with residents concerned about all kinds of things. And often, different groups of residents opposed each other, depending on the issue." I sighed. "Even after a few years of being in office, I can't get used to 50-percent of the people being mad at me because I didn't vote the way they wanted me to."

"No wonder you're always so busy! When we were watching the meeting, I asked Bob if he ever got to see you anymore." Margaret laughed. "He said, 'Oh yes, I see her every first and third Mondays—on TV!'"

I smiled. "Thank goodness he has a sense of humor with the crazy hours I keep." Bob understood my commitment to my practice and civic duties and took care of the home front as best as he could. He was still very much into cooking.

One evening, I was going through my big trustee binders, and Bob was relaxing on the couch, reading an issue of Bon Appétit. He looked up.

"Hey, do you remember when your mom made shrimp with cucumbers?" He asked.

"Umm, no, not really, why?"

Putting down the magazine, he said, "I don't know, I just thought about it. I remember liking it. I didn't know cucumbers could be so good, cooked."

"She cooked cucumbers? I only knew it as eaten raw. Hmmm, yes, I remember now but have no idea how she did it. I'll find out," I said.

"I'll ask her," he said.

"No, that's okay, I'll find out."

"No, really, I'll call her now." Bob insisted.

I shrugged.

A few minutes later, he told me he was going to my parents' house on Saturday to learn how to make shrimp with cucumbers.

"What? How come? I'll go with you."

"You don't have to. You said you had a lot of meetings this weekend, so I'll go. Don't worry—I'll do a good job!"

That next Saturday night, late, I hadn't heard from Bob or my mother, so I called her.

"Hi—how did it go? Is Bob still there?" I asked.

"Susie, hi! No, he left about a half-hour ago—he'll be home soon. Oh my gosh, he was so funny. Shrimp with cucumbers is so ordinary, how come all of a sudden he wanted to learn how to make it?"

"I don't know. I'm swamped, and I guess Bob figured if he wanted to eat something special, he'd have to cook it himself. How did he do?" I asked.

"Fine! He's so nice that husband of yours. He followed my instructions and did a good job. He's very patient and wanted to do it right, and it turned out oishi! You'll like it. I kept a little for your father's and my dinner, and he's bringing the rest home. I haven't made that in a long time, so it was fun cooking it with him."

"Thanks for teaching him." Bob was rarely receptive when I tried giving him any cooking instructions, but he raved over learning from my mother—go figure.

"Oh, don't mention it, I'm glad he's interested," she said.

When Bob got home, he couldn't wait to heat the meal for us. The kids, as usual, were out with friends, so it was just the two of us.

"Wow, this is delicious!" I said. The cucumber had an ever-so-bit of crunch, and the shrimps' mildly tart, yet sweet flavors filled with umami made the meal delicious. "So, how'd you make it?"

"Well, you know your mom, she doesn't measure, so it was hard figuring out how much of everything she used. But I estimated as best as I could and wrote it down." He pulled out his folded sheet of notes.

"First, I combined about two tablespoons each of sake and soy sauce," he read. "Then I added grated ginger, I guess about a teaspoon, the same amount of finely minced garlic, and about a teaspoon of sugar, with a couple of pinches of dashi granules, and mixed it all up. That's what I marinated the shrimp in."

"Mmmm sounds good." I ate as I listened to Bob go into great detail about how he made the meal.

"Let's see, I think I got it all," he said, looking up from his notes. "Yes!"

"It's delicious, Chef Bob. I love it."

"Since the kids don't eat shrimp, I'm gonna substitute it with chunks of chicken next time I make this," Bob said.

With a little hot rice and some steamed carrots, we feasted on Bob's excellent Japanese meal.

During one of the public Village meetings, the board discussed a variance regarding the demolition of grassy parkways in the neighborhood so the adjacent building owners, who didn't want the hassle of parkway maintenance, could extend the concrete sidewalk to the curb and install cast-iron tree surrounds. I was opposed to this proposal because the project required replacing permeable green space with impermeable concrete, thus adding more rainwater discharge demands on our underground stormwater system, as well as put the health of trees at risk. And I didn't want this action to set a precedent in the Village.

Weeks later, I ran some errands not far from my parents' place. I was behind schedule that day but decided to stop in and see them for a quick visit. My world moved and changed regularly, but everything about my parents and their home seemed to stay the same. I found being with them cathartic.

"Ahhhh, Susie, what a surprise to see you! Are you hungry?" my mother asked.

"No," I said, looking at my watch. "I can't stay long. I wanted to drop in to say hi. Where's Dad?"

"He's in the basement working on another one of his projects. Let me make you some *udon*."[33]

"No, please don't bother. I wanted to drop in for only a few minutes. Then I have to go—I have so much work to do at the office."

Before I knew it, I found myself sitting at her kitchen table as she prepared udon for me. Her shimmering, savory broth of dashi infused with bonito flakes, with its mild sweetness of mirin against an ever-so-light touch of sesame oil and shoyu, the soft, thick and chewy udon noodles, all topped with cubes of tender chicken and a garnish of chopped green onions, practically brought me to tears. I ate her udon with abandon.

"How are the kids doing?" she asked.

"They're both fine. Jonathan's majoring in Biochemistry and minoring in Chemistry—he's also hooked up with other musicians, so he's happy in Boulder. Kristin is enjoying college life in Minneapolis and finally declared her major—and guess what she picked?"

"I don't know—what?"

"She decided to major in Japanese with a specialty in linguistics! She'll learn all about our culture, language, and she'll even learn to read and write Japanese." I smiled.

"Ahhh—Susie, will she?" Reaching out her arms, she clapped her hands once and bowed. "Where did she get that idea, out of all the things she could have picked?" My mother asked.

"I guess from you and Dad, who else? She sure didn't get it from me!" I said. "Ahhhh, hard to believe how grown-up they are. In a blink of the eye, the kids will graduate from college. Time is moving fast."

"Just wait, it goes faster, the older you get," she told me. "How do you like doing your work for Oak Park?" my mother asked.

"I enjoy it. But I go to so many community events, and it's sometimes tough to juggle all that. But everything is okay."

"Is the group mostly women?" she asked.

"No, right now, I'm the only woman on the board."

"Oh, no. Susie, be careful what you say to the men. You have to be very careful."

"Mom, things are different than when you were young. At work, I'm often the only woman in construction meetings. Don't worry—I'm doing okay."

"You know, men don't like to be told what to do."

"Okay, Mom, I'll be careful." I laughed.

Oh boy, if I ever told her some of the things I've had to say to contractors, she'd flip out.

"I hope they're not mad at you," she said.

"Who? What do you mean?"

"You know, the men in your Oak Park group," she said. "But even if they're mad at you, you did the right thing. Keep being strong, Susie!"

"Mom, I don't understand. Why do you think the board is mad at me?"

She took out an article she'd clipped from the newspaper and handed it to me. I was surprised to read the Chicago Tribune had picked up the board discussion regarding the demolition of the grassy parkway, highlighting me, by name, as the sole dissenting vote that easily passed 6-1.

"You stood up to all those men! Keep doing that. Not one of them took your side, and you voted against them anyway. I'm so proud of you," she said.

I smiled.

Well, well—so my my mother is a feminist!

Time continued to elude me. Maintaining a high level of focus to fulfill the urgent responsibilities of Trustee work, my architectural practice and family was a constant challenge. Every bit my adversary I'd never beat, Time was in total control of me, dictating its demands, mocking me when I fell short of expectations, and parceling out its minutes, hours, and days at its discretion.

Driving to a meeting one morning, I passed a Starbucks and saw several people sitting outside, under the sun, chatting with friends, reading the newspaper, or simply relaxing as they savored their coffee. Looking at my watch, I bristled feeling grumpy.

Don't these people have to get to work or anything? It would take a miracle for me ever to have time in the middle of the morning to casually sip a cafe latte under the sun. Achhh—I'm jealous.

Toward the close of my four-year term as Trustee, I toyed with the idea of running for re-election.

"Bob, some people approached me and asked if I would be interested in running for re-election." I casually said.

Bob was silent.

"Did you hear me? What do you think, should I run for—"

"I heard you!" He interrupted.

He remained silent but cast an expression I had never seen in all our years of our marriage. It wasn't a glare, nor anger, and certainly not, "Oh, how nice."

He spoke. "You're not serious, right?"

"Well, I thought..." I paused, searching for words.

"Are you serious?"

I never brought up the idea again, and graciously stepped down when my term expired.

After more than twenty years of school and work, an opportunity for a buyout presented itself to me. It's difficult to sell a service business such as mine—a few computers, some office equipment, the soft assets of ongoing contracts, a diverse portfolio, and goodwill was about all there was to sell—so when I received an offer, I went for it.

I vaguely remembered hearing bustling activity downstairs but dismissed it and fell back asleep. Bob had gone to work, and the air was still. The morning sun coming into our bedroom awakened me, but its angle was unfamiliar. It was after 9 a.m., hours later than my usual wake-up time, and I heard birds chattering.

My eyes opened wide.

Oh my gosh. I'm retired. How can that be? I'm only forty-eight!

It was the first day I would not have any meetings, or go into the office, or review big binders full of Village ordinances. I walked downstairs to the kitchen.

What shall I do today? Maybe nothing. Or I can garden. Or maybe do a load of laundry.

It was early spring with temperatures still brisk, but sauntering down our tree-lined street, I saw the sun peeking through tree branches that had not fully leafed-out, kissing swaths of bright yellow daffodils and cobalt blue scilla that blanketed the broad lawns of Oak Park.

Spring: a new beginning, indeed!

I turned the corner at Lake Street and arrived at Starbucks.

"Can I help you?" the barista asked, his face expectant.

I never did get the hang of this part. I took a deep breath.

"Yes. I want a decaf Americano, extra strong, not that large size, the smaller one," I said, pointing. "Yes, that one, and I'd like non-fat milk with a pump of vanilla. Oh, yes, and don't fill it to the top because I'll need some ice to cool it down a bit."

"Whip or no whip?"

"Uh, excuse me?" I asked.

"Do you want the milk whipped or not whipped?"

"Oh, no, not whipped."

"That it?" the barista asked.

"Yes, thank you."

"Tall decaf double single pump vanilla skinny no whip stirred room Americano pleeeze!" he called out.

Sheesh.

My coffee was perfect. I stepped outside of Starbucks and found an unoccupied chair. And there, I spent my mid-morning leisurely sipping my Americano, relaxing under the warmth of the sun.

During those first few weeks of retirement, my Swiss Army Cavalry watch, stubbornly integral with my wrist for so many years, began to lose time, so I took it to Marshall Field's watch department as I always did when it needed a new battery.

"Hi, I'd like a battery replacement," I said, handing my watch to the jeweler. "I might as well get a new watchband while I'm at it. Where are your black leather ones?"

"Over there." He pointed and began to inspect my watch.

"This is pretty old," he said. "I can change the battery, but it looks like you might need a new movement."

"Huh, interesting," I mused. "How much will that cost?"

"I'll have to send it to our watch repair department to get an estimate. It'll be expensive, probably more than what you paid for it in the first place. It'll take at least two weeks to fix if they have the parts."

"Thank you, no," I said.

On any day in the past, I couldn't have possibly managed life without my watch. But now, I chuckled at the irony that the timepiece, to which I was so indebted, had stopped working at precisely the time in my life when I no longer needed it.

Sweet. It seemed like the perfect closure.

Time slowed down, and days seemed longer, nights unending, and weeks went unplanned and unscheduled. But after a few months of having such an abundance of time, a craving so unattainable in years past, I grew restless.

"Bob, I hate to admit this, but I'm stuck, and I don't know what to do with myself. I'm afraid I'm too young to be retired. I have no sense of purpose. I'm a mother whose children have their own lives in college, an architect without an office, and a wife who has nothing to do. I spent all my adult life defining myself, and now, I don't know who I am anymore."

He thought for a minute. "Are you thinking of getting a job?"

"No, I don't think so. I love that I don't wear a watch anymore or need business cards! If I got a job, I know I would find myself with little or no time to do things I want to do. And I don't want to go there again."

"Well, so, what is it you want to do? What did you always want to do, but never had the time?" he asked.

"That's the problem—I don't know. I need to find something challenging, something that will help me get reacquainted with my creative self and fill me up with satisfaction."

"How about piano lessons? You've been saying for years how you want to do that someday. Guess what? It's SOMEDAY!"

That was a scary idea. I'd be testing myself, my wits, memory, skill, out in the open—like a flashlight casting its light, or darkness, on me.

But he's right. I guess it's now or never. I was so tired of hearing myself grouse about not having enough time for piano lessons, and now was a perfect time.

"I'll do it!"

Walking into the home studio, a pleasant room with its centerpiece, a Steinway grand piano, I met my new piano teacher, Joe Cisar. Tall and slim with brown hair, he welcomed me with a warm smile. After a few minutes of meet and greet chit-chat, Joe got down to business.

"So, what brings you here?" he asked.

"I took piano lessons through my junior year in high school but haven't played since then, and I'd like to start again," I answered, paused, and unartfully blurted, "And I want to play Beethoven!"

Joe nodded. "What kind of music did you play?"

"Let's see, classical mostly, Beethoven, of course, Mozart, a little Strauss, and also popular tunes like Hatari's 'Baby Elephant Walk' and 'Moon River.'" I felt relaxed until his next dreaded question.

"Why don't you play something for me so I can get a sense of where you are with your music?" he asked.

Oh my god!

His request sent a shockwave through my body and with the speed of a glissando across the keyboard, cold and numbness ran from my neck and shoulders down into my arms and hands, feeling as if they had turned into thick, rubber clubs, while at the same time, my scalp was icy-hot and tingling.

Performance anxiety. It reared its ugly head like a predator with its prey. As a child, I had played the piano with reckless abandon, not caring about the world's view of how I sounded. But somewhere around my teen years, becoming more and more self-conscious about my abilities or rather, inabilities, not liking how my playing sounded, along with being an unfocused teenager, I quit taking lessons. That's where my psyche got stuck and after all these years , my demon, performance anxiety, presented itself with more fury than I had remembered.

In fits and starts, I played the last piece I'd worked on when I was in high school, Mozart's Sonata in C major K. 545. I could hardly breathe while my shaking hands banged out Mozart's magnificent composition. Finally, to my relief, after too many measures of pure agony, Joe, in his calm, thoughtful, and measured voice, interrupted my playing.

"That's fine," he said. "I think working with a diverse repertoire will help improve your technique. We can start with a Beethoven bagatelle." He left the room briefly.

Joe returned with a copy of the Sechs Bagatellen No.1 and sight reading the music, he played it for me. I was blown away by the piece and Joe's exquisite playing.

Does he honestly think I'll be able to play that?

"I think you'll also benefit from some Chopin Preludes," he said, playing without looking away from the score. He continued, "I'll write down the name of the book's publisher you should buy. And we can even explore some jazz piano if you like."

Still reverberating from my disastrously raucous Mozart performance, I left Joe's studio exhausted and ambivalent over my hour with him. I was drained. It was a pretty sad situation if my performance anxiety kept me from playing even in front of my piano teacher.

Over the next few months, I practiced for hours every day, feeding my insatiable appetite for trying to make music again. But my results were disappointing. As an adult student, it was difficult reconciling the conundrum of hearing my awkwardness at the keyboard, compared to the glorious sounds Joe created in his studio and on stage, and those I heard in concert halls.

After several months of lessons, Joe patiently listened to me attempt to express each of the voices of Bach's Invention No. 8, F Major.

You poor thing! How can you stand listening to me butcher this piece composed by the Maestro?

But always the professional, Joe's skillful teaching, patience, and willingness to hang in there with me helped instill some self-confidence. And together, over time, we tackled the works of Bach, Chopin, Schubert, Mendelssohn, Stravinsky, Scott Joplin, some jazz—and of course, Beethoven.

I sat at my piano one morning working on a new piece.

"I'm taking the car, Mom. I'll be home around six," Jonathan called out to me. He was home from college for spring break and generally informed me of his plans rather than asked for permission.

"Okay, have a good time," I said without looking up. When I heard the door latch close, I realized Jonathan was gone.

Oh man, I didn't even think to ask where he was going. Was that bad of me? He's growing up so fast.

Playing classical piano again was like reuniting with a fine old friend. Listening to music moved me, sometimes to tears, and making music filled me with satisfaction and joy. I diligently practiced as if I was trying to make up lost time for the decades my old Lyon and Healy had sat dormant. With all the time in the world, I enjoyed life. Time suspended itself for me, and I seized my music.

"Hi, Mom," Jonathan said to me later that day, looking puzzled. "Wait. You were at the piano when I left this morning, and now it's almost nighttime. Were you there the whole day?"

"Ha! You know, I once told Dad that I loved studying music so much, I could play the piano all day, but didn't think I meant it literally. I guess I did after all!"

֍

Bob's career was in full bloom, Kristin and Jonathan had graduated from college and lived independently—Kristin in Minneapolis and Jonathan in Boulder. No one ever told us that when kids go to out-of-state schools, they rarely return home, especially when their schools are in such great states. We asked them if they were planning to come back to live, and I heard them say, "Well, no!" or maybe it was, "Hell, no!" Either way, they stayed in their beloved new states.

Our nest was officially empty. We decided to downsize from our home in the historic district of Oak Park to a Chicago loft condominium in an odd little neighborhood holding a strange past.

Skid Road was a term believed to have originated in the 1800s in the Pacific Northwest, where the logging industry cleared a path or "road" for large logs to slide on wood skids from the forested hills, down to the lumber mill. The area around the road was populated with makeshift housing for loggers and often attracted rowdy indigents. During the Great Depression, the term evolved into Skid Row throughout the country, including an area west of Chicago's downtown Loop. Here, train lines converged and railroad workers and indigents, frequenting its many bars and brothels, "flopped" in cheap, single resident occupancy hotels. In 1966, an infamous drifter, Richard Speck, was apprehended on Skid Row at the Starr Hotel after brutally slaughtering eight nursing students.

Over twenty years ago, in the late 1970s, the city razed a parcel of land ridding the flophouses, bars, and the Starr Hotel, marking the beginning of the city's urban renewal program. Coexisting within the edges of Skid Row were structurally viable commercial properties. Many of the one, and two-story manufacturing plants, storage buildings, and warehouses were in disrepair or abandoned and lay in static repose as if in a fetal position. This area west of the Loop, now aptly called the West Loop, was where Bob and I had decided to settle.

The world was on the threshold of its next millennium, and we began our new life in the city. Our building, circa the early 1900s, once serving as paper storage for a Chicago newspaper, was carved into several adaptive reuse loft condominiums.

"Bob, look at our neighborhood." He joined me at our window. "It's so barren, desolate."

"Yeah, almost eerie," he said. "except the prostitutes don't think so."

"Prostitutes? I've had to step over a few drunk guys passed out on the sidewalk, but not prostitutes."

"You're not paying attention!" Bob laughed.

We loved the edgy, primal rawness of the city. Across the street from us, wind whooshed through the broken windows of an abandoned structure, a condo for pigeons of sorts, and sometimes for no apparent reason, a flock of these two-legged creatures would suddenly take flight out of every fenestration they could find. Throughout the land around us, small scruffy bushes defiantly poked through cracks in the sidewalks and vacant parking lots, dotting the urban landscape like mournful shrubs in a desert.

One night, I awakened to the sound of a woman who seemed in distress. I picked up the phone.

"911, how can I help you?" a female dispatcher with a deadpan voice asked.

It was about midnight.

"Yes, hello, I keep hearing a woman's voice under my condo window, and I think she's in trouble," I reported.

"Name and address."

I gave her my information.

"What makes you think she's in trouble?" The dispatcher asked.

"Well, I'm not sure, but she keeps saying, "Oh, that hurts, stop it. You're hurting me. You're hurting—"

"Honey," the dispatcher interrupted, "how long have you lived in this neighborhood?"

"About two months," I said.

"Uh, huh," she scoffed. "I'll dispatch a car." Her voice, once deadpan, suddenly sounded animated and amused. She hung up.

Okay, so I'm not the savviest city dweller—yet.

In the morning, I explored the northern part of West Loop, the iconic meatpacking district on Fulton Market Street. The area bustled with a cacophony of whistling men wearing white, blood-stained butcher's coats, guiding semi-truck drivers inch their rigs back and forth into their designated loading bays. Truck deliveries to wholesale fishmongers and produce purveyors, and beeping front-end loaders filled with wooden pallets, added to the daytime bustle. But at night, I later discovered, Fulton Market was still, desolate, and sat in deafening silence.

Near our condo, however, nighttime brought a different story. Greektown, a small area within the West Loop, is where Greek restaurants line Halsted Street and cast their intoxicating fragrances of saganaki (oopah!), spit-roasted gyros, and wood-fired ovens. I noticed restaurant customers often parked on or close to the block we lived and walked to Halsted Street happily chattering and laughing, anticipating the delightful theater of Greek dining and feasting on their favorite dishes. And walking back to their cars after a great evening of fun, good food, and drink, they always seemed to be in the merriest of spirits. There was a lively, positive energy in the air, despite our neighborhood's withering surroundings.

The festive mood of Greektown against the blight, grit, and tension of its streetscape was the classic backdrop to the sanctuary Bob and I had found in our new loft. Its wide-open spaces, exposed steel girders and columns, and natural light flooding through the north-facing window wall, added to the exquisite incongruities of urban living, evoking a sense of adventure to our neighborhood and our new life.

Both Kristin and Jonathan came "home" to visit us for the weekend to see our new digs.

"Cool! It's different." Jonathan was the first to speak. "How do you like it?"

"We love it! What do you think, Kristin?" Bob asked.

"Awesome. But it doesn't seem like a place you'd like, Dad, coming from our traditional Oak Park house, and all. I could see Mom liking it, definitely, but I'm surprised you do."

"Yeah, when we first started looking around, I wasn't sure moving to a loft was the right thing to do. But when we saw this building, I was sold. I love it here!"

"Did you design the space, Mom?" Jonathan asked.

"Well, what you see is the basic layout we'd seen in the drawings at the developer's office, but I made modifications. This unit hadn't been built-out when we were negotiating our purchase, so there was time for me to make changes. In fact, in the middle of the night, I sat up and realized, since this is a two-bedroom unit, there wouldn't be a place for each of you to sleep if you came home at the same time. So, the next morning, I drew up plans to build that loft space above the guest bedroom," I pointed upward.

"The developer accepted the changes, we negotiated a new price, and his contractor did the construction, so it all worked out."

"I'll sleep up there!" said Jonathan.

"Okay, you can use the futon sofa—it's pretty comfortable."

"I figured you'd live in a real loft someday, because of all the walls you kept taking down in our house," said Kristin, smiling. "I think it's great you guys made the move—it's so cool. Hey, by the way, when I was driving down Jackson Boulevard, I passed a building a couple of blocks away from here with a Hubbard Street Dance Center sign on it. Is that where The Hubbard Street Dance Company is?"

"Yes! They moved their studios to this neighborhood a year ago. I'm going to sign up for ballet classes there. Maybe you were too young, but do you remember I used to take lessons from them when I worked on Hubbard Street?"

"No, I don't remember," Kristin paused. "But, I'll sign up for classes with you!"

"That would be great—I guess I'll finally get you back into ballet after all!" I laughed.

It was so lovely having our kids' approval of our very untraditional new home.

Before moving from Oak Park to the city, we'd donated my old, faithful Lyon and Healy piano and had our newly purchased, pre-owned Steinway grand piano delivered to our loft. I was working on Chopin's Prelude No.15 in D-flat Major, Op. 28. With our high ceilings, warm amber hardwood floors, and exposed brick walls, my piano's rich, deep tones and brilliant, high tones filled every corner of our new place. I felt like a pianist playing in a concert hall—always a crazy fantasy, but fun to imagine. My playing, though, was still erratic, and I never knew which "self" would sit down to play.

Will Dr. Jekyll or Mr. Hyde show up today?

Consistent adeptness at the keyboard was not my strong suit, but I persevered and continued to practice like nobody was listening.

"I can't wait to see your new loft!" Margaret said over the phone. "And when can I come and hear you play?"

"Arghhh! Margaret, I'm so sorry, but I can't play for you. I don't know what's wrong with me, but I still can't play in front of anyone," I confessed.

"Even if I sat in the corner, and you can pretend I'm not here?" She laughed. "My stepmother used to play her piano every day, and I loved listening to her. Those were some of my fondest childhood memories."

If only I could play for people—maybe one day.

꙳

During nice weather, Bob and I spent much of our free time in our "extra" room—our balcony, enjoying our urban landscape all summer long. A frustrated gardener without a garden, I created, admittedly, an over-the-top environment filled with flowers and plantings in our tiny outdoor space.

Pink and white petunias, tall, lemon-yellow South African marigolds, pink geraniums, and green spikes filled the flower boxes secured on the top rail of our balcony—and vinca vines and Wave petunias spilled out of the boxes, like the rush of a waterfall.

In large pots sitting on the floorboards, I planted chartreuse sweet potato vines, white agapanthus, tuberose, and Scarlet Runner Beans. The bean plant vines grew vigorously to twelve feet or longer in no time, bearing clusters of dainty red flowers. As the vines lengthened, I wove them in and out of the balcony's vertical rails, creating a living privacy screen. By mid-summer, ten-inch long green beans dripped from our balcony "walls."

While on our balcony, soft breezes joined us, bringing their telltale breath of where they had been. On some days, they arrived from the west, bringing their sweet, buttery, definitely evocative, cozy fragrance of fresh-baked bread coming from the ovens of Bays English Muffins Company just three blocks away. Since 1933, Bays family business continued to make their muffins using Minnesota spring wheat, potato flour, whole milk, Wisconsin AA butter, and pure Hawaiian cane sugar. Their aromas were delicious.

On other days, the breezes perked me up. "Ahhh, chocolate!" I would say, taking a deep breath through my nose as I faced the sky.

"Blommers must be cooking today," said Bob. Blommers Chocolate Company, the largest cocoa processor and chocolate supplier in North

America, was located just a few blocks east of our loft. When their cooks cooked, they gave us the gift of their labors—the treasured fragrance of semi-sweet chocolate in the air.

Sitting on the balcony one crisp early morning, enjoying a robust cup of coffee, a small group of elderly Asian women entered my field of vision. As they passed by, my mind suddenly and inexplicably whispered a fear I didn't know I'd had. They strolled across the street, close to each other, touching, smiling, quietly talking, all having dark hair, all wearing dark clothing. I leaned forward.

Who are they? Where could they be going in this neighborhood?

One of the women had trouble keeping up with the rest, and the group slowed their pace for her. Transfixed, I stood up. As they continued to walk away, their images getting smaller, more granular, and finally dissolving into the labyrinth of the city streets, I squeezed my eyes to clear my vision, hoping to get one last glimpse of them. But the women were gone. Like the rolling, expanding, vibration of a timpani drum, heat swelled in my eyes and face, then down into my chest and stomach. They reminded me of my mother and her five sisters, and in my mind, my mother was the woman who had trouble walking.

Oh, how silly. Why would that upset me? My mother, except for some knee issues now and then, was perfectly healthy, and so was my father.

But still, the troubling image lingered dormant in my head.

"One hundred teacups." Dr. Strawn, my undergraduate pottery professor, had remarked that his teacher in Japan, a master potter, told him that if he wanted to be a serious potter, he needed to make one hundred teacups.

In a rented space at Terra Incognito, a pottery studio in Oak Park, I sat making one hundred teacups, not that I considered myself a serious potter, but because Kristin had moved from Minneapolis back to Chicago and was getting married. I would make the teacups as wedding favors for our guests.

Having been away from pottery for many years, I knew I'd need to make at least an extra fifty teacups figuring I would reject some, and possibly lose a few through the firing. Using white stoneware clay, I made my teacups, all relatively uniform in size. After the cups were bisque-fired, I bathed them in a translucent, blue-green celadon glaze. As I loaded the cups in the kiln, I placed some near the gas discharge burner—those cups received a soft kiss from the flame during the firing, resulting in a delicate blush of pink on their sides.

It felt great to be back in a pottery studio, albeit for only enough time to make Kristin's teacups. I loved the smell of clay and fellowship with other potters.

Kristin and her husband's wedding was lovely—she, absolutely beautiful, and he, proud and handsome. The traditional, columned reception hall of the Chicago Historical Society was a perfect backdrop for their ceremony. As a wedding gift, Margaret made an exquisite cake with handmade fondant flowers trellising down its four tiers. A string quartet played during the pre-ceremony, reception, and dinner, and Joe, my piano teacher, and cellist Richard Yeo played Chopin's Sonata for Cello and Piano, G minor Op. 65, 3rd movement during the wedding party processional. Paula Cisar, Joe's wife, sang a soprano solo during an interlude of the ceremony. After dinner, a disk jockey played songs (hardly any of which I could identify) as everyone danced and had a fun time.

A week before the wedding, I unpacked a sealed package that held the wedding dress I'd worn thirty years earlier when Bob and I married. I cut the fabric around the prettiest parts of the dress and sewed pieces together to create an envelope that would hold my journal—the book filled with letters I'd written to Kristin with my thoughts, my love, and pride I had for her as she was growing up. The last thing the envelope needed was a closure that would be a pretty button. As I sewed, I thought of my mother. I then understood what she meant about how satisfying it was to sew on a button.

I gave the journal to Kristin on her wedding day.

Where did all that time go?

"You've got to be kidding me!" Bob said. "How can you suddenly decide to go back to work? I thought you were happy being retired. You've spent the past three years doing what you love most, your music, pottery, what's going to happen with all that? What's your point?"

A former client at Governors State University (GSU), a campus in the far south suburbs of Chicago, had called me and asked if I would be interested in applying for their newly created position of university architect. The metaphoric three-sided table of a construction project includes a place for the client, the architect, and the contractor. Always on the architectural side of a project, the prospect of being on the client side intrigued me.

"I said many times that I thought I was too young to be retired. I'm only fifty-one years old. Yes, I love my life right now, but the idea of working within my industry in a different capacity pulls at me," I told Bob.

"Okay, if you say so. If that's what you want, then you should go for it," Bob said with uncertainty in his voice.

I went through the GSU search process, was offered, and I accepted the position that would later evolve to Associate Vice President of Facilities.

GSU was like a small town with friendly people, where I often received a welcoming wave from my grounds staff when I drove through campus. The university was on seven hundred and fifty idyllic acres, including academic buildings, world renowned Nathan Manilow Sculpture Park, organic farmland, an Environmental Research Preserve of protected woodlands, and ponds that served as a migratory stop-off for wildlife. The environment was an astounding contrast to my city life, and I considered myself lucky to live in both worlds.

I loved my job. It was fast-moving, fluid, strategic, tactical, requiring quick thinking for temporarily stabilizing sudden facility breakdowns, to long-range planning for permanent solutions. The campus was in constant need of fixing. Whether it was an ice-cold flood caused by a burst frozen water pipe in the middle of winter, or a fresh air supply breakdown in the cadaver lab in the middle of summer, and every possible problem in between, I was ultimately responsible for the fix. And together with architects, engineers, contractors, and my staff in the planning and construction of new buildings, I thrived. I was energized.

But it wasn't just my work that energized me—it dawned on me that societal change had happened since I was an entry-level architect.

My direct report supervisor of grounds had retired, and for a few months, while I searched for her replacement, my grounds staff reported directly to me.

"Hi, Susan, it's Shawn," my groundsperson said on the phone.

"Hi, Shawn, how're you doing?"

"I'm fine, but my kid is sick, and my wife has to go to work. We take turns in situations like this and it's my turn today, so, I won't be able to make it to work."

"Not a problem," I assured him. "I hope it's nothing serious!"

"Nah, just a cold, but daycare won't accept kids that are sick," he said.

I wished his child well and hung up the phone.

Well, well, well. A father calling-off because of his sick kid was unfathomable back in the day. Yes, the world was a better place.

My department's conference room was spacious, with a conference table that sat ten people, easily accessible lateral archive files for reference, a pull-down screen for electronic presentations, and a communicating door from my office, and one from the main office area. My direct reports, supervisors of administration, architecture, housekeeping, building engineers, grounds, carpentry and electrical, and their staff were knowledgeable professionals committed to their work and the university.

My team and I sat in our conference room developing tactics to avert a situation we thought could be imminent. I listened intently to their concerns, and together we developed a Plan A solution. Before our break, I told them our next task would be to develop a Plan B back-up.

"We'll strive to execute Plan A," I said, "but there are so many moving parts to this situation, and we have to anticipate the unexpected and pivot on a dime if needed. That's when a hybrid of Plan A and Plan B will save the day."

Planning was my strong suit. "Anticipate the unexpected" was my mantra, and always have a Plan B. Everything in my life was going perfectly. But I should have listened to my own advice and had a Plan A and B.

My parents were healthy, active, retired, and living a peaceful, happy life. My mother, at seventy-nine years young, puttered around her kitchen, and my father, at eighty-one, raised hibiscus, cactus, aloe plants, and succulents with great success in his sun parlor off the living room, but never grew plantings outside. One Father's Day, Bob and I built an urban, postage-stamp-size vegetable garden for him in their side yard. Each year after that, my father increased the garden's footprint, and he and my mother reveled in his harvests. Japanese eggplant, Japanese cucumbers, Chinese green beans, tomatoes, zucchini, and shiso were just a few of his crops, and my mother cooked delicious farm-to-table meals using his treasures. His angst over his tomato plants, however, was an exception to his otherwise idyllic little urban farm.

My father and I were weeding his garden one morning. "Oh, Dad, look, that squirrel's sitting there looking at you. How cute!"

"That squirrel's a troublemaker!" he growled, stamping his foot on the ground and waving his arms. "Get outta here!" The little critter scampered away. My father showed me a tomato.

"Look at this. He takes one or two bites when they're nice and ripe then leaves it on the vine."

I laughed. "How do you know it's that squirrel? Maybe it's another squirrel, or maybe it's a possum or a raccoon."

"Nah, it's him. One day he took some bites out of my tomato and left it on the stairs for me to find. I know it's him!"

"Do you know how hilarious you sound, Dad? I think he's sweet. He was giving you a gift."

"Achhh!" he scoffed.

Unsuccessfully, he tried wrapping his tomato plants in chicken wire cages, and even wrapped individual, almost-ripe tomatoes in mesh nets to foil this rogue rodent. He waited on his porch for the bandit to attempt another heist, ready with his fishing net to catch it red-handed (what he would do with the squirrel if caught, I do not know), but alas, the vermin eluded him, and the taunts continued. Although my father feigned disgust, I believe he had respect for the cunning thief and conceded to its victories.

When they had more veggies than they could eat or give away, my mother made jars of umami-rich *tsukemono*, pickled vegetables, to cleanse the palate and add color and crunchy textured side plates to her meals. She soaked them in a shoyu, sugar, rice vinegar, dashi base, or a spicy miso sauce and marinated in the fridge for a few days.

Shiso, from the mint family but with its unique fragrance and taste, is known for its abundance of antioxidant, antiviral, and antibacterial properties. Its shape is similar to an elm tree leaf but broader at the base with deeply serrated edges and grew either green or purple. My father had a purple shiso patch that re-seeded itself every year, and my mother picked the larger leaves for her tsukemono.

One day my mother called me on the phone. "Susie, you have to come over and pick up some vegetables from our garden—we have so many! When can you come?"

It would be hard to break away from home that coming weekend. I had so much work to do for the university and had planned to spend those few days putting together a PowerPoint to present to the university's board of trustees.

"Uh, Mom, I uh—" I stalled.

"Can you come over Saturday? I'm afraid they're going to get over-ripe," she said.

Arghhh!

"Okay, I'll come in the morning."

When I arrived, she gave me a pile of fresh, firm Japanese cucumbers, bright green extra-long, just picked Chinese green beans, and shiso leaves wrapped in damp paper towels.

"I'm going to teach you how to make shiso tskemono." she said.

Oy vey, I've got so much work to do at home!

At her kitchen table, she said, "First, wash the leaves, pinch off the stem, and put them in between paper towels to dry as I did, do you see?"

she asked me. "Now take one raisin—"

"Only one?" I asked.

"Yes, only one. Wrap the raisin in the leaf. No, not like that!" She laughed. She centered the raisin near the broad end of the leaf, folded the bottom edge over the raisin, then alternately folded over each side of the leaf, rolling it upward until the tiny bundle reached the top. She then inserted a toothpick to hold it securely.

"This is so much work, Mom!"

Who's got that kind of time?

"That's okay, keep making them, you'll be glad. I'm going to send these home with you, but remember to let them sit in the fridge for a couple of days."

She placed the little wrapped morsels in a jar of her sweetened soy and vinegar marinade and brought out a jar of tsukemono that was ready to eat, along with hot rice. With my chopsticks, I took one of the tiny bundles and brushed it against the rice to soak up excess marinade then put it in my mouth. I breathed out through my nose to capture all the subtle flavors from my tongue. I sensed the minty, basil-ish taste of the shiso leaf and the raisin's burst of sweetness, slightly fermented by the marinade, and together with the delicate chewiness of the shiso leaf against the soft texture of the raisin, they sent my taste buds into full umami satisfaction mode. I ate a small bit of hot rice to settle down my palate and took another shiso bundle.

"This is incredible. I didn't expect a single raisin, and shiso leaf could pack so much flavor! Oishi!"

She laughed. "I told you it was worth the work."

※

Kristin and her husband had a beautiful baby girl, Alexandra, who instantly became the love of our lives. My parents, Bob, and I visited them to meet our new grandbaby. Holding Alex for the first time, I arranged her, so the side of her head was against my heart, and she instinctively nestled and conformed to my body—I wanted her to hear and feel my heartbeat. Her intoxicating baby smell, warmth, and her newborn baby sounds brought the same euphoria I had when I held baby Kristin for the first time.

"She's so beautiful, look at all that hair!" I whispered. "I love her. And I love you, Kristin, you did a good job."

"I love you too, Mom. I had no idea how much love a baby brings. I'm so happy."

It was my mother's turn to hold Alex. She and my father looked at each other and exchanged some Japanese words that I didn't understand, but Kristin did, and she smiled. I put my arms around my mother and Kristin as my mother held Alex. My mother, daughter, granddaughter, and me. Four generations of women. Life was good.

During the next few years, Bob and Alex became great buddies. When she was big enough to kneel on the counter stool, she liked making cookies with him.

Sitting in the living room one morning, I skimmed through a pile of cookbooks looking for inspiration for vegetarian or vegan recipes, and Bob flipped recipe cards digging for cookie recipes as Alex watched.

"Found it!" he said. "Alex, do you want to make Mrs. Fields Chocolate Chip Cookies today?"

"Okay!" Her eyes were wide with excitement.

Bob put one of my white chef's aprons on her, oversized for her little three-year-old body, but he folded and gathered it, and wrapped the strings around her several times to keep the apron in place.

"There. I think that'll work," Bob said. "Wait, hold this big wooden spoon, I want to take a picture of you. Okay, smile! Got it!"

They happily chattered away, adding ingredients, mixing, and stirring until Bob had a realization.

"Uh, oh, something's not right."

"Something's not right, Gaga?" Alex asked.

"Looks like we have to go to the store and buy some more ingredients."

"What happened?" I called out.

"I don't understand, I've made this recipe so many times, but for some crazy reason, the batter is weird—and runny."

"Ewwww! Can't help you," I said, "baking's not my thing. You gonna make a new batch?"

"I think I can fix what we have. But I have to go to Dominick's. I'll take Alex with me."

"I'll go with you," I said, "I need some things for tonight's dinner."

Bob bundled up Alex in her winter coat, hat, and mittens, and we trudged through the snow on that bright, brisk morning, pushing her stroller for the three-block walk to the grocery store. When we arrived, Bob transferred Alex to the shopping cart baby seat, and I took the stroller to use as my food cart. I headed for the produce department when I heard Bob call out.

"Oh look, Alex, there's Margaret. Margaret!" He waved to her, smiling.

I turned back and joined them.

"Hi, Bob! Hi, Susan, and look how big Alex is! Shopping today, huh?"

"Margaret, you're the baker," Bob said. "Alex and I just made a double batch of Mrs. Fields Cookies, but the dough is thinner than I remembered when I made it before. I'm sure I followed the recipe. What do you think—did we have a bad batch of flour or oatmeal?"

Margaret pondered. "You double batched it, and it's too runny?"

"Yeah!" he said.

"Did you double batch the wet ingredients, but forget to double up on the dry ingredients?"

"Oh. I'm sure I doubled up on everything. Well, I'm pretty sure I did."

Margaret started laughing. "Are you sure?"

Bob paused and said, "Okay, Alex, it looks like we gotta go to the baking aisle and start all over." He turned around the shopping cart, and off they went.

Margaret and I laughed.

"Such a surprise to see you—I didn't know you shopped at this Dominick's," I said.

"Oh, no, I usually don't, but I had time before my client meeting, so I thought I'd grab a few things I need for home. How are you doing?" she asked.

"I'm good. I was heading for produce. I want to start making more main meals with vegetables instead of meat, so I'm making a vegetable soup tonight, and some veggie sides."

"Are you all gonna be vegetarians, then?"

"Nah, you know me," I said. "I like to reserve the right for a nice steak once in a while. And besides, Bob, the carnivore man, would never stand for it. I want to see if we can ease into more plant-based entrees. I've seen documentaries and read a lot about the benefits of plant-based food. Bob and I are getting older, thicker around the middle, and I want to eat healthier—you know, fewer carbs and calories, less fat."

"That's a good plan. I know I should do that, but I love my meat too!" Margaret looked surprised when she saw her watch. "Oh my gosh, Susan, I've gotta get to my meeting. So good seeing you!"

"Okay, bye, have a good one!" I waved.

That evening, I made a hearty soup of seasonal root vegetables of parsnips, carrots, and potatoes, along with celery, onions, collard greens, great northern and kidney beans, tomatoes, and green beans. Sautéing the wedge-cut onions in a few tablespoons of extra virgin olive oil, then the beans and chunky-cut veggies, brought out its brilliant colors and earthy fragrances. Adding vegetable stock, a bit of balsamic vinegar, bay leaf, some dried oregano, and spices gave the soup a depth of flavors. Before serving, I added a handful of peas to perk up the soup's color even more. A side dish of stir-fried cubes of Japanese kabocha winter squash (including its skin) finished with some sizzling teriyaki sauce, and a bowl of hot brown rice accompanied the soup.

"Dinner's ready! What do you think?" I asked Alex and Bob.

Alex brought her face close to the soup. "It smells good!"

"What about meat?" Bob looked forlorn.

I laughed. "The beans and veggies will give us the protein we need."

"Yeah, but, but—" he stammered.

"I can throw in some meat in tomorrow night's leftovers. I just wanted to experiment with cooking a meal without meat. It's good, isn't it?"

"I guess so, what kind of meat will you throw in?" he asked.

"Chicken, I suppose."

I figured by tomorrow night; he might forget about the meat I promised.

I think our new way of eating will work—fingers crossed.

"Dad, you need to exercise. Why don't you walk more? Get some fresh air," Dennis, an emergency department doctor, suggested. I completely agreed. We were at my parents' place.

"Why should I exercise? I don't believe in exercise. The body is like a machine—the more you use it, the faster it will break down."

At age eighty-seven, my father was lean, spry, and pretty healthy, so it was difficult to argue his point. We laughed at his flawed theory, but years later, after battering our knees with running, golfing, and such, both Dennis and I agreed, maybe our father had been on to something.

A month later, Dennis called me.

"Susie, Dad was admitted to the hospital."

"What? What happened? Is he okay?"

"He's doing okay. Mom called me this morning and said she was worried about him. She said he wasn't himself—always tired and had been in bed for five days, so I went over there." Dennis continued, "He was responsive but pale, lethargic, and I thought he looked dehydrated, so I called 911."

"Are you at the hospital now? And how's mom?" I asked.

"No, I was with him all day, but now I'm with Mom at her place, and she's okay. I'll go home soon."

I called my father at the hospital.

"Dad, how are you? How do you feel?" I asked.

"Everyone is making a big deal over me. I'm fine. Are you coming?" He asked.

"Yes, do you need anything?"

"Let me talk to Bob." I gave Bob the phone.

I heard Bob say, "Yes, yes, I do. Oh sure. Okay, see you soon."

"He wants me to bring my electric razor," Bob said.

"Hey, why couldn't he just ask me?" I thought. "Such a funny guy."

When we arrived at the hospital, my father was reading the newspaper and was in good spirits. He looked a little pale but sounded good.

Well, that was a quick recovery!

During my father's twelve days in the hospital, all lab tests, his CT scan, and EKG were normal. But he fainted during his time there, which was enough to justify a little longer stay.

When the hospital doctors thought our father was ready to go home, Dennis took exception to their discharge orders. Having been in bed for five days at home and another two weeks in the hospital, Dennis reasoned, our father was too weak to come home and suggested he get transferred to a rehab center to gain more strength. The hospital agreed.

During the transfer process, my father's heart stopped. He ceased to live. One minute his eighty-seven-year-old heart pumped, and the next minute it didn't.

His sudden death was a shock, as I never anticipated his life was in danger, before or even while he was in the hospital.

"All tests were normal," *they* said.

"He's fine," *they* said.

"He'll be going home soon," *they* said.

At my last visit, we chatted and kidded around, and he was alive and well—and then he wasn't. I felt blindsided.

How could I have been so stupid? At eighty-seven years old, he was sick, rushed to the hospital, and fainted. Why did I not worry? I worried about everything at home and work. Why not my father? Where was my Plan A and Plan B?"

My mind was cruel to me. I should have thought of different scenarios that could occur, given my father's age. My parents' presence was always positive, safe, supportive, and they never changed—even though I aged, they seemed to stay the same. I had a blind spot of denial and never thought about their death.

"How could I be so stupid?" I asked myself over and over. There was nothing I could have done to alter his outcome, but I could have said, "Dad, I love you." Not—"Luv-ya-Dad, g' bye!" as I did after visiting him in the hospital. Regrets fell heavily on me.

※

I stayed with my mother after my father died.

"Mom, should we talk about Dad's memorial service?" I carefully measured my words.

"Okay."

"Would you like a Buddhist service, or—"

"Oh, Buddhist, yes, Buddhist," she said.

"At the Midwest Buddhist Temple?" I asked.

"Hai. Yes."

Although my parents were not practicing Buddhists, their parents were devout, and I believed my parents lived their lives as their parents, with compassion and sympathy for others, truthfulness, and peace.

I don't recall ever going inside the Midwest Buddhist Temple but had admired it from the outside many times. Built in 1971, in Chicago's Old Town area, its low-slung combination hip and gable roof, the symmetry of the grand staircase aligned on the centerline of the structure, and a tiny but lovely Japanese garden, was as I envisioned a traditional Buddhist temple would look.

In the *Hondo*,[34] the fragrance of incense, reminding me of green tea, was comforting and calming. The soft sound of the *kansho*[35] bell signaled the beginning of my father's memorial service, and like my parents, the ceremony was simple and humble.

We chanted. I was unfamiliar with the purpose of chanting and found it somewhat arcane, but chanting the words from the service book, in a low, somber voice, I felt my father's presence.

My mind drifted to the past to my teenage years—

"Would you like *ochazuke?*"[36] I remembered my father once asked me.

It was the summer before I went away to college. After spending the evening with my friends, I came home and found him sitting alone at the dining room table, watching TV. It was nothing unusual—my father was a nighthawk. My mother had gone to bed, and Dennis was still out with his friends so, I decided to keep him company.

"Yes, I would love some," I answered, getting up.

"No, you stay and watch the show. I'll bring it to you," my father told me.

To some, that would have been a lovely fatherly gesture. But in our house, my mother always served my father, and in her absence, that was *my* job. I was bewildered by his earnestness to serve me ochazuke but gladly accepted his offer.

Rummaging through the kitchen drawers and cabinets, he created sounds—not a percussion concerto, like my mother smoothly performed, but more like an improvisational, modern score. I heard a whoosh of water and a sudden clunk of a teapot landing on the stove's burner. The high-pitched beeping of the microwave announcing the heated rice was ready, the rattle of the refrigerator door opening, and thumping when it closed, and the clink and clatter of dishes and chawans made a symphony of sounds that made me smile. And then—silence. The absence of sound piqued my attention, and with raised eyebrows, I wondered what was happening.

After a few minutes, my father came into the dining room with a tray of two chawans of hot rice, a pot of green tea with roasted brown rice kernels, two pairs of chopsticks, and an assortment of tsukemono, which my mother always kept handy in the fridge. He poured the tea over the rice and placed each dish of tsukemono on the table, along with the chopsticks and a small porcelain shoyu dispenser. The tea's fragrance was spellbinding, and the tart smell of the tsukemono made my mouth water.

He did this for me on many nights that summer, until I left for school. Those were the last times he and I shared quiet moments like that, and I wondered if they were my father's way of saying he'd miss me when I leave. And I missed him now.

Bob and I spent the night with my mother after my father's service. She was understandably exhausted, as were we, so we all went to bed early.

The next morning, I was awakened by my mother's percussion concerto. She was making breakfast, as she had every morning for the past sixty years, while married to my father. Her beautiful sounds swept me with sadness. I joined her in the kitchen, and we hugged.

"Mom, are you okay?"

She didn't reply.

"Mom?" I asked again.

"I have to make breakfast. Bob will be hungry when he gets up," she said.

"Okay, I'll help you."

A few days later, I saw a folded American flag lying on my parents' dining room table. In the tradition of U.S. military protocol, my mother had received it to honor my father's service during WWII. I remembered when my father and I had made a flag case together in his workshop, years earlier, for Bob's deceased father, Ken, also a WWII veteran. I found the original drawings and specifications I'd prepared for Ken's flag case and gave them to a local woodworker who would make a case for my father's flag—it would exactly match the one my father and I had made for Ken. When the woodworker sent me the finished case, I folded the flag into the iconic triangular shape, nestled it into the new cherry wood flag case, its final resting place, and Dennis presented it to our mother. My father would have been honored.

Over the following months, my mother remained indifferent and unfocused. Fully turning my attention to her trying to fill her emptiness, I barely took time to grieve, myself, over my father's passing. I had to be strong for her. Maybe tending to her needs was my way of filling the void in my own heart.

"Mom, would you like to spend some nights at our house?" I asked over the phone.

"Oh no, Susie, I have too much to do here," she answered.

"How about just a few days? We can cook together and maybe do some shopping. Bob can pick you up tomorrow—is that all right?"

"Okay, but I don't want to stay too long."

The next day, I heard Bob call out, "We're home!" he said, as he and my mother arrived at our loft. She had brought a small bag of personal items and a shopping bag filled with kitchen stuff for cooking.

"I thought we could make a simple soup, Chawanmushi. Do you remember what that is?" my mother asked.

"The egg custard soup? You haven't made that in a long time!"

She nodded. "We can make it today."

Helping her unpack her bag of pots, pans, dishware, and ingredients for that night's meal, I laughed, "What's all this? Y'know, mom, I do have a pretty well-stocked kitchen."

She continued to unpack.

"Oh? Do you have dried shiitake mushrooms?" she asked, smiling.

"No, not really," I confessed.

"Sake?"

"Uh, uh." I sighed.

"Chicken, shrimp, spinach?" she asked as she pulled them out of her shopping bag.

"Well, no, but I could have easily run to the store for them!"

"Kombu?" she asked.

I took a deep breath, rummaging through my cabinet. "Yes! Here's some, you gave it to me a while ago!"

"Bonito flakes?" She looked at me.

I sighed. "Uh, no, no bonito flakes."

"Do you have carrots, a lemon, and eggs?"

"Yes, I have all of that!" I felt redeemed, finally.

"Okay, let's cook," she said.

"Can I help?" asked Bob while inserting a CD of Chopin Preludes and Etudes in his stereo system.

"Of course!" My mother smiled. "Here's the chicken breast. I already took off the skin and washed it, so you can cut it like this." She cut a sample to show Bob—it was roughly a half-inch cube. "And also, soak the shrimp in cold water so it'll finish defrosting."

"Susie, can you make a quart of dashi? While you're at it, soak the mushrooms in hot water. Put a heavy bowl on them, so they don't float to the top."

"Okay," I said.

I knew the dried mushrooms needed at least a half hour's soak in water for reconstitution, so I took two large ones out of the bag and got them started first. For the dashi, I cut a five-inch square of dried kombu, wiped it with a damp cloth, and with my kitchen shears, cut it into roughly four equal strips, and added them to a quart of water to heat. Just before the water boiled, I removed and discarded the kombu strips, and I threw in a few cubes of ice to keep it from boiling. Then I added a cup of dried bonito flakes to the kombu water, stirred, brought the stock to a boil, and removed it from the burner. When the bonito flakes settled to the bottom of the pot, I strained it through a cheesecloth bag and discarded the bonito.

As Bob and I carried out our tasks, my mother washed and cooked a bunch of fresh spinach, and when done, she cooled it under running water. After draining, she extracted excess water by squeezing the spinach, forming it into the shape of a log, and cutting it into four, equal sections.

"Bob, sprinkle some sake and shoyu, chotto, on the chicken," my mother instructed.

"Okay. How much sake and shoyu?" Bob asked.

"I don't know, about a teaspoon of each. And let it sit for a while, ten minutes, then drain it."

"Dashi's done!" I told my mother.

My mother poured about a teaspoon of sake, two teaspoons of shoyu, and a sprinkle of salt into the dashi. "Heat it, stir, then let it cool down." She told me.

"I marinated the chicken and drained it. What next?" Bob asked.

"Thank you," my mother said. "You can shell the shrimp now but keep on the tail! Do you know how to take out the vein?"

"Yes!" he was proud to say.

"Susie, the mushrooms are soft and ready," my mother said. "Cut off the stems and put them in a freezer bag. They're too tough to eat, but they'll be good added to soup stock the next time you make it. And slice the caps into strips, okay?"

"Hai!" I said, smiling.

"You sound like your mom!" Bob teased.

We all laughed. It was good to hear my mother laugh. Being in the kitchen made her happy, helping her forget her despair even for those few moments. Our kitchen, open to the rest of the loft, was 'U'-shaped, with a long counter and base cabinets on one side, the dishwasher, sink, and fridge on the other, and a full, six-burner range at the bottom of the 'U.' Sensing each other's presence in space, we moved around the kitchen without so much as an inadvertent bump—and with the music of Chopin in the air, we found our flow.

My mother cut the outermost skin of a lemon, being careful not to include the bitter white pith below. Stacking the peels, one on top of the other, she sliced through them lengthwise, cutting thin strips for garnish. She then peeled a skinny carrot and cut it, crosswise, into about quarter-inch-thick round disks.

"Okay, Bob, Susie, watch me," she told us. She cracked five eggs into a large bowl and with chopsticks, pierced the yolks and mixed them. "I'm not beating it, just mixing it, chotto, enough to blend the whites and yolks." She slowly stirred the cooled-down pot of dashi broth into the bowl of eggs and mixed it. With a metal mesh sieve in one hand and the bowl of dashi/egg mixture in the other, she poured the mixture back into the pot through the sieve, and stirred it.

"Put those in each of the chawans," she said, pointing to the platter of carrot rounds, mushroom strips, spinach, chicken cubes, and shrimp.

Bob and I evenly divided those ingredients into the chawans, and my mother ladled in the dashi/egg broth, within about a half-inch of the rim. She loosely covered the top of each chawan with aluminum foil.

"Susie, will all the chawans fit in your fish poacher?" my mother asked. I got out the poacher and we decided they would all fit.

"Put the steamer rack and water in the poacher, and when the water comes to a boil, we'll put in the chawans and cover the pot," she told me.

About fifteen minutes later, she lifted the foil of one of the chawans and inserted a toothpick into the soup. "Not done yet," she said. "When the toothpick comes out clean, it'll be ready. Set the timer for another five minutes." In the meantime, she brought out rice she'd made, and some small dishes of tsukemono.

After five minutes, she had me test it. "Clean! Look, Mom." I showed her the toothpick.

"Hai. Looks good."

My mother carefully took out the chawans from the steaming poacher using oven mitts.

We each had individual chawans. I lifted the foil, and a puff of the steam with a tantalizing aroma immediately wafted out of the bowl. I saw corners of the carrots, mushroom, chicken cubes, spinach, and the tail of a shrimp peeking out from a thin veil of liquid broth above the blanket of smooth, silky, egg custard. The soup was hot, so I let it sit, and its fragrance continued to intoxicate me. Finally, I ate. The chicken, so tender it practically melted in my mouth, and the broth had deep, complex notes of the sea against the earthiness of the mushrooms, carrots, and spinach—all bursting with umami. Still very hot, we ate delicately, relishing each bite.

"Mom, this is so good!" I said.

"Well, you two made it oishi." My mother seemed content.

"Mmmm. Delicious!" Bob said.

Although my mother said it was a "simple soup," we had cooked all afternoon, given the time it took my mother to give us our lessons on cooking. We ate and talked and laughed throughout our meal.

After dinner, I played the piano for her—Beethoven's Sonata No. 8, C minor, second movement, Adagio cantabile. It is a reflective movement, and probably wasn't the best piece to play at that time in my mother's life, but I think I may have a disability of sorts—musical long-term memory loss. I could only play what I was working on at the time.

With all my performance anxiety issues, playing for my mother brought me comfort. It seemed so natural, and I heard my music flow smoothly. When I finished, I felt calm.

"That was beautiful, Susie. I'm so glad you're playing again," she said.

"Did I ever thank you for all those years of lessons I took? I know they were expensive. Toward the end, you wouldn't let me quit, but now I appreciate your insistence—thanks, Mom."

{

Dennis and I were relieved when our mother decided it was time to sell her apartment building and move to The Breakers, an independent living, senior citizens retirement community on the north side of Chicago. Located on the site where the grand Edgewater Beach Hotel once graced the shores of Lake Michigan, my mother, Dennis, Jane, and I looked at a two-bedroom apartment that had an unimpeded view of the lake and Lincoln Park.

"So, what do you think?" I asked as we toured the apartment. "Look at your bedroom. It's so big, and your sewing area can fit right in front of the windows."

"It's nice, I guess," she responded. "Is the apartment big enough for the whole family to come for dinner?"

"We can make the second bedroom a den, and it can double as a guest bedroom," I said. "And if we install a set of French double doors on this wall," I pointed, "the second bedroom would open to the living room, so when the family is here, we can sit in either room, and we'd still be all together!"

"Okay." My mother perked up a bit.

It wasn't until The Breakers' manager took us to lunch in their dining room, a two-story space with a glass ceiling that let in the brightness of the sky, when my mother seemed to envision her new life there.

"Oh, it's beautiful in here," she remarked. "And the food is delicious!"

Transition to life without her husband was sad and painful. At eighty-five years old, it took time, but she worked hard at integrating into her new community.

A few weeks after moving into her new apartment, she told me, "I wake up in the morning in time to see the sunrise over the lake. I pretend I'm looking at the ocean in Hawai`i, and that makes me so happy."

Every morning when I drove to GSU, I saw her sun at the same time, and that made me happy.

Over the following few years, my mother made warm, caring friends who adored her and seemed to want to protect her from sadness. People were fascinated and attracted to her innocence and her genuine interest in them. With the help of her new friends, her high-spirited personality began to come back. She and her friends had meals together and attended all the day trips of shopping, tours, lectures, live shows, and concerts The Breakers had to offer.

My mother loved to swim and when she discovered the building's pool, she and her new friend, Josephine, went swimming together every morning. My mother was a good swimmer, doing many laps each day, and I thought the company of her new swimming partner helped her stay on track. Josephine and her life partner, Dr. Bill Onoda, a medical doctor until he retired, were a Japanese couple whom my mother adored. Bill read newspaper articles to them over breakfast every day and explained its gist.

"He's so smart and so nice. He's such a gentle man," my mother said of Bill. "Most of the time, I don't understand what he's talking about when he explains the articles, but he doesn't give up and keeps trying!" She laughed. It was a beautiful sound that I heard more and more often.

※

Demands of my job left me little time to spend with my mother, but I thoroughly enjoyed the occasions that I did manage to visit her.

Through the sloped glass roof of The Breakers' well-appointed, white-tablecloth dining room, the clear sky showered its light all around my mother, her friends, and me as we talked, laughed, and enjoyed our Saturday afternoon lunch. Shirley, one of my mother's bold, outspoken friends, was uncharacteristically quiet during our lunch conversation.

"Shirley, you're not eating, don't you like our lunch today?" asked one of the ladies.

"I'm fine," Shirley said.

"Oh, I was just thinking you were so quiet and I—"

"I'm fine!" she repeated. Then Shirley turned to me.

"So, Susie, how long have you been at the university?"

"About ten years."

Barely finishing my answer, Shirley asked me, "And how is it going?"

I sensed an interrogation coming. "Stressful and keeping me very busy," I said.

"Busy? Uh, huh. Too busy to visit your mother?" Shirley snapped.

Suddenly, the bright sky around us seemed to go gray, my face flushed, and my mouth went dry. I took a deep breath and heard my voice slowly reply, "Umm, my campus is over two hours from here during rush hour, so visiting my mother after work is very difficult. I try to come on weekends."

"Weekends!" Shirley scoffed. "Before today, when was the last weekend you were here? How come you can't visit her more often?"

I felt my body shrinking into my chair. Silence hovered over our table, and like a bulldog protecting her young, Shirley did not spare me.

"Well?" she asked again.

I turned to my mother, expecting a reassuring kind of smile of, "Don't listen to Shirley, she just likes to make trouble sometimes," but instead, her gaze cast downward. To me, she looked as if she was—embarrassed.

One of the ladies at the table broke the awkward silence, her voice straining to be cheerful, asked everyone's opinion about what dessert would be nice to order.

Did Shirley let the cat out of the bag? Did my mother tell Shirley I don't visit her very often, and now Shirley was out to right my wrong?

I was the one who deserved embarrassment and was horrified that my mother looked so uncomfortable.

⸘

Time unrelentingly nipped at my heels with meetings, project planning and delivery, budgets, union negotiations, and dealing with any problem evenly remotely associated with facilities. My job required 24/7 on-call accessibility during evenings and weekends.

Although the university closed between the Christmas and New Years' holidays, I was at home immersed in writing a paper, *Climate Action Plan for Sustainability for GSU*. The report was due at the beginning of the new year for submittal to the American College and University Presidents' Climate Commitment, an organization in which the president of GSU was a member. The plan included metadata supporting proposed tactics to eliminate the university's net greenhouse gas emissions in specific areas of both physical and academic operations. The paper also committed to making research and educational efforts to help reverse global warming.

I was consumed with my writing when dark thoughts muscled into my mind.

It's the holidays. Why am I spending my precious days-off doing this? What about my family, my mother? Time was beating me again. Shirley was right to question me.

I loved my job but unable to juggle all aspects of my life as I had in the past. Was it the commute, and at sixty-two years old, had I less energy to spare? I did not have a nine to five jo—my Blackberry was always on "ON," and my laptop at home remained fully charged, beckoning me to continue my work at night, and there I was, shackled to my work over the holidays.

The haunting scene years ago, of the elderly Asian women I once saw from my balcony, crept into my head—

They strolled across the street, close to each other, touching, smiling, quietly talking, all having dark hair, all wearing dark clothing. One of the women had trouble keeping up with the rest, and the group slowed their pace for her.

As I recalled the image of the Asian women, my mind transposed those women with my mother and her five sisters, Norma, Margie, Nobuko, Se, and Aiko. All the sisters slowed their pace, so my mother, who now used a walker, could keep up with them.

Was the scene a prophecy?

Back then, I had neither the will nor the insight to understand the haunting scene's simple message: my mother would not always be physically or cognitively able, nor will she live forever. The question of purposefulness faced me. Was my life's purpose, at this time, to work at the university, enhance my career, and earn a paycheck? Or was it to nurture my mother and give her assurance that she still had an essential place in the world? My mother taught me so much all my life, and I continued to learn from her. She was my mentor, my inspiration, my lifelong anchor, always there to cheer me on in whatever venture I embarked, and I was missing the gifts of wisdom she still had to offer.

Always so tangled up with never having enough time for all the things I needed to do, I realized it was she, at ninety years old, who was running out of time in a different and frightening kind of way. A binary choice faced me squarely: do I stay at the university, or do I leave? She and I had little time to waste.

I decided to retire.

᛭

Each of Chicago's four seasons are glorious: spring's mild temperatures and defiant awakening of flora and fauna after winter's ravage; summer's riot of colors of lush, green trees, prairie grasses, flowers blanketing lawns and dotting balconies, and distant white sails slow dancing on

Lake Michigan; autumn's photosynthetic alchemy beckoning bright red, orange, purple, and yellow from the green leaves of its grand trees; and even winter's dramatic and unpredictable turbulence.

One cold winter day started with pure cerulean skies, intensified by the contrast of bright, white, powdery snow covering roofs and grounds, and the black and gray rough-textured bark of angular, leafless trees. Then within minutes, the sky suddenly changed as if a watercolorist took her soft-haired hake brush and mopped the sky. Using her pensive Payne's Grey watercolor, the artist skillfully twisted her brush, showing off the pigment's dramatic gradation of colors ranging from striations of steel gray to deep, ominous blue-black, that would be clouds of threatening snow.

Bob was at work, so it was only Tony, our fifteen-pound, apricot-colored cockapoo, and me at home.

We're in for snow—how I love days like this.

I shuddered as I crossed each side of my cardigan sweater snuggly around my torso and continued to watch mother nature put on her show of wizardry in the sky. The melancholy music of Erik Satie's Gymnopedie No.1 playing on the stereo matched the gray day I saw through the window. One of the disadvantages of living in a loft with exposed brick walls, tall ceilings, and a north-facing view was the chill that hung in our apartment throughout winter. But I had Tony to warm me.

"Tony, where are you?" I called out in a singsong, high-pitched voice. "Tony?"

He sauntered over to me. "Yes, here I am!" I imagined he was thinking. Seeing his long, droopy ears, his brown, button eyes, and black gumdrop nose always made me smile—how could I not? Tony's hair, silky soft with relaxed curls, was inherited from his poodle mother and cocker spaniel father. His hair did not have a grain direction, so I could stroke him up and down, side to side, or in circles without any complaints from him. We had a symbiotic relationship—he loved to be pet, and I loved petting him.

The coldness of outside faded away when I picked him up and held his body against mine. He snuggled up against me, and my hands and chest warmed up immediately.

On an unseasonably pleasant winter afternoon in January, Margaret met Tony and me in the park near our loft. The air was cold but windless, and the sun shone brightly.

"Hi Tony, oh you're so cute, but you already know that don't you?" Margaret said as she gave him an ear rub.

"Tony, sit," I told him. I sighed. "Go on now, sit—*Tony, sit!* Say hi to Margaret."

Tony sat and waved his paw at Margaret—it was more like a swat.

"Good boy." I gave him a treat.

"Oh my gosh, Tony, you're so smart!" Margaret turned to me. "I wish I'd brought Sophie with me. I think she and Tony would get along so well."

Sophie was Margaret's miniature schnauzer. Black and silver, Sophie's coat was smooth, shiny, and ever-so soft. With her soulful, round, onyx-black eyes, and uncropped ears that tipped downward, she brought happiness and comfort to Margaret. But Sophie was as rambunctious as Tony, and I'm not sure either would relinquish their "alpha" crown to one another, but we often talked about getting them together. Who knew what our crazy pups would do to each other?

"So good to see you, Margaret. How were your holidays?" I asked, hugging her.

"I was so busy! I had tons of cakes to bake and decorate, and pastries to make for parties, receptions, and my family. I'm exhausted and can barely get my energy back."

She sounded tired. As Margaret continued to talk about her holidays, I noticed long afternoon shadows of nearby buildings zigzagging on the park's snow-covered berms and walkways. Between those dark shadows, the sun cast its warmth on the surface of the snow bringing it alive with a mesmerizing, spellbinding metamorphosis when flecks of ice were neither frozen nor melted. Instead, the snow's surface was fluxing, shivering, shimmering, and glistening like the magical image I saw in my pottery firings. This was the moment I sought, not in a high-fire kiln, but in the cold of winter. It was the true *glint of the sun on the ice*. My heart leaped.

I was about to point out this visual feast to Margaret when she jarred me back into our conversation and asked, "So, Susan, what do you think?"

"I'm sorry, say again?"

"I said I've had an earache for more than a month, and when I swallow, it feels like there's a piece of glass stuck in the back of my tongue. It's painful! What do you think it is?"

"Gosh, I don't know. Maybe it's strep throat," I said. "A month is a long time to be in pain. Have you talked to Dr. Forbes?"

"No, not yet. I better call her," Margaret said.

Dr. Janet Forbes, both Margaret's and my primary care physician, would know what to do. Margaret made an appointment.

The following week, Margaret called me. "Dr. Forbes spent a lot of time with me as she always did. She examined my throat and said some tissue, deep in my throat, caught her attention, so she wrote an order for a CT scan of my head and neck, and recommended I see an Ear Nose Throat specialist."

Ice water suddenly ran through me.

Why would Dr. Forbes order a CT scan for a routine sore throat and earache?

⸘

"Squamous cell carcinoma at the base of your tongue, stage 3, maybe stage 4 cancer," otolaryngologist[37] Dr. Louis Portugal said. Soft-spoken, articulate, and professional, the doctor held our complete attention.

I was with Margaret in the exam room at the University of Chicago Medical Center (UCMC). After examining her throat and reviewing the results of her CT scan, Dr. Portugal was reasonably sure of his diagnosis.

The doctor said many things in our conversation, but the words, "squamous cell carcinoma, stage 3, maybe stage 4 cancer," hung in my mind. We were stunned. Speechless.

Then Margaret broke our silence.

"Will they cut out my tongue?" Margaret asked, her eyes filling with tears.

Dr. Portugal's answer was an emphatic, "No. At UCMC, we've found great success with chemotherapy and chemoradiation for these kinds of cancers."

"This can't be happening to me, Doctor. I've been through chemo and radiation before, and I can't do it again. I'm sixty-five years old now, and I can't do it!"

Over fifteen years earlier, Margaret had breast cancer, but with great courage, mental, and physical strength, she prevailed. At that time, I was deeply involved with my family, the Board of Trustees, and my architectural practice. We kept in close contact via the phone during that time, but with much regret, I had little time to spend with her otherwise. It was incomprehensible she was facing another battle with cancer.

"Let's take it one step at a time," said Dr. Portugal. "You'll need a biopsy that can confirm or deny this diagnosis. There are risks to any invasive procedure, including biopsies, but without it, we won't know for certain if the mass on your tongue is cancerous and if so, its extent." He continued, "Margaret, are you willing to go through this first step?"

"I don't know, Doctor, I guess so. It's just that I never dreamed I would have to go through this again," she said, putting her head in her hands.

Before we left the office, the doctor said something about how we ought not to go overboard on the Internet regarding this diagnosis. I smiled weakly, knowing full well that the first thing I would do when I got home would be to go on Google.

We were silent during our drive home from Dr. Portugal's office. Margaret, now divorced, had two grown sons and I knew that as young adults, her sons were busy building their own lives. I was resolute to walk this journey with her.

I'm retired, and I have time to help her. She can't go through this by herself.

I spoke. "Margaret, when you had breast cancer, I felt bad that I couldn't set aside more time for you."

"That's not true. You brought food to my family and me, and I remember you drove me to some of my radiation sessions. You did a lot!"

"I could have done more. I should have done more," I insisted. "Let me be your advocate this time. If you'd like, I can go to your doctors' meetings with you. Would you want me to do that?"

"Oh, Susan, would you? I can hardly think when I'm with doctors. My mind goes blank, and I can't process what anyone says. Oh my god, I can't believe this is happening to me— again!"

When I was with Margaret, I felt strong. I wanted to be her rock. But when I got home, my heart ached, and my stomach twisted in fits of anxiety. I was sick with fear for her.

A few days later, I sat in a small room at UCMC with Margaret's sons, Daniel, the oldest, and Merrell. Both young men were well-mannered and courteous, but in disbelief about their mother. She was in the operating room, having her biopsies taken. We waited.

Finally, Dr. Portugal knocked on the door and came into the room, looking solemn. I introduced Daniel and Merrell to the doctor.

"How is my mother?" Merrell asked.

"She's fine. Your mother is in the recovery room now, and you should be able to see her soon."

Dr. Portugal continued, "We took two types of biopsies, a frozen section, and a permanent section. We were able to get results of the frozen section very quickly while your mother was still under anesthesia. Her CT scan, what I observed in my earlier examination, and the frozen section concur with our suspicion that your mother has squamous cell carcinoma of her tongue."

"What about that other section, the permanent section? What about that one?" Daniel asked.

"The permanent section requires a week to ten days to analyze, but in the meantime, we'll begin putting a treatment plan in place. If the permanent section concurs with our diagnosis, then we can start treating your mother right away."

We were all in shock. Before this meeting, our conversations about the prospect of Margaret's initial cancer diagnosis were just words. Now they were a reality.

"This seems surreal, I'm trying to absorb it all," Daniel said.

"I don't know what to think. How will this all turn out? Will my mother live?" Merrell interjected.

"We must think positively. Your mother will need that to get through a difficult treatment. And to answer your question, Merrell, yes, we are confident she will live," Dr. Portugal answered.

"Doctor, Margaret is a pastry chef. She needs her tongue to function for her livelihood. Will she be able to continue her work? What are the next steps?" I asked.

"We'll assemble an oncology team who are very knowledgeable and experienced with this kind of cancer. The team will be able to answer your questions. But be assured, UCMC has found a treatment protocol that balances their patients' quality of life with the rigors of cancer treatment," the doctor explained.

"What's the success rate of the treatment?" Daniel asked, "Is everything going to be okay?"

"Yes, she will be okay," Dr. Portugal said. "UCMC's rate of success is high, and I believe we caught your mother's cancer in time. I'm confident she will become cancer-free."

After Dr. Portugal answered all our questions, he left us to gather our thoughts. Daniel and Merrell later spent time with their mother as she recovered from the procedure.

After that, I accompanied Margaret to most meetings with her doctors and acted as her advocate and scribe. I needed to be mentally and emotionally present for her, as that was all I knew I could do to help her purposefully. I emailed summaries of the day's medical meetings and procedures to Margaret and her brother, Michael Mayer, who forwarded the reports to the family and close friends. It was a communication system that worked well for us, allowing the avalanche of technical, procedural information, and schedules to be put in writing, sparing Margaret from having to repeat her status over and over again to those who asked.

"Bob," I said one morning, "I've been searching on Google, and there's so much out there on squamous cell carcinoma of the tongue: articles, support groups, photos, medical treatments, natural treatments, diagnoses, prognoses. It's terrifying and exhausting. I feel like my head is going to explode."

"If it's upsetting you too much, you need to stop looking at those sites," he said. "You're going to make yourself sick. Just listen to what the doctors have to say and stop the searches."

I sighed. "Easier said than done. I have to learn everything I can. I can't stop myself."

The more I discovered what was in store for Margaret, the more her future became a blurry puzzle, and the pieces didn't seem to fit. Medical terms like biopsies, frozen sections, permanent sections, CT scans, planning scans, so different from my everyday language, made little sense to me. We needed to know the big picture of her treatment timeline. When will it start? When will it finish? And most importantly, when will Margaret be cured?

It was as if someone took puzzle pieces from different puzzles, piled them on the floor, and said, "Have at it!" I wasn't sure I was the right person to act as Margaret's advocate, as I had neither a medical background nor experience in these kinds of life-changing matters.

I visited Margaret one afternoon at her home. Sophie sat close to me as I petted her—her round black eyes slowly closing and opening in complete relaxation, and whenever I stopped, she put her paw on my hand, reminding me I needed to continue. Margaret and I smiled, watching her.

"We've been friends for more than twenty years, and I love you," I told Margaret. "I'll stick with you through your journey, but I don't know that I'm the right person to help you in a way you need and deserve."

"I love you, too, and just being with me has been helpful. I don't know who else can do what you're doing. You've kept me calm when all I want to do is scream! Stick with me, yes please, stick with me."

We cried and hugged.

"I've been researching my cancer, and it's terrifying. Oh my god, so scary. I can't sleep, and sometimes, I can't stop crying." Margaret continued to sob.

"Listen, remember when Dr. Portugal warned us not to get too wrapped up on Internet searches or chat rooms because conditions of others have nothing to do with your set of circumstances?"

"I know, but I want to know what's going to happen to me, and everything I read is so awful, I can't stand it."

"And that's why we have to have confidence in your doctors. They have real-life survivors who are living normal lives after treatment. Dr. Portugal told us we have to stay positive about this cancer. He emphasized that point."

I was trying to convince myself as much as Margaret. In spite of what I'd told her, I continued my exhaustive searches. After collecting complex and contradictory data, I realized Dr. Portugal was right, and I finally stopped my "research." But not before reading *LIFE, ON THE LINE A Chef's Story of Chasing Greatness, Facing Death, and Redefining the Way We Eat*. It is a memoir about world-renowned Chef Achatz and his business partner restaurateur, Nick Kokonas. Chef Achatz had walked his road to healing from squamous cell carcinoma of his tongue, the same cancer Margaret had. During his cancer treatment at UCMC, Chef Achatz continued his incomparable creations at his restaurant *Alinea*. And through his journey to wellness, he and Kokonas had opened their second restaurant, *Next*. Chef's recovery was long and painful, but his success in beating his cancer gave Margaret and I hope that she, too, would recover and resume her life and profession as a pastry chef.

Lying in spoons one night, Bob and I were in bed having our last conversation of the day.

"I don't know what to do," I said. "I'm so scared for Margaret. My head is full of worries, and I can't let go of them. I can hardly ever fall asleep—I can't tell Margaret, but I'm spent. I feel like I have nothing left to offer her."

"How is she doing?" Bob asked.

"She's consumed with fear."

"Be there for her. She needs you to be strong," he said.

"But what if I can't be strong? Then what?"

"You are strong. You don't have to worry about that. You have no control over Margaret's cancer, but I know you'll support her. I know it," he said, hugging me.

Bob was who kept me steady. With all my worries for Margaret, there was no one I felt I could just "let go" with, other than him. He was my safety net, and his hug comforted me.

But as I drifted to sleep, there appeared the long-ago image of waves below me as I stood precariously near the edge of the wooded bluff of the Evanston Art Center.

I'm falling!

My tightened body flinched, and my eyes opened wide to erase the image.

A lot of my conversations with Margaret were over the phone and usually at night. It was difficult for me to comfort her when I was so worried myself, but I tried my best.

"Could you tell me a story about your mother?" she asked me one night.

"What kind of story?"

"I don't care. A conversation you had, a funny story, a sad one. Anything. I want you to talk about her."

"Well," I cleared my throat. "I used to work with a fellow whose world was rocked to its core when the doctors told him and his wife, their newborn baby had a disability that would be life-long. I didn't know if I should send a gift and a happy card for their new baby as if everything was perfectly fine, or let it go for now and not impose on them. I asked my mother what I should do.

After thinking briefly, my mother said, "Well, baby needs clothes!"

Unencumbered by pesky, unimportant sidebars of a situation, my mother always had a knack for getting to the core of issues. "I have no idea why I made this such a complicated decision. Of course, a newborn baby is a joyous occasion and of course, a baby needs clothes, no matter what the circumstances. Why didn't I think of that?" I said.

Margaret laughed. "I know, we always torture ourselves in that way, don't we? We have to be more like our pups and live in the moment, one day at a time."

"Yes, we do," I agreed, realizing that my overwhelming worry wasn't doing Margaret or myself any good. I resolved to take it one day at a time—for Margaret.

In between visits with Margaret, her doctors, tests, and late-night phone conversations, I spent days and evenings with my mother. I called her one morning to see if she wanted to get together.

"Hi, Mom, I was thinking of coming over. You free?" I asked. I heard loud music in her apartment—Middle Eastern music, it seemed.

"I can't hear you, who's this?"

"It's *Susie!*"

"Who?"

"It's *Susie!*" I laughed.

What in the world?

My mother answered, "Oh, Susie, I can't talk right now. Gabe is teaching me how to belly dance!"

"What do you mean?" I asked.

"I have to go now. I'll call you later." She hung up.

Oy vey!

Later that afternoon, I called her again.

"Hi—so, who's Gabe, and why is he teaching you belly dancing?" I asked.

"Gabe is my massager. I told you about him. Oh, it was so much fun!"

"Mom, why did your massage therapist teach you belly dancing? He's supposed to give you a massage."

"Oh, he did, and I told him how much I love to dance, so after the massage, he taught me to dance. He's from Egypt."

"He's a male belly dancer?" I asked.

"Yes! He said in Egypt, it's common. Why don't you come over the next time he's here, and he can teach you, too?"

"I dunno about that."

"Oh, Susie, you need to be open to new ideas. Belly dancing's fun!"

We laughed.

No way.

Then I thought of my elderly mother, belly dancing in her apartment with a young Egyptian masseur.

Well, maybe one day. God, how I loved her.

Spending more time with my mother than I had in the past, I noticed her cognitive skills seemed to be somewhat in decline, in subtle but curious ways.

One day, we were on our way to her ophthalmologist.[38]

"Let's go this way, no, no, that way," my mother said as we walked down a corridor.

"No, wait, over there, let's go over there. Oh, my goodness. Nothing looks familiar!"

"Mom, let me ask at the information desk."

"Oh, I'm so *baka!*"[39] She feigned laughter, but under her breath, I heard her say, "I don't understand, I've come here so many times . . ."

Inside the doctor's office just past the receptionist's desk, she saw an impressionist style painting at the end of the hallway. She walked up very close to it, stopped, and said, "sakuda."

"Pretty, isn't it?" I asked. It was a painting of a tree with a broad habit filled with pink blossoms.

Squinting, she examined it intently and whispered, "Sakuda. Yes, sakuda."

"What's sakuda?" I asked her. But she was focused on the painting and didn't answer me.

I didn't know what she was talking abou—it looked like a magnolia tree to me, but I didn't argue with her. When I got home later that day, I Googled "sakuda" and found that it was a surname, which didn't ring any bells for me.

She just hasn't been herself lately. Maybe I'm imagining it.

I was determined to fix whatever wasn't right about my mother's health. During my ten years at the university, I was responsible for "the fix" of all things related to buildings and grounds, and I seemed to carry that charge into my personal life. I thought my mother needed to start using a part of her brain she had never used in the past.

"Mom, would you be interested in learning to play the piano?" I asked.

"Oh no," she said. "I could never do that."

"I can teach you. I know you can learn."

I brought my portable electronic keyboard to her place, set it up, marked the letters of the keys, and told her we would start with one of

Mozart's 12 Variations on "Ah vous dirai-je, Maman," K. 265 (300e.)

"Huh? What?" she squealed. "Oh, Susie, that's silly, I can't play Mozart!"

I giggled. "Mom, don't worry, the variation we'll work on is also known as 'Twinkle, Twinkle, Little Star!'" We both laughed long and hard.

I taught her to play with her right and left hands and had her sing as she played.

"I never dreamed I could ever play the piano!" she exclaimed with childlike enthusiasm.

"I knew you could do it, Mom."

It was fun, albeit challenging, still, we persevered and she was laser-focused on her studies.

On days I wasn't with her, she phoned me to show off her playing. She was astounded with her progress and talked about how difficult it was, but it was clear she delighted in playing. Her memory of the music and hand coordination vastly improved after just a few weeks, but suddenly and inexplicably, she lost interest in playing.

"I get that, Mom. My progress at the keyboard hit a brick wall many times. Let's let it go for a while, and we'll come back to it later," I told her.

I had a lot of ideas to help her. There was an art room at The Breakers, and I could teach her how to make pottery. We could start with pinch pots, and then coil pots, and maybe I could even teach her how to use the potter's wheel. We could play card games, and, ah, yes, we could work on puzzles!

I purchased some simple, wooden puzzles of large, colorful shapes and numbers. I believed working on them would be satisfying and help her gain confidence. During a visit with her, I turned over the puzzle board, and the pieces tumbled onto the table. I gave her a puzzle piece, the number 'one,' but she seemed confused.

"Mom, everything all right?" I asked.

"Susie, what am I supposed to do with this?"

"Oh, I'll help you. Take this puzzle piece, number 'one,' and put it inside the shape where you think it'll fit."

She held the piece and turned it sideways and tried to push it in, and then upside down, diagonally, but nothing worked. I guided her hand to make the puzzle piece upright. Still, she could barely get it in place. With my hand on hers, we finally succeeded.

"Good, Mom. Let's try it again." I asked her to remove the puzzle piece. "Now, try to put it back in."

"Oh, Susie, I don't know what I'm doing," she whispered.

She struggled and was unable to figure it out. I guided her hand again, and eventually, we managed to get all five numbers in their proper places. It wasn't her declining eyesight or her arthritic fingers that made it so difficult for her. It was her logic, analytical skills, and memory that escaped her. Stunned at the extent of her inabilities, I became anxious and fearful. We worked with that puzzle several times, with the same results.

When I got home at the end of the day, Tony greeted me robustly as if I'd been gone for weeks. He followed me into the bedroom, and I got down on the floor and wrapped my arms around him, my tears flowing.

How could this be? Our conversations are perfectly lucid. I had no idea she couldn't process something as simple as a child's puzzle.

Like an impatient toddler, Tony usually tried to wiggle out of hugs that lasted too long, but this time, he remained still and rested his chin on my arm, letting me hold him as I cried.

Once I understood and accepted that parts of my mother's brain were operating on such a different level, my anxiety and fear seemed to release itself, and I somehow found the patience I never knew I had.

Maybe she needs to revisit activities more familiar to her.

Cooking was a significant part of my mother's life, her purpose, but since living at The Breakers, she'd had her meals in their dining room and rather enjoyed not having to do the day-to-day cooking she used to do.

"Mom, when I come over tomorrow, can you help me wrap wontons?" I asked over the phone. "I told Bob I would cook some for him."

"Oh, yes, of course! Do you have all the ingredients?" Her voice was bright and cheerful.

"Yes, I'll bring over everything. Okay, I'll see you tomorrow around 11 a.m. Don't eat lunch downstairs, okay? We'll wrap extra wontons and make some soup."

At her apartment the following day, I combined the ground pork and the rest of the ingredients in a bowl.

"Mom, did I put in enough green onions?"

"Mmmm, I think you could use more, chotto, just a little. Did you put in water chestnuts? And shoyu?" she asked. "What about garlic, ginger, and sesame oil—what else, oh, how about miso?"

"Yes, yes, got it all."

"Oh, Susie, I have some frozen shrimp. Get it and thaw them in cold water, then we'll chop it up and put it in with the pork.

"Great, okay."

After I mixed all the ingredients, I put a small bowl of water on the table, laid out some wonton wrappers on a cutting board, and put a dollop of the pork and shrimp stuffing on each of the wrappers.

"Here you go, can you wrap some up?"

Like riding a bicycle, my mother took care of the task at hand post-haste. Except for having a little trouble handling the delicate wrappers due to her arthritic fingers, she did a great job. Then we made soup of chicken broth with a touch of dashi granules and shoyu, dropped in a few wontons in a separate pot of boiling water, and when done, put the wontons in the soup. We garnished the soup with green onions and enjoyed our lunch of wonton soup.

"Oishi!" she said as she dipped the wonton in a little sauce of dry mustard, water, and shoyu.

"Instead of deep-frying the wontons, I think I'll make soup just like this for Bob tonight. He'll be so happy. Thanks for helping me."

Over the following weeks, we played simple memory games about people and events past and present and ventured back to her piano lessons. She was even able to have some success with the puzzles.

But I knew my mother's puzzles were not the only ones that needed putting together.

⟡

Margaret and I walked through a series of underground, white-walled corridors at UCMC. I could hear echoes of our footsteps on the hard tile floor. We were going to meet her oncology team members for the first time: Radiation Oncology Specialist Dr. Daniel Haraf and Medical Oncologist Dr. Victoria Villaflor.

We arrived at the reception area where Margaret introduced herself to the receptionist who guided us into a windowless, but friendly and comfortable conference room.

After waiting for a few moments, the two doctors joined us. Mid-aged, medium height with brown hair, and the more sedate of the two, Dr. Haraf was forthright, pulled no punches, and was a let's-get-down-to-business kind of guy. His charm was a little dry—still, his sense of humor helped "break the ice." Dr. Villaflor seemed Dr. Haraf's junior. She was tall with long dark hair she'd worn in a low ponytail and had a warm, approachable personality—her smiles came easily. The two doctors were the yin and yang of a perfect team. We were relieved this UCMC team brought their experience and knowledge of the successful treatment of Chef Grant Achatz.

We had a friendly meet and greet conversation, then got down to the dreaded subject of Margaret's cancer.

The doctors were professional, aware of Margaret's condition and status, and very respectful and compassionate about her concerns. They knew of Margaret's breast cancer treatment at the, now defunct, Michael Reese Hospital. Since UCMC was the keeper of official Michael Reese files, they had access to her medical history.

"Margaret," Dr. Haraf said, "your permanent section biopsy came back positive, so your tongue cancer is again confirmed. We recommend that we begin treatment as soon as possible. It involves chemotherapy and chemoradiation."

"You're familiar with chemotherapy?" asked Dr. Villaflor.

"Yes, unfortunately, yes, I am," Margaret replied.

"So, you know it will cause nausea, and you'll lose your hair?"

Margaret nodded, a tear falling down her cheek.

"And you'll likely have joint and body pain, but we have medications that will help ameliorate the discomfort," Dr. Villaflor added.

"Yes, and radiation will cause a sore throat that may cause painful swallowing, but there are pain relievers for that as well," said Dr. Haraf.

Dr. Villaflor interjected, "Eating is so important, Margaret. You'll have to eat to keep your body well nourished."

"You'll temporarily lose function of your taste buds and salivary glands," said Dr. Haraf. He continued, "And some foods you eat may taste awful, or in some ways, you might taste nothing at all. But you have to press on and eat," Dr. Haraf cautioned.

The mere mention of taste buds sent Margaret into a state of horror. She turned to Dr. Haraf.

"What about my taste buds? Will they be destroyed forever? I need them—I'm a pastry chef and can't lose them!"

"They'll only be affected temporarily. We know you're a pastry chef—Dr. Portugal told us. And we know the importance of careful radiation and chemo calculations not only for your life but also for your professional livelihood. We have had success with other patients who have had cancer similar to yours."

"I don't know what to say. I've been trying to prepare myself for this news, but I'm still in shock. What's the next step?" Margaret asked.

The doctors concurred that before treatment could start, Margaret would need a few more scans, including a Positron Emissions Tomography (PET scan), to determine, on a cellular level, if cancer was in one or both nodes near her throat. If both nodes were affected, she would be considered a stage-4 cancer patient, which would qualify her to participate in a UCMC clinical trial.

"I know all this is overwhelming," Dr. Villaflor said, "but please be assured that with the protocol we're developing for you and the circumstances of your cancer, we're confident you'll become cancer-free."

"Oh my god, oh my god, Susan!" Margaret's voice was a strained whisper as we walked down the lonely corridor after the meeting. She struggled to hold back tears. "What am I going to do? How can I lose my taste buds? And all that pain they say I'm going to have! I can't believe this is true." Her face was taut, eyes full of tears, and her hands were trembling.

We stopped walking and stood next to the corridor wall. I wrapped my arms around Margaret and held her tightly.

"Margaret, Dr. Haraf said the *temporary* loss of taste buds. You'll be able to taste again. Your taste buds will come back," I whispered.

"I feel lost. Oh my god, what am I going to do?" Margaret cried.

I faced her. "You're a fighter, a survivor. I know that, and you have to too. You'll get through this! Do you choose to fight this battle?"

"Well, I guess so, but what other choice do I have?"

"You can always choose to give up if you want to."

"No, I won't give up." She straightened her shoulders.

"Then let's fight it—you're a strong woman. We'll get through this!"

This was not the picture puzzle we wanted, but Margaret was a brave soldier and accepted the challenge. More puzzle pieces were added to the pile, leaving an abundance of questions for us to ask and answers to ponder.

Over the following weeks, the oncology team developed her treatment strategy. First, she would have one session per week of outpatient chemotherapy for six weeks. Once completed, her treatment would then include five days of inpatient chemotherapy and radiation therapy, followed by nine days of rest during homestays. This five-day/nine-day cycle would repeat itself for ten consecutive weeks.

Finally, a schedule!

We were getting a better handle on the actions needed, where and when they would happen, and when they would end.

Margaret had a loving family and many devoted friends, and our lives would intertwine with hers during those days she would be at home. And we would give her 24/7 assistance as needed. Margaret's brother, Michael, prepared spreadsheets of her at-home dates so we would know who would be staying with her and when. And we would implore, beg, and cajole her to eat. But how and what she would eat remained a mystery.

I felt helpless as I learned the immediate effects of Margaret's cancer treatment, knowing there was nothing I could do to help her. The hospital will provide the nutrition she needed during each of her five-day inpatient stays, but meals during her home stays were yet undetermined.

One morning, it dawned on me. *I can cook for Margaret!*

She'd be home for nine days, times two meals/day, times five weeks equals ninety meals, which rounded up to one hundred meals for Margaret.

I was an on-again-off-again vegan, so preparing plant-based foods was familiar to me. Our granddaughter, Alex, now ten years old and spending the weekend with us, meekly asked as I planned the night's dinner,

"Nana, are we going to be vegans today?"

I answered, "No, not today, Alex."

Relieved, she smiled and helped me cook vegetable fried rice, beef teriyaki, and grilled root vegetables—an excellent meal for our little omnivore.

As an architect, I saw my built environment in many ways: color, texture, dimension, context, structure, form, and function. And this would be my compass as I thought about the kinds of meals I would cook for Margaret. I am not a chef, but I like to cook and eat healthy. And I decided my meals for Margaret would be mainly plant-based purees with garnishes of meat for additional protein.

One evening, I began to experiment with foods, so Margaret could taste-test them before she started her cancer treatment. I went through the fridge, looking for the treasures I'd bought from Whole Foods. Seeing the vegetables piqued my imagination and the possibilities this cooking experiment would bring. My excitement grew.

Like a surgeon, I washed and dried my hands before putting on my disposable vinyl gloves, then washed my gloved hands.

Even though all the veggies were organic, I soaked them in lukewarm water with a dash of dishwashing liquid and scrubbed everything, including the greens, and rinsed them thoroughly. This process wilted the greens, but since I would thoroughly cook everything anyway, wilting was not a problem.

I boiled the greens, saving the water they were cooked in to use as a thinning liquid for some of the purees. After the veggies roasted in the oven, I prepared them for puree. Using a blending stick, I pureed each vegetable separately, then poured each one in its own container. I stepped back to inspect them.

Wow!

The veggies showed off their brilliant, supple, vibrant colors to me. I was blown away. Lined up on my counter, they looked like an artist's palette. I did this food experiment just before Margaret's cancer treatment commenced, so she could still taste.

I called her.

"Hi, how're you feeling today? Am I calling too late?" I asked Margaret.

"Nope, not too late. My sister-in-law, Marge, came in from Colorado to visit me, and we were chatting. I feel good!"

"Great, say, would you two like to stop by my place tomorrow? I made some puree samples for you to taste test."

"Oh, I'd love to! Can we come in the morning, around 10?"

"Perfect, see you then."

Looking back at my "artist's palette," I was awed by the humble red beet casting its evocative, fresh, earthy scent of a farm field after a summer rain and its vibrant magenta color as beautiful as a fine Merlot; the pliability and soft, creamy smoothness of asparagus; the bold, deep greenness of pole beans with their fresh, clean grassy fragrance; and the cheerful, sweet brightness of carrots.

I sighed with satisfaction.

The next morning, I placed the small bowls of sample pureed veggies in an arc, mimicking an artist's palette:

> Red (sweet red bell pepper)
> Magenta (red beets)
> Shades of orange (carrots, sweet potatoes, and butternut squash)
> Yellow (golden beets)
> Shades of green (green pole beans, broccoli, asparagus, collard greens)
> White (parsnips)

Margaret and her sister-in-law arrived, and I guided them into the kitchen.

Margaret beamed. "Oh. My. God! They're beautiful! I've never seen anything like this, Susan, what vegetables are they?"

I identified each and asked, "Would you like to taste them?" I put two spoons near each bowl to avoid cross mixing of the colors. They tasted each veggie.

"Delicious—did you add anything to the vegetables? Salt, pepper?" Margaret asked.

"No, no spices, nothing. Too risky because it might hurt your throat."

"They taste like pure, real food and so flavorful. I can't wait to eat your meals, Susan!"

Knowing that Margaret appreciated the taste and beauty of the samples of vegetables, I felt I could continue my meal planning for her.

Later that night in March, I began to design and cook one hundred meals for Margaret. As I completed each type of meal, I wrote notes, took pictures, and safely filed them away. I decided when situations settled down, I'd review, organize, and write about my process. But for the next few weeks, my focus was to finish the meals.

⸘

"I can't go through with it. I hate these kinds of scans. I'll hardly be able to breathe, and I'll feel my heart beating too fast, I know it."

We were on our way to UCMC for Margaret's scan. A self-professed claustrophobic, she was nervous and anxious.

"You can do this, Margaret. I'll be right next to you for part of the procedure."

We entered the cold PET-CT[40] scan room together and faced a large, doughnut-shaped machine and a long narrow bed that would slide back and forth through the doughnut to scan her.

Margaret climbed onto the bed, and the technician prepared her for the scan. He went to his glass-walled control room to test the sound system, so he could remotely communicate with Margaret. I sat near her head and did all the talking, to help distract her from sounds made by the doughnut. The machine did make a racket, and I wasn't sure she could even hear me.

"Margaret, I'm here with you. My mother asked me to give you her best wishes for this test. Did I tell you about her experience with a PET-CT scan? My mother thought it was pretty scary, too, but pretended she was on a lifeboat adrift at sea and thought if she moved, her boat would tip over, so she stayed real still. She pretended those awful noises were sounds from a big ship that was coming to save her. That's how she found a way to get through her scan by imagining other, more pleasant things. My mother asked about Sophie. She had a dog when she was young..."

And so on, and so on. My mother had never had a PET-CT scan that I knew of, and I don't think she even had a dog when she was a kid. Still, I knew Margaret liked hearing stories about my mother, so I made them up and kept talking mindlessly.

After the first part of the scan concluded, the technician asked me to join him in his control room, after which he completed the second part. Margaret remained still as required and successfully got through the whole procedure.

"I'm so relieved that's over—it was awful," Margaret said on our ride to her place.

"You did great! You said you couldn't go through with it, and you did—congratulations!"

I was relieved, too, and it was uplifting to see this accomplishment behind her. This scan was the first of many steps toward her cancer outcome, and she did a great job under stressful circumstances.

After a full day with Margaret at the hospital, I was happy for her but exhausted and drained. I couldn't wait to get home and collapse on the sofa—maybe take a nap and dream about lifeboats and my mother.

※

My legs heavy and shoulders bearing too much weight of the day's events, I looked forward to that nap. I was so tired I was barely able to climb the stairs to my loft. As I approached the front door, I heard the phone ringing inside and managed to muster the energy to get to the phone. My coat still on and keys in hand, I picked up the phone.

"Aunt Susie? Aunt Susie!" The voice was thin and strained.

"Lisa, is that you? Are you all right?" I asked.

"Aunt Susie, something terrible happened to Grandma, and the ambulance is taking her to the emergency room!"

My stomach sank. "I'll go to the hospital right now. Don't worry, Lisa, I'm sure she'll be all right."

I learned later, Lisa, Dennis's daughter, had visited my mother earlier on that chilly March afternoon. They'd sat chatting in The Breakers' comfortable lobby. As Lisa was leaving, my mother had suddenly become disoriented and lost consciousness. Lisa quickly called for help, and paramedics were soon on the scene.

When I arrived at the hospital, I found my mother in bed, looking pale, sleepy, confused, and disheveled in an oversized hospital gown.

"Oh, Susie, you're here. What happened?"

"You fainted Mom, and the doctors are trying to figure out why. Don't worry, you're in the hospital now, and you're going to be fine." I didn't have any other answers for her.

After a few minutes, my mother looked up at me in surprise.

"Oh, Susie. When did you get here? What happened to me?"

My heart skipped a beat. I'd never seen my mother with such a short-term memory lapse before.

"Mom, we're not sure, but the doctors said everything would be all right."

My thoughts went back to my father in the hospital six years earlier, when *they* said he would be fine; *they* said all his tests were normal, and *they* thought he'd come home soon. I got scared. Is my mother facing the same imminent fate as my father?

No! Everything will work out. Everything must work out.

I spoke to her doctor later that day. He said he wasn't sure what caused my mother's fainting episode but noticed a significant presence of amyloids in my mother's CT head scan. I didn't understand the relevance of amyloids in her brain, but the news unsettled me.

I spent days with my mother in her hospital room, keeping her company and meeting with doctors. I slipped out briefly to take care of household tasks and touch base with Margaret, then returned to my mother to stay overnight with her. Her private hospital room was spacious, received plenty of natural light, and had a couch that converted to a guest bed.

Bob was surprised to see me when he came home from work one evening.

"How come you're here?" he asked.

"I needed to take a shower, get some fresh clothes, and take a break.

I can't stay here long—I need to get back to my mother," I said, slumped in the cushions of our couch.

"Are you all right?" He reached over me to turn off the TV.

"I'm fine," I said.

But I'm not fine—I felt I was on the edge of the wooded bluff, fearful about Margaret, and now my mother.

"Is your mom okay?" he asked.

"I think so, but she's changed. She seems so distant. Either that or she doesn't comprehend—I don't know which would be worse. I'm so scared something terrible is going to—Oh, I don't know what I'm talking about. Everything will be fine."

"I'm worried about you. Why don't you stay home tonight? I'll cook dinner, and we can have a nice glass of wine," he smiled.

I smiled back. "Sounds tempting, but I can't. I have to go to my mother. I'll take a rain check, okay?"

"You got it!" Bob gave me a hug that I wished would never end. I went back to the hospital.

The doctors discharged my mother after a week. They suggested an around-the-clock caregiver for the next three months, followed by an evaluation of her strength, balance, and cognitive skills. I was pleased she was finally going home, but I knew her life would be very different. I contacted The Breakers and asked for referrals for caregiving services.

The transition from her coveted independent and socially busy life to a dependent one was difficult, but she worked at accepting her new challenge. Adjusting to having someone in her apartment 24/7, though, would not be easy. After several temporary caregivers came and went, the caregiving service finally found a person who was available for a three-month assignment. Corrine, a woman in her fifties, slim with black hair, was chatty, very assertive with my mother, and seemed to know what she was doing.

"Hi, Corrine! Hi, Mom, how're you?" I asked, arriving at my mother's apartment one morning. We'd planned to have breakfast together in The Breakers' dining room.

"Hi, Susan, we're fine," Corrine answered for the both of them.

"Mom, are you ready to go downstairs?" I asked.

"Hai. I have to put my shoes on."

"Don't forget, we're going to take a walk outside this morning," said Corrine.

"Oh, thank you, but my son is coming this afternoon, and he's going to take me for a walk." My mother smiled.

"Well, I'm taking you today. Your son can take you another time."

"Okay." My mother whispered as her smile disappeared.

I took Corrine aside and said, "She looks forward to Dennis's visits and their walks together. You can walk with her another time, okay?"

"Susan, I do this all the time. I think your brother is a little too close to the situation, and I should walk with her today."

What the hell is she talking about?

When we arrived at our table in the dining room, I asked my mother, "Are you happy with Corrine?"

"She's okay." My mother said, sinking into her chair.

"Mom, she seems very stubborn, and you're always so quiet when she's around. Are you all right?"

"I don't want to make trouble with her."

"Finding the right caregiver takes a little time—the service knows that. Do you mind if I ask them to find another person?" I asked.

"I'm afraid I'll get in trouble with them. What if the service doesn't send me anyone else? Then Corrine will be mad at me."

"Can I just ask them?"

"If you want. But don't make any trouble, Susie!"

"Okay, I won't," I assured her.

I talked to the caregiving service, telling them I didn't think Corrine was the right fit. They had no problem with that, and within a week, they had another caregiver for my mother.

"Hello, I'm Editha," she told my mother and me when she arrived at the apartment. Soft-spoken, likely in her mid-years, small and compact in stature, with dark hair—I liked her gentleness. I took her suitcase and put it in the guest room.

"Come in, come in!" my mother said, her eyes twinkling, and her smile was broad. "Are you Filipino?"

Editha laughed. "Yes, how 'bout you?" she asked.

"I'm Japanese, but I was born in Hawai`i!" my mother said proudly.

"Oh, Hawai`i! I've been to Hawai`i—it's beautiful over there."

Editha and my mother bonded immediately. I smiled, listening to them giggle and getting to know each other. Thus, was the start of a friendship between my mother and her new, primary caregiver. Over the next few days, my mother's humor, self-confidence, and high spirits began to come back.

I was pleased to find that Editha was also firm when necessary. I arrived at my mom's place one day, just as my mother was getting up from her nap.

"Susie, when did you get here?" my mother asked.

"Only a few minutes ago," I said.

"Oh, I was so tired this morning," my mother said.

"Are you rested now?" Editha asked.

"Yes, yes, I'm fine!"

"Good, then it's time to work on your physical therapy, okay?"

"Editha, I thought you were going to say it's time for lunch," my mother laughed. "I think I'll sit for a while and wait for mealtime."

"No, you need to work," Editha said, smiling. "Get strong! Come on, let's exercise."

"Okay, and after that, we'll all go downstairs for lunch."

Editha winked at me.

My mother's resolve to work toward good health remained solidly intact. She diligently followed her physical and occupational therapists' instructions during their sessions, as well as working on her own and with Editha. Always optimistic and positive, my mother struggled to maintain those attributes that served her so well in life. But with Editha's help, she persevered.

Since my mother's unexplained fainting incident, she had a plethora of wellness and follow-up doctors' appointments. Maneuvering her walker was challenging, but always the happy warrior, she soldiered on without complaint.

Whenever Dennis came to visit, he put our mother through her paces. They took long walks through nearby Lincoln Park, and when she complained she was tired, he insisted they walk a little farther.

Feigning exasperation, she once said to me, "He's so bossy, that Dennis!"

"It's no use arguing with him, so do as he says. He's a doctor after all," I said.

My mother's progress in strength and balance was evident, and I knew she was grateful for Dennis's time and attention.

When it came to walking inside her apartment, however, she ditched her walker and instead, steadied herself by putting her hand on the wall.

Each time she did this, I implored, "Mom, please use your walker! There's nothing on the wall to grab if you lose your balance."

Sometimes she heeded my pleas, but she usually just smiled, and like a defiant child, continued using the wall for stability. It was futile to argue, but I never stopped urging her.

One day over lunch in her apartment, my mother suddenly looked at me.

"You were born left-handed, you know, and your father and I switched you!" She beamed with pride.

With my eyes wide and mouth full of food, I pushed out a high-pitched sound. "Hmmm?" I swallowed. "What do you mean?"

"When you were a baby, you always grabbed things with your left hand, so we kept putting everything in your right hand, and then you became right-handed—it was amazing!"

"What? Mom, are you sure?"

"Yes, I'm sure. We switched you!"

"But, Mom, you're not supposed to—I mean, kids who are switched, are…"

Okay, let it go.

"Thank you, Mom," I mumbled.

When I got home that night, I started to teach myself to write with my left hand. I was startled at how fast my left hand picked up its new charge. Being an actual lefty brought up all kinds of questions about my left-right brain function, but those ponderings would have to wait for another time.

For all of my parents' amazing qualities, this was one of the first times I wondered, "What in the world were they thinking?"

Margaret went through a flurry of investigative tests, including a regular CT scan, to update her original one that showed signs of cancer in the first place. She also had a CT Simulation scan, that allowed the doctors to determine the location and extent of the tumor.

After reviewing the results of her tests and scans, the doctors gave us bad news and good news. The bad news: cancer was in both of Margaret's nodes, which placed her in a stage-4 cancer group. The good news was this: as a stage-4 cancer patient, she indeed qualified for participation in a UCMC clinical trial.

The protocol for the trial was complicated. Generally, if, after the fifth week of the six-week phase-one powerful chemotherapy treatment, her tumors reduced by at least 50-percent, her phase-two radiation field would be diminished from the traditional range, sparing more taste buds and salivary glands. That was, obviously, of utmost importance to Margaret.

"I feel lucky I qualify for the clinical trial, but—" she said.

"But what?" I asked.

"I can't stand the thought of the cancer being in more places than my tongue. Oh, I don't know, do you think this is good news?"

I thought for a minute. "I know it's a little weird to be happy your cancer is stage-4 but just think, the clinical trial may save more of your taste buds."

"That makes sense. Achhh! It's all so confusing," she said.

Clearing this hurdle helped the doctors plan future logistics of Margaret's treatments, and piece by piece, the puzzle took on more clarity and hope.

A week later, I stayed with Margaret at UCMC as she received the first of six chemotherapy sessions. It was a blur of activity filled with discussions with doctors, nurses, physician assistants, technical staff, and a nutritionist. I took copious notes, but it was too much to digest at the moment, and I hoped that once I transcribed those notes in an email to Michael, it would make more sense. The barrage of information, with little time for comprehension, raised more doubts about myself as I attempted to advocate for Margaret. I thought I had a handle on the puzzle, but once again, nothing seemed to fit.

In the following days after her first chemo session, Margaret made her way through CT scans and blood work, and we attended a bunch of meetings with health care providers. At night, we had endless conversations about the days' events.

"How are you feeling since your chemo?" I asked.

"Not bad, actually—just tired."

"Nausea, Margaret?"

"No, not really. The meds they gave me are doing its job. But honestly, I dread the thought of losing my hair. I've decided to have it shaved before too much falls out. I've been looking at wigs and found one that's a baseball cap with bangs and a ponytail attached to it. I think that would be cute!"

"Oh, yeah! That's great, especially with warmer weather coming up. I can't wait to see you in it."

Changing the subject, I asked her, "How's Sophie doing? Does she know you're going through a hard time?"

"Oh, Susan, I don't know what I'd do without her. When I talk to Sophie or cry, she looks at me like she understands. I love her so much. She's such good company and knows how to make me laugh, too."

I never understood the fuss dog owners made over their pets until Tony, the first pup I ever had, became part of my family. I got what Margaret was saying. I knew how they touched our souls in an inexplicable but palpable way—especially during times like these.

"Don't talk. Just listen!" Over the phone, I could hear my mother's voice quiver with frustration, sounding like she was on the verge of crying.

"But, Mom—"

"I don't want to hear you. I just want you to listen to me. Shirley lifted her nose and snubbed me when I first moved here, and I don't like that."

Shirley was an attractive woman, always well-dressed, and at ninety-plus years old, she was friendly, articulate, with a mind sharp as a tack. Soon after getting to know my mother, she'd become one of her most devoted and caring friends.

"But, Mom, that was five years ago. When you first arrived at The Breakers, Shirley didn't even know who you were. Maybe she was just careful about who she became friends with." I was trying to help her see another point of view, but my mother would have none of it. She insisted on focusing her angst on an incident way back in the past.

This was not the first time my mother expressed agitation during the past few weeks, each time taking me by surprise because it was so out of her character. I didn't understand why, all of a sudden, she would spin herself into a cycle of negativity—it just wasn't like her.

We hadn't raised our voices with each other since I was in high school. I felt awful. I was trying to offer my mother another viewpoint, and my efforts were unwelcomed. There I was, trying to fix a situation that didn't need fixing. She wanted me to hear her feelings without me trying to fix anything.

I later learned that uncharacteristic agitation was a sign of things to come.

Sitting in my kitchen, Kristin sighed and said, "I wish there was something I could do for Margaret."

"I know what you mean, I feel pretty helpless too," I said.

Kristin's eyes grew big. "Do you think Margaret would like to meet my abbot? Maybe he can help her meditate to settle her through the cancer treatment." Kristin was studying Buddhism at a temple in Chicago and was very engaged in her newfound spiritual discoveries.

"Yes! I think she'd like that. I'll call tonight and ask her."

Margaret welcomed the idea, so Kristin coordinated a date with the abbot.

The next week, Margaret called me. "Oh my god, I had such a great day with Kristin today! She brought me to her temple, and I got to meet her abbot. He had such wisdom about my cancer treatment, and I feel like I have renewed strength."

"I'm so happy for you! What did he say? How did he help you?" I asked.

"He said Buddhists respect all living things, and I need to respect and love myself, cancer and all because cancer is living cells in my body. We meditated together, thinking positive thoughts to usher and guide cancer out of my body."

"Wow. You know, Dr. Portugal mentioned to us many times about thinking positively toward your health and the cancer treatment, remember?" I asked.

"I know, and I think there's something to that. I feel so empowered now. I feel like I finally have some control over my life, in so many ways. I feel there's hope!" Margaret continued. "And then afterward, Kristin took me to San Soo Gab San. It's a Korean restaurant, and she ordered all these small plates of incredibly delicious, spicy dishes. I'd never tasted anything like it before—they were great. With my radiation coming up, I'm not sure how much longer I'll be able to eat spicy foods, so I tried everything on the table, and it was so much fun—and I used chopsticks!"

"She knows how to pick the best dishes, and everything tastes so much better using chopsticks," I said. "Margaret, I'm so happy for you. You sound great!"

A few days later, Kristin told me about her Buddhist studies and how she was engaged in sutra copying meditation. "I put a thin sheet of tracing paper, about thirty inches long, over a sutra called the Heart Sutra, and with a calligraphy pen, I carefully traced the aphorism, in silence and awareness. By doing that, I blocked out the world, and that's why it's considered a form of meditation."

"How long was the sutra? How much time did it take you to finish it?" I asked.

"Hmmm, it was pretty long. I think I worked on it for a couple of weeks but not continuously, just a little at a time."

"Kristin, remind me, what was the purpose of the Heart Sutra copying meditation?" I asked.

"It's a form of practice meditation for a family member, and the abbot would read our sutra, then pray and meditate for that family member. But I asked the abbot if I could trace the Heart Sutra and dedicate it to Margaret, and he agreed."

When completed, Kristin gave the abbot her Heart Sutra scroll, rolled, and tied with a ribbon. I knew that the abbot's prayers and meditations would work for Margaret, especially if my Kristin was involved.

≀

Later that week, I visited my mother and had invited Margaret to join us.

"Hi, Susie." My mother was in a happy mood and welcomed me with a hug.

"Guess what, Mom," I said, taking off my coat. "Margaret's coming here too!"

"When, right now? Oh, I better clean up the house."

"Your house looks fine, don't worry." The phone rang, and she picked it up. It was the front desk telling her Margaret had arrived. "She's here!" My mother had a big grin and waited for the knock on her door.

"Margaret! So good to see you! How do you feel?" My mother said as they hugged.

"Very well, and how are you?"

"I'm fine. Kristin told me about your visit with the abbot, and I can't wait to hear all about it. Would you like some tea?" my mother asked.

"I'll make it," I said.

"I'd love some," Margaret said. "You must be so proud of Kristin, studying Buddhism."

"Oh, yes!" My mother beamed. "My husband and I considered ourselves Buddhists, I guess, because our parents were, and I'm so glad Kristin's learning about it. And I'm happy you went to meet the abbot. How did it go?"

"It was wonderful. I loved it. The abbot helped me sort out some things about my life and my cancer. He taught me about being positive. I was so grateful for his words."

My mother smiled. She loved that Margaret appreciated the Japanese culture and way of life and was happy that she had opened her mind and heart to the abbot and his Buddhist teachings.

"Positive, yes, very important. You have to be positive and strong," my mother told Margaret.

I felt comforted as I heard my mother and Margaret talking together. The two had known each other for more than twenty years since the kids were pre-teens, but this was the first time I realized they'd developed this spiritual bond all along. Both their lives were changing so quickly now, in so many different and uncertain ways, and they'd become kindred spirits.

A few weeks had passed when my mother asked, "How's Margaret doing?"

"Her cancer treatment has gotten tough since having so many chemo treatments. She suffers from pain and feels blue almost all of the time. I'm so scared for her." I paused and noticed my mother seemed to be barely listening to me.

"Mom, are you okay?" I asked.

Tears welled in her eyes, and she said softly, "Be strong for her, Susie. She needs you to be strong."

Why I burdened my mother with such news about Margaret, I'll never know and wished I could take back those words. I realized there was a boundary line, and I had crossed it, so from then on, I told her only good things about Margaret's journey, of which there were many.

My mother tried to protect me from harm all my life, and I knew it was my turn to protect her from Margaret's sadness, pain, and grief.

Another significant milestone for Margaret approached, but I cautiously avoided speaking about it with my mother—just in case.

"I can't sleep at night because my body aches so much." Margaret's voice was low, flat, empty. I could barely hear her over the phone. "My joints hurt, and I always feel like I have the flu. I don't know how much longer I can go on like this."

"Margaret, do you want company? Can I come over and visit?"

"No, I want to try to sleep. I'm so sick and tired of all of this."

"We have a meeting with Dr. Villaflor tomorrow. Are you going to be able to make it, or shall I call and reschedule?" I asked.

"No, I'll go."

Margaret and I spoke very little the next morning as we sat in the patients' reception room. She fell in and out of a light sleep while waiting to see Dr. Villaflor. We were about to find out if her tumor had shrunk. I shifted in my chair, sneaking peeks at the clock above the receptionist's station, and anxiety mounted as the appointment time came and passed.

What if the tumor didn't shrink more than 50-percent? What if it didn't shrink at all? What if—

Margaret had had her fifth of six chemotherapy sessions during this first phase of her cancer treatment. If the tumor diminished more than 50-percent, Margaret could expect to receive a narrower field of radiation during her second phase of cancer treatment, which would spare some of her taste buds and salivary glands.

"Margaret?" I whispered. "The nurse is waving us in."

"Okay." She groaned as she stood up.

Although Dr. Villaflor had a natural cheerfulness, today, her smile was extra big as she greeted us. I answered her smile with one of my own.

"Margaret, I have good news! Your tumor reduced by 52-percent!"

"It's half the size it used to be?" Margaret asked without emotion.

"Yes, the chemo is doing its job, and we're pleased with the results." The doctor beamed.

Dr. Villaflor continued, "But the final word will come from Dr. Portugal after he examines you. I've set up the meeting, and he's expecting you."

"Thank you. Thank you for the good news." Margaret stared straight ahead.

"Fantastic news, thank you, Doctor! See you again soon!" I waved good-bye.

After we left the doctor's office, I turned to Margaret. "Are you okay? The news was what we hoped for, right?"

"Yes."

I knew something was bothering her, but I figured she would share it when she was ready. We made our way to otolaryngologist Dr. Portugal, who was there for Margaret at the beginning of her journey into tongue cancer. He had already received the good news and welcomed us warmly.

"Good morning!" He smiled. After we settled in, he turned to Margaret. "Let's have a look at your throat, okay?"

She nodded.

Examining her throat, he said, "I'm happy to say, your tumors appear visibly reduced!"

Margaret was silent.

Touching her shoulder, I asked, "Margaret, this is such great news, isn't it? Now your radiation field will be reduced!"

She turned to the doctor. "Yes, this is great news. Thank you, Doctor."

As we walked toward the parking lot, a quiet stillness hung in the air between us.

"I don't know what to say," she said. "I know I should be thrilled, but I'm not. I still have to go through radiation and more chemo, and then what? This whole thing keeps going on and on—I'm exhausted, and I feel so crappy! You and the doctors have been so supportive, but right now, and I don't feel relieved. I feel beaten. I'm so sorry, Susan."

"Awww, Margaret, you don't have to apologize for your feelings. They're yours, you own them, and no one is allowed to take them away from you. You don't have to feel relieved right now if you don't want to. Give yourself a break and let yourself feel whatever you need to feel. But at some point, remember Dr. Portugal's and the abbot's advice, that we need to keep working at being positive, okay?"

"I know, I know, but it's so hard. I'll try, I promise."

A few weeks later, I drove Margaret to the hospital for her first week of phase-two cancer treatment. It involved five-days of inpatient, twenty-four-hour chemotherapy, and two radiation sessions a day. We arrived on the floor designated for head and neck cancer patients and reached her assigned room.

We explored her accommodations.

"Nice," I said. "It has good natural light, and it's clean and private. What do you think?"

"It's okay, I guess," Margaret said.

Staff came in and out, and friendly patients stopped by to chat.

"That was so nice of that man to visit you. He was so friendly.

What did he say his name was?" I asked Margaret.

"I don't know, I forgot. I guess I better pay better attention from now on." Margaret cracked a smile.

The environment was positive and upbeat. Patients were very open with their health experiences and interested in Margaret's situation, not in an invasive way, but rather with a sense of camaraderie. Margaret was a little tentative, but I hoped good things would come from all this.

The scene reminded me of the times Bob and I took Kristin, and a year later, Jonathan, to their college freshman dorm rooms for the first time. I felt a sense of happiness and sadness. Happiness, because each was embarking on a journey, their own, meeting new people, growing, and learning new things. And sadness, because those milestones marked the fulfillment of one of our primary purposes in life: to raise our children and guide them through their lives as best as we could. We wanted them to grow in their own ways, and we knew it was time for us to let go.

I walked with Margaret on her journey—that was my purpose—and now she would meet other patients who walked that same path, and who could truly support and empathize with her fears and achievements. I knew it was time for me to give her space and let her grow and learn from them.

Margaret's first five-day stay of inpatient treatment chemoradiation went smoothly, and she called me one evening from the hospital.

"Susan, the food here is not edible. It's overcooked, and all I taste is whatever additives the kitchen uses on the food. I know you're cooking for my homestays, but I'm wondering, could I have some of those meals while I'm here in the hospital?"

"Of course, you can. Your brother, Michael, will be visiting you tomorrow, and I'll ask him if he can pick up some of the food packets on his way to see you, okay?"

"Thank you so much. I can't wait! I remember when you made samples, and I came over to taste them. Your meals tasted like real food, and they're so beautiful too!"

The following afternoon, Michael, Margaret's brother, arrived at my condo building and called me from his car. I went downstairs and met him at the front door.

"Susan?" he asked.

"Michael? It's so good to finally meet you," I said.

"I know me too. We've talked and emailed so many times, and it's nice to meet you in the flesh!"

"Here are a few meals for Margaret. Tell her to heat it gently—too fast or too hot will make them melt into a puddle. And tell her 'hi' for me."

"Okay, will do." Michael and I spent a few minutes of meet-and-greet and caught up on Margaret's status.

"I better get these meals to Margaret. Let's talk again soon!" He turned and headed for his car.

After Margaret's five days of inpatient treatment, her son, Daniel, took her home and stayed with her for a few days. When I visited, I found her dazed by her medication protocol. While in the hospital, the nurse tracked and administered her meds, but now that she was at home, it was her responsibility. She was required to take a dozen medications at various times of the day and dispensed in different ways, making the whole ordeal very distressing for Margaret.

"The nurse explained all these medicines before I left the hospital, but how am I supposed to remember what she told me? Oh my god, I don't know what I'm doing," she cried.

I reviewed the nurse's notes, and their complexity was pretty ridiculous. I was surprised the hospital sent her home to fend for herself without a safety net. Cancer patients who undergo chemotherapy can often have "chemo-brain" that may temporarily leave them with information processing difficulties and memory loss. Margaret was experiencing it all.

Looking for patterns and intersections of each medication, I developed an Excel spreadsheet daily log, delineating each hour she needed to take each med. After going through some rough drafts together, we came up with a final schedule that required a simple "checkmark" in the designated box when she took each medication. The log allowed Margaret to feel confident about knowing what meds she needed to take and when to take them. It also served as a road map for others who helped Margaret during her homestay, so they could remind her, when necessary, what meds were due.

Even though Margaret had made new friends at the hospital, she welcomed my help, and I had to admit, it felt good to still have a purpose.

༺

"I can't hear people very well when they talk," my mother told me, "especially when they talk fast and all at the same time—it's so *yakamashii!*⁴¹ I sit there like a dummy. I never know what's going on." She sighed, rubbing her hands together.

So, for her ninety-first birthday celebration, Bob and I had a low-key event in our loft, as I thought my mother would like. Her hearing loss, I believed, was part of the reason why she felt so detached. If only she would get hearing aids, but my urgings fell on "deaf ears," so to speak. She simply didn't want them.

We cooked some of her favorite comfort foods that night: grilled teriyaki chicken, namasu salad, roasted vegetables, and nishime. Dennis and Jane brought Peking Duck from our mother's favorite Chinese restaurant, and sushi from Mitsuwa Market, her favorite Japanese grocery store. Kristin, her husband, Michael, and daughter, Alex, came with andagi, the Okinawan donuts my mother loved, and Lisa and her fiancé, Matt, brought the birthday cake.

My mother missed her other grandchildren. Our son, Jonathan, and Dennis's other children, Kevin, and Julie and her husband were unable to come because they lived and worked out-of-state. Still, my mother was in good spirits on this day.

"Oh, everything looks so oishi. You folks shouldn't have gone through so much trouble," she said. "Kristin, did you make the andagi? It looks so good!"

"Yes, thanks, Grandma, I hope you like it."

"You're ninety-one now," Jane said. "We had to have all your favorite dishes!"

"Hey, Mom," Dennis chimed in, "I'll be coming over to your place with a *Prunus Incisa Little Twist*,⁴² soon." He chuckled.

"Ahhh—Dennis, what's that?" My mother asked.

"A cherry tree! I'll plant it in one of your garden boxes." he beamed.

"Sakuda? Are you teasing me, Dennis? Where did you get the sakuda from?" my mother asked.

She's repeating that word, sakuda, again.

"Hey, wait a minute, a sakuda is a cherry tree?" I asked, but they were too immersed in their conversation.

"I'm not teasing you," Dennis said. "I ordered it from the nursery where I buy all my plants and trees, and just got word it arrived. If we have a mild spring, it might even bloom this year."

"Oh my gosh. A sakuda—I never dreamed I'd ever have one. I can't wait!" My mother was elated.

I'd remembered when she stopped at the painting in her eye doctor's reception area, transfixed, and she'd said that word, "sakuda," again and again. I broke away from the party. I Googled "cherry tree" instead of "sakuda" as I'd done the day she kept repeating that word. Reading about the cherry tree, I learned that in Japan, spring flowers of the sakura (pronounced, sa-ku-da), bloom everywhere en masse. The pure white or pink blossoms symbolize clouds, and its fragility and short life remind the Japanese of the beauty and impermanence of our lives.

If I'd spoken even a little Japanese, I would have known the "r" in a word is pronounced like a "d." What caught my attention, though, was the part about the 'impermanence of life.'

Did she think about the impermanence of life? Why?

After we finished our feast, Kristin brought out her andagi, Lisa placed the birthday cake in front of my mother, and we all sang a hearty version of "Happy Birthday" to her.

A few days later, Dennis planted the sakura in one of my mother's designated planters in the rooftop garden area at The Breakers. As chilly as April was, my mother, bundled up and visited her tree every day to meditate. She wanted our family and Margaret to view its beauty when the blossoms came. She loved that tree. She revered not only its beauty and symbolism but also for the fact that her son planted it for her.

May was a hectic month for my family. We all celebrated Mother's Day with my mom, and great-granddaughter, Alex, would perform in her piano and ballet recitals and also perform traditional Asian dancing at the Buddhist temple. And I planned a bridal shower for Lisa and

Matt, who were getting married soon.

With my mother's vision and hearing disabilities, along with struggling to get about with her walker, I worried all those activities would wear her out.

"Mom, maybe we should skip some of Alex's dance performances. I'm sure she'd understand."

"No, I don't want to skip it. I want to go," she insisted.

"We could still go to her ballet and piano recitals, but the Asian dance recital is later in the evening, and you might be too tired."

"I want to go to all of her recitals!"

"But Mom—"

My mother interrupted me, "I'm going to *all* of them!"

Through sheer tenacity and love for her family, she attended all the events and experienced everything she could with us, and for us, in her own brave and noble way.

Sitting in her living room one afternoon, we listened to a tape of classical Okinawan folk songs playing on her boombox. My mother sat behind her walker, eyes closed, both arms raised, slowly waving with the beat of the music.

"Oh my gosh," she said, suddenly opening her eyes. "I just remembered how I used to dance with my father. I forgot all about that until just now!"

"When did you dance with him?"

"When I was a little girl. We danced at parties."

"What kind of parties, Mom?"

"All the farmers on my father's farm got together and had a party with food and music, and I danced with him. It's been such a long time since I'd thought about that," she whispered.

"Mom, how old were you?"

"I don't know, I can't remember. I'm so tired—I think I'll take a nap now," she said, her voice barely audible. She got up, and instead of using her walker, she put her hand on the wall to steady herself.

I jumped up. "Mom, use your walker, please," I said, bringing it to her. She ignored me and kept walking toward her bedroom, her hand moving slowly against the wall, leaving its imprint along the way.

༄

As busy as the month was for me, it was seemingly quiet for Margaret as she settled in for her nine-day homestay. Merrell, her youngest son, spent the day with her, but in the evening, after he'd left, she developed a mild warmness, not a fever, just warmer than usual. Later that night, her warmness turned into a full fever, and Daniel rushed over and took her to the ER.

For the rest of May, Margaret was in the hospital as doctors tried to bring down her fever and determine the source of the infection. Her advancing cancer treatments, pain in her mouth and throat, along with her temperature, made eating impossible.

"Susan, I can't eat your meals anymore. I need a feeding tube," Margaret told me over the phone. "With all the meds I'm taking, I've been trying to keep track of my calories, protein, and supplements, and it's too confusing for me to do any longer. The feeding tube will have everything I need. I know you worked hard at making my meals, and I'm so sorry, but I have to stop eating them!"

"Oh, Margaret, don't worry! The important thing is, the feeding tube will keep you strong."

The fever continued.

༄

Before being released from the hospital three months earlier, in March, my mother's geriatrician had recommended she come back to the hospital three months later to take tests for a neurological assessment.

I was in the reception room, waiting for her to finish her tests. It was a long, two-hour process of verbal, reading, and memory exercises. When she came out, my mother's eyelids were heavy, and her shoulders bore a burden of despair as she joined me.

"I don't think I did so good." She had tears in her eyes.

"There's no such thing as doing good or bad, Mom," I said. "Those were assessment exercises to help the doctors decide what therapies were necessary to keep your atama working properly."

She nodded, but I'm not sure she was convinced.

Editha was waiting for us when we arrived at her apartment. When my mother saw her, she perked up.

"Editha! I'm so glad to see you! Oh, we had such a busy day."

As Editha made some tea for us, she said to my mother, "Tell Susie about your dream."

"No, no, she doesn't want to hear about a silly dream," my mother said.

Editha insisted.

My mother spoke slowly.

"I had a dream—

"I heard a knock on the door in the middle of the night, and it scared me—

"I opened the door, and it was your father—

"He came to visit, and told me, he mi—he missed me."

A heavy sense of heartbreak swept through me. It had been six years since my father had died. What does this dream mean? Does she know something, I don't? I was beginning to feel myself unhinge—I felt lightheaded.

I'm too close to the edge of the bluff—I'm going to fall!

Take a breath. You can't lose it right now.

My mother and I hugged each other tightly, longer than usual—the kind of hug two people share when one of them is departing for a trip. Tears filled my eyes, and I tried my best to hide them. She tried to hide hers too.

The hospital discharged Margaret, but two days later readmitted her with another fever. The doctors couldn't seem to get a handle on its recurrence. She was able to continue her chemoradiation for the most part, but the on-again-off-again fever slightly delayed her treatment schedule.

Margaret's otherwise strong will had worn down.

The early morning June sun warmed me, and I reveled in the nursery, alive with crowds of people picking out treasures for spring plantings. The strong scent of dirt, flowers, and greenness was intoxicating. I felt small looking up at the tall metal racks of flowers surrounding me—each shelf holding the sweet faces of violas and pansies, trays of pink, white, and burgundy ruffled petunias and a rainbow of colorful geraniums.

"Let's see," I thought out loud. "Pink geraniums and a mix of pink and white petunias will be good. Her sakura will bear white blossoms and pink center, so this planting will work. Perfect, she'll love it!" After paying for the flats of flowers and a couple of bags of potting soil, I loaded them into my car and headed for my mother's place.

Taking a circuitous route through the neighborhood, I reached Lake Street. A gritty part of town, Lake Street's diverse urban life of abandoned low-rise buildings, crumbling concrete sidewalks, and old streetlights coexisted with hip restaurants, clubs, and a sprinkling of upscale residential buildings. It's a fascinating mix of complexities and contradictions—an urban floor teeming with the life cycle of the city like a forest floor sustains an ecosystem of varying stages of decomposition and new, emerging life.

Flanking each side of Lake Street, rows of closely spaced, tall steel columns held up the elevated train tracks above, known in Chicago as the "L." The thick layers of paint protect the columns from rust that could undermine the steel column's strength, much like bark protects trees' underlying cambium, the tender part of the tree rich with living, growing cells.

While a forest floor receives dappled sun through a canopy of trees, Lake Street's urban floor receives slices of the sun through spaces between the wood ties of the "L's" tracks. For a pedestrian, these diagonal streaks of the sun add a dynamic rhythm to the urban landscape. But while driving, these slices of light creates a mesmerizing, almost hypnotic strobe effect like an old vintage film. As a train rumbles overhead casting its shadow below, dusk momentarily falls through the air. When the train passes, the vintage movie continues.

From Lake Street, I followed construction detour signs and turned onto North Post Street to enter Chicago's iconic Lower Wacker Drive. Iconic, because its dramatic environment of concrete columns and low, dimly lit, leaky ceilings supporting a network of downtown streets above, often shows up in many of Hollywood's chase scenes. While it feels like an underground tunnel, incongruous views of the Chicago River can be seen hugging the road with each twist and turn. Lower Wacker is a perfect way to smoothly navigate under the busy downtown streets and avoid dozens of stoplights, heavy traffic, and ubiquitous pedestrians and cyclists.

After ten minutes of travel, I took the north ramp onto another Chicago icon—Lake Shore Drive. I'd traveled this route many times. The contrast of Lower Wacker's murky, hovering environment, meeting Lake Shore Drive's sudden burst of daylight from the big, blue skies of the city, and dark blue waters of Lake Michigan, always made my heart leap—every single time.

Views along Lake Shore Drive of sandy beaches, shoreline parks, flowers hanging from the overpasses, joggers and cyclists along the foreground, and distant white sails stitching together heaven and earth at the lake's horizon, made Chicago sparkle. After driving north for a bit, I exited at Foster Avenue and onto Sheridan Road to reach my mother's building.

When I arrived, I loaded the flowers and bags of dirt onto a bellman's cart and took the elevator to the rooftop garden. Landscaped with trees, shrubs, rolling mounds of grass and flower beds, the rooftop also provided designated raised planters for those residents interested in gardening. My mother and Editha waited for me as they sunned themselves near the sakura Dennis had planted for her birthday.

"Hi!" I said.

"Hi, Susie!" they called out in unison.

After our hugs, kisses, and smiles, Editha and I got to work. My mother watched and chatted as Editha and I planted the flowers around the sakura. When we finished, we all stepped back from the planter and admired our instant garden.

"It's beautiful," my mother said. "I promise I'll water the flowers every morning." She looked at her watch. "Oh dear, Editha! We have to go, or I'll be late for my manicure!"

"Okay, Mom. Don't forget, I'm going dress shopping for you tomorrow, and I'll bring them here in the morning," I called out as they scurried off.

"Hai. Thank you, see you then, Susie." she replied.

I stayed behind. Clearing up the spoils of gardening, I thought how lovely that my mother treated herself to mani-pedis. She never dreamed of indulging in such luxuries when my father was alive.

The next morning, in the cool, air-conditioned store, I slid hanging dresses across the rack's chrome rod. "Too bold. Too dark. Ah, yes, here's another one she'll like," I whispered. After making my purchases, I went to the shoe department and found a pair that would complement any of the three dresses I'd selected.

My mother loved it when I shopped for her in the past, and was always giddy as a schoolgirl when picking off the fluffy white tissue paper from the top of the shopping bag that held her treasures below. But today will be special.

She'll choose which dress she wants to wear to Lisa and Matt's wedding next month. She's so excited about going—but whatever dress she chooses will probably need some alterations. That won't be a problem—we have plenty of time for that. Okay, all set.

I looked forward to seeing my mother's eyes light up as she tried on the dresses.

When I got to the car, I placed her dresses, protected in a long, zippered garment bag, on the floor of my trunk, and put the shopping bag that held her shoes on the passenger's seat.

I drove east toward my mother's place when my mind hit a roadblock.

What about Margaret? I would probably spend all day with my mother and wouldn't have time to visit Margaret in the hospital. I knew she was feeling blue.

I had to make a choice. I turned and headed south to UCMC in Hyde Park.

Margaret, still with her persistent fever, had spent several weeks at UCMC. I arrived in her room and found her looking tired and lethargic. She only had a few more weeks of treatment left, but her bruised spirit wore her patience thin.

Her treatment seemed to go on forever. Yet looking back, it felt like just yesterday when we sat in Dr. Portugal's exam room and jarred into the world of squamous cell carcinoma. Throughout her ordeal, Margaret had faced her unknown future head-on and kept pressing forward with determination. But on this day, she felt defeated.

"Hang on as long as you have to," I urged. "You're almost at the finish line, so keep up the good fight," I told Margaret.

"I know, but I'm so tired of all this. Tired of pills, tubes, needles, and I don't know how I can do it any longer," she said.

I was at a loss for words, but then I realized what she needed.

Yes, just listen.

My cell phone rang. It was Bob, his voice calm but strained.

"Susan, a doctor called and told me your mother was in the ER at Swedish Covenant Hospital. He wants you to come immediately. I think it's pretty serious, and he wants your mother's DNR. Should I fax it to him?"

Images of my mother, Editha, and I laughing and talking as we planted her garden just yesterday, flashed through my mind. Do Not Resuscitate—that can't be. There must be some misunderstanding!

"Should I fax it to him?" Bob asked again.

"Yes—yes, thank you."

"The doctor wants to talk to you, so I gave him your cell number," Bob said. "Go to your Mom, but be careful driving. Susan, did you hear me? Be careful, okay? I'll take a cab and meet you there."

"Okay." The call ended.

"Margaret," I whispered, "my mother had a setback, and I'm sorry, but I need to leave right now."

"Is she okay?"

"I—I don't know. I'll call you when I find out."

As soon as I slipped out of Margaret's room, I power-walked through the hospital corridors, narrowly escaping collision with people, carts, and wheelchairs. When I got outside, my pace broke into a sprint to my car. Instead of feeling hot from the run, I was cold, my muscles tense, heart beating out of control, and breath heavy. It was a fight for time, and I was in soaring flight to reach my mother.

While driving from UCMC on the south side of Chicago to my mother's hospital on the north side, I received a call from the same doctor who'd spoken to Bob. He told me my mother had a massive stroke, and her situation was grave. He didn't know how much time she had. The doctor said something about a significant brain-bleed and I should come as soon as possible.

"I'm on my way. Yes, of course, thank you very much." I said.

My head was empty of cohesive thoughts and filled with raw fear as I raced through the streets.

The doctor didn't know how much time she had.

Time for what? Her dresses are in the trunk of my car, and she's going to Lisa and Matt's wedding next month. Will she recover in time for the wedding?

Then, a moment of horror.

"Mom, wait for me!" I yelled aloud as I drove. "Please, Mom, don't let go, I'm almost there. I'm so sorry. I could have been with you. I should have been with you—I'm so sorry! Please don't let go! Don't let go!"

By the inexplicable grace of implicit memory, I managed to drive eighteen miles on the highway, and then weave in and around local streets to get to the hospital. How I got there, I'll never understand.

Don't let go. Don't let go.

I arrived at the hospital's emergency department. I saw my mother connected to monitors and IVs, and a flurry of health care providers in and out of her ER cubicle. The room was cold, and the lights above so bright and icy-white, they cast a blue hue over her. I held her hand and whispered in her ear that I was with her, and she slowly opened her eyes. She tried to talk to me, but the sound of her voice was not hers. It was low and gravely, and her words garbled. I sensed she wanted to know what happened. "Don't worry, Mom, be strong. You fainted, and you'll be all right." But everything was not all right.

My mother was dying.

The following day, Dennis's and my family sat vigil at my mother's bedside. Throughout our stay, at least one of us held her hand. Jonathan later arrived from out of state and spoke to her. She opened her eyes ever so briefly and closed them again. Although paralyzed on the left side of her body, her right hand was strong, and she held it around ours, in a very firm grip as if telling us, "Do you see? I'm still strong. Don't cry for me. Everything will be okay."

Dennis and I continued our vigil, taking turns spending the night with her. As the days passed, her grip waned to a gentle wrap. When I talked to her, tearfully, she responded with a light squeeze, her thumb stroking the base of mine, back and forth, as if to comfort me.

At night, the air in her room was static, cold, and dark. The granular shadows of monitoring machines loomed around her like hooded monks in prayer. A neon green line on one of the monitors spilled its hideous hue on all that surrounded it, including my mother. The hypnotic line transfixed me. It zigzagged, up and down and across the screen, repeating its pattern over and over, as it beeped with no particular tempo.

Don't stop moving. Don't stop beeping.

After hours of watching the green thread, I laid my head next to my mother and placed her hand on my face. I heard only the rhythm of her breathing.

As my mind rested, I slipped into another world where my mother and I talked and laughed together again. My heart leaped as long-ago images visited me—wrapping my arms around my mother's soft, body; my childhood sunbaths; my mother teaching me to float on my back for the first time—

We were in a calm lake, and I felt the warmth of her hand under the small of my back holding me up, my arms and legs flailing.

"Mommy, don't let go, don't let go! I'm going to sink!" *I'd cried out.*

I'd heard a hint of a giggle from her. "Don't worry, Susie, I'm holding you—you won't sink. I won't let go until you're ready, I promise, I won't let go," *she'd said.*

Eventually, I'd relaxed—and floated. I felt the sun's glow on my face and the lingering, warm imprint of where my mother's hand used to be after she slowly let go.

That dreamy world ended in harsh abruptness when a nurse entered the room. She left the door wide open, letting in a sudden rush of sounds from the corridor: chatter of officious voices; a rolling cart with a bad wheel that groaned on the hard, vinyl-tile floor; and the smell of powdered eggs and overheated coffee. Brushing past me, the nurse claimed the room as her own, flipping on ugly fluorescent lights and snapping up the window shades with a flick of her wrist. In an instant, white-hot daylight spilled into the room like a steelworker's kettle pouring out its liquid metal. I squeezed my eyes shut and instinctively put my hands up, palms out, in a defensive pose to protect myself from the shards of bright light accosting me.

"How are we doing today?" the nurse asked no one in particular.

I squinted, allowing only a thin sliver of light into my head, and forced my mouth to mimic a smile, but did not answer her question.

Not looking up from her clipboard, she said, "I see you and your brother requested your mother's transfer to Midwest Palliative and Hospice Care Center today. I'll place the order, and an ambulance will pick her up in a couple of hours."

I nodded. Still unsure what my mother had heard or processed, I turned to her.

"Mom, you've been through so much, but we're going to move you one more time to another facility—it'll be quieter. The ambulance will take you, and I'll meet you there."

I wasn't sure what a hospice center could offer that a hospital generally did not but was told it was the best thing for her right now.

As we waited for the ambulance, my thoughts wandered. The right side of my mother's brain had bled, so her whole left side was paralyzed.

When she recovers, I can be her helper. My hands will be her hands.

But she's not going to recover—you know that.

I closed my eyes tightly. Exhausted, I surrendered. Intellectually, I understood my mother's stroke was massive, and recovery was unlikely. Still, emotionally, I couldn't imagine my life without her. I needed more time.

"Your ambulance is here," the nurse said.

I asked one of the ambulance attendants to keep me in his rearview mirror, as I was unfamiliar with the area where we were going. He told me he would, and he did, as we navigated city streets. But once we got onto the Edens Expressway, the driver seemed to ramp up his speed to breathtaking levels, weaving from one lane to another, making it impossible for me to keep track of him.

"What the hell! He's driving too fast! She'll fall out of the gurney. Slow down!" I yelled, gripping the wheel tighter as if that would make him hear me. I began to sweat but felt like ice water ran through my body. My heart raced, and I couldn't catch my breath.

I'm going to lose her. I don't know where I'm going!

Finally, catching sight of the distant ambulance exiting the expressway, I somehow managed to follow it as its image appeared and disappeared through the trees of a circuitous winding road. When I arrived in the parking lot of the hospice center, I saw the ambulance attendants wheeling my mother's gurney into the building.

I parked my car and ran to the hospice center. I was breathless. I caught a glimpse of the attendant pushing my mother's gurney into the elevator just before the doors closed.

She was safe.

PART II

Evening cherry-blossoms:
I slip the inkstone back into my
kimono
this one last time
　　—Kaisho[1]

Must she?
She must.
But I need more time.

{

I inspected my mother's darkened room and saw its soft-yellow walls and an oversized beige, leather reclining chair in the corner. Along the wall across from her bed, was a small, upholstered sofa in quiet tones of beige, yellow, rose, and pale willow green. Cherry-stained wooden Venetian blinds tilted slightly, let the sun's narrow slits gently tumble onto the dark-stained hardwood floor. An incandescent lamp on her bedside table cast a warm glow on her relaxed face. The stark contrast of the hospital's cold, visually harsh environment to this tranquil setting of simplicity, with its soft colors and smell of fresh linens, brought me immediate relief.

So, this is hospice.

For the first time in many days, I felt my neck, shoulders, and back begin to release its tension, and I was able to breathe deeply.

{

"If a person doesn't want to talk about something, then don't ask. That would be nosy and rude," my mother told me when I was a child.

I adhered to her instructions throughout my life, for the most part, even though I had simple questions for her.

"Why did you change your birth name to the Anglo name you have now?"

"Why did Dad pick Chicago for his studies?"

"How did you feel when you moved from Hawai`i to Chicago, leaving your father and sisters whom you loved so much?"

"Why do we have so few Japanese family friends?"

I didn't know the answers, and time had run out for those and other questions I never asked. My mother's stories would be left untold. I knew who she was from a daughter's point of view—from my experiences with her and within the sphere of a child's egocentrism. I never imagined who she was as a woman, until now. What did she think, how did she feel about her life outside her role as a mother? I wanted to know all the answers to my questions, but it was too late.

I searched deep into my memory of forgotten remembrances and images of my mother. Reading books about the nisei, second-generation of Okinawan descent like my parents who lived in Hawai`i, I learned how complicated and conflicted their lives were. During and after WWII, the nisei were wrought with discriminatory, painful, and disrespectful, if not unconstitutional, incarceration of their fellow Japanese American friends by their American government. And they were shunned with disdain by many Caucasian Americans. The American society, bringing the nisei shame and embarrassment, made it all too difficult for many nisei to discuss. It's no wonder that sansei, third-generation like me, were left with silence from our parents on even simple questions.

I stitched together what I knew, learned, and imagined, and assembled what my parents never told me to fill the hole of their complex silence. I'll never know whether the following vignettes align with truth, but thinking it through, and writing them down helped me express who I thought my mother was, not she, as my mother, but she, as a woman.

The young woman grew despondent during the past three frigid, sunless weeks. Whenever she looked out of her fourth-floor apartment window, it seemed as if a thin, gray, gauzy veil hung in front of it, like a filter through which she saw her world. A pretty snowfall had overstayed its welcome—once a fluffy white blanket that covered the ground had turned into hardened mounds of ash-gray ice, flecked with dirt. It was a scene as cold and grainy as a melancholy, black-and-white photograph.

But finally, the sun shone brightly, and she saw color again. "Susie, it's time for your sunbath!" she called out to her three-year-old daughter. The mother laid her thick futon, a wedding gift made by her mother-in-law, in front of the window where the sun, like a shining flashlight, lit up a small patch of the hardwood floor in her chilly apartment. She placed a pen and writing paper next to her.

"I haven't written to Aiko in a long time. It's a good day for that," she thought, "but first, Susie needs a sunbath."

Unbuttoning Susie's sweater, the little girl asked, "What about Dennis?"

"Your brother is too old for a sunbath, and anyway, he's playing with his friends today." Dennis, three years older than Susie, undaunted by the ice, snow, and freezing temperatures, eagerly explored their new neighborhood, finding it a mysterious, exhilarating contrast to their previous home in Hawai'i.

She continued to take layers of clothes off Susie. First, the thick, wool sweater then the long-sleeved flannel shirt, corduroy pants, and finally the leggings, leaving her daughter in just her underwear, sleeveless t-shirt, and socks. Susie shivered until she stepped onto the futon and into the sun's warmth where her mother sat waiting for her. The toddler curled up on her mother's lap, feeling the softness of her mother's body and the gentle rhythm of her mother's voice, listening to stories read out loud and hearing the Okinawan folk songs her mother quietly hummed.

The young woman watched her daughter's heavy eyes slowly open and close. Susie's little hand, at first tightly clinging to the soft, satin-lined ears of her well-worn, pink and white rabbit, then relaxing, slowly let her rabbit tumble onto the futon, as she slipped into her *afternoon nap. The mother was grateful for the sun's elixir of health, abundant in Hawai`i, and so elusive during Chicago's winter. It didn't matter that the window's glass through which the sun shone blocked the vitamin D health benefits that she wanted so desperately for her daughter. It didn't matter that it was twenty degrees outside. It didn't matter that she was five thousand miles from her beloved home in Hawai`i. All that mattered that very moment was she, her husband, and children were together in Chicago, and Susie could finally have a sunbath.*

She thought about her Hawai`i—where she was born, grew up and married, where their two children were born, and where her deceased mother was laid to rest. She ached for her aging father and five sisters with whom she was very close and who prayed for her return. She was homesick and sad. She wrote a letter to her youngest sister, Aiko. And her tears fell. The warmth of the sun, her napping daughter, and her tears lulled her into a light sleep.

⸘

Having discovered the fertile soils that supported an abundance of sugarcane, pineapples, fruits, flowers, and vegetables, American plantation owners, many of whom were descendants of Caucasian businessmen and missionaries, desperately needed cheap laborers to sow their land. These plantation owners became significant beneficiaries of the U.S. government's decision to annex Hawai`i's treasure of islands and relax immigration laws.

Eight years after annexation, Sukenori Higa and his brother, Kamanaka, immigrated to Hawai`i from Okinawa, a small island southwest of mainland Japan. A year later, their youngest brother, Shingo, joined them. Like the thousands of immigrants from Southeast Asia who descended upon the Hawaiian Islands, the brothers worked long days on a sugarcane plantation, laboring under the island's beautiful but searing sun. They endured the plantation owner's harsh, discriminatory, abusive, and sometimes torturous practices. Six years after his arrival in Hawai`i, Sukenori married Kame, also from Okinawa, and together they worked on the plantation. The Higa families saved their small earnings allowing them to leave the plantation, lease land, and operate their fields. Perseverance and hard work were the cultures of Okinawan immigrants, and farming was their trade.

On occasion, the farmers would put down their tools, gather their families, and feast on their harvest prepared in the Okinawan cooking tradition. Goya champuru—bitter melon lightly sautéed in oil with homemade tofu; tender sliced pork stir-fried with fresh eggs; colorful stir-fried vegetables; steamed purple Okinawa potatoes; rice; roasted pig; fish caught from the pure ocean waters of Hawai`i; seaweed and cucumbers marinated in a sweet and sour rice vinaigrette; and for dessert, andagi donuts. To the Okinawans, their meals were humble and straightforward, but the world later learned, this was a diet that supported generations of people having the longest lifespan on earth.

Not only did the farmers and their family feast, but they also danced throughout the night. A little girl named Humiko loved dancing with her father, smiling and talking, their raised arms swaying slowly, gracefully, under the moon in the summer night's air, to the soulful folk music of the sanshin, a three-stringed Okinawan instrument, and the low, rhythmic beat of drums.

"WHAT IS YOUR NAME? DO – YOU – UNDER – STAND – ENGLISH? WHAT – IS – YOUR – NAME?" The teacher's voice was louder than necessary.

The bashful seven-year-old girl, in perfect English, replied.

"My name is Humiko Higa."

"What?" he asked. "Did you say Foo-mee-koe?"

"Humiko," she answered.

"Whoo-mee-koe? Well, I've never heard of such an ugly name, and it's too hard for me to remember. Your name is now——" The teacher paused and thought for a minute. He continued. "Your name is now Helen. Helen HEE ga." The teacher had the authority to assign an Anglo name to his Asian students. Being able to think, on the spot, of a convenient new name beginning with the letter "H," the same letter *as the girl's birth name, he felt quite satisfied with himself. He couldn't hide a hint of a smile.*

"Yes, Helen, like Helen of Troy, the beautiful Greek goddess. Such a perfect name befitting this pretty little Jap girl," the teacher thought.

Later that day, Humiko swallowed deeply as she tried to maintain composure while speaking respectfully in Okinawan to her mother. Troubling her mother, who farmed the fields all day, was to be avoided as much as possible.

"Mother, I prefer being called my real name, but the teacher made up his mind," the girl said, her eyes, hot with tears, were cast downward. To the girl, an Anglo name was disrespectful and a rejection of her parent's culture and their proud Okinawan heritage.

"Humiko, you must obey your teacher. Go along with whatever he wants and don't ever make trouble," her mother said.

Her mother understood that this was the American way. So, it would be, the girl would be called Helen at school, but at home, her parents continued to call her Humiko, and to her sisters, her nickname would be "H" for short.

Sukenori and Kame had six daughters, and in between the girls, three sons did not survive. All the children were born in Hawai`i, then a U.S. Territory, thus their nationality was American. At birth, the parents gave their children traditional Okinawan names, but when they entered school, Anglo names were thrust upon them by their Caucasian teachers, priests, and nuns.

The couple's firstborn daughter, Shizuko, was re-assigned the name of Norma; Humiko (Helen) was second; then Toyoko (Margie); Nobuko (Nancy); Setsuko (Agnes); and the youngest girl, Aiko (Jeanette). That was, indeed, the American way.

It was also the American way for Okinawans and other Asian minorities to defer to haoles, even though Asians were the majority population. Helen understood the power of the people who could not only arbitrarily re-assign names to children, but also affect their place in society. Helen's immigrant father, Sukenori, was not allowed to purchase land but could only lease it from wealthy landowners who imposed unfair fees on his crop. And when Norma married an immigrant man from mainland Japan, she lost her U.S. citizenship.

But discrimination didn't just come from Caucasian Americans. Children of mainland Japan heritage enjoyed teasing Okinawans as well. On many days, Helen tried comforting, with little success, her younger sister, Nobuko, when she came home after school crying from taunts of "Okinawa ken ken—buta kau kau!"

Buta means "pig" in Japanese, and "kau kau" means "eat," thought to be a part-Hawaiian, part-Japanese phrase. Although the direct translation, "Okinawans eat pig/pork" was harmless, the epithet was translated and meant as derogatory: "Okinawans eat pig food (kitchen scraps, pig slop)." Many Okinawans, indeed, raised pigs, considered a dirty job of low status, albeit often lucrative.

Helen learned to tread lightly in her world, navigating discrimination's complicated and challenging course with deferential mindfulness. And she never, ever made trouble.

While working at Love's Bakery, Helen (Humiko) Higa met Bassett (Toshiyuki) Uehara, the young man who would later become her husband. He was re-assigned the name of Bassett, a seemingly cruel joke by his teacher, who likely named Toshiyuki after her Bassett hound dog. Like so many children, Bassett wanted to keep his birth name, but during those times of war and Anglo hierarchy in Hawai`i, he knew keeping his name would be dangerous.

Bassett served honorably as a sergeant in the U.S. Army during WWII and was in Honolulu, protecting America during the Japanese attack on Pearl Harbor. When he re-entered civilian life, he found discrimination against Okinawan and Japanese Americans pervasive in Hawai`i and the West Coast. He believed he would find more opportunities further east on the U.S. mainland, remote from Pearl Harbor. Maybe, just maybe, he thought, discrimination would be less so.

After Helen and Bassett married and had their two children, Dennis and Susan, Bassett moved to Chicago for studies in electronics at DeVry Technical School and sent for his family when he settled.

In 1952, when Helen, Bassett, and the children reunited in Chicago, a city of people vastly unlike herself and those she left behind in Hawai`i, Helen realized, with the war still fresh in the minds of Caucasian Americans, she and others of Asian descent were regarded with suspicion and hate. It was a time of hurt, shame, and embarrassment, but the couple persevered in their efforts to raise their children as best as they could. Talk of discrimination and inequities of life rarely passed their lips, and at no time in front of their children.

Helen and Bassett were never comfortable with their Anglo names. Their re-assigned names did not reflect who they were meant to be at birth, their being, their roots. Helen reluctantly accepted her name, but Bassett did not. Upon arriving in the city, he felt empowered when he picked his new name, "John."

Living in their new Caucasian world, John and Helen obeyed society's unwritten rule: Assimilate, do not congregate. They complied, hoping to shield their children from retribution and unpleasant experiences they'd had. John and Helen settled in an all-white neighborhood on the north side of Chicago, and there, the family maneuvered through their lives.

When asked the ubiquitous question by curious strangers, "What's your nationality?" Helen, whose nationality was American, knew that question was euphemistic for, "Are you Chinese or Japanese?" Helen always replied that we were Japanese. She knew that truthfully claiming our Okinawan heritage would be too complicated for curiosity seekers—after all, "they thought we all looked alike anyway, so what's the difference?"

Discrimination was no stranger to Helen. Fearless, with a touch of defiance, she decided to fight hate with love. She became a self-appointed ambassador for her proud culture and her Hawai`i birthplace—a land some considered exotic and mysterious. She fulfilled this role through cooking for her new Caucasian friends and their families in Chicago. But her meals were not just about food. With patience and perseverance, she cooked for her friends' hearts to nurture their minds and spirit for acceptance of her culture. She introduced them to delicious flavors and intoxicating fragrances. Knowing they might be hesitant to try new foods given its departure from their meat-and-potatoes palate, she took special care to make her meals beautiful—cooking for their eyes.

I sat next to my mother, holding and rubbing her feet under the covers. Looking up, I saw her hospice doctor, Dr. Jason, standing at the doorway of her room.

"Her feet are so cold. Is there something we can do to warm them?" I asked.

Tall and lean with dark hair, he smiled and came into the room. He pulled the blanket back slightly to look at her feet. When she'd gotten her mani-pedi a few days earlier, she'd picked the same pinkish-salmon color for her toes to match her fingernails.

Oh, her feet are so lovely, so sweet.

"Do you see the red mottled splotches on her ankles?" The doctor's voice was soft and kind. "That mottling of red will expand upwards, and when they reach her knees, it's one of several signs that will tell us Helen's time may be near. Don't worry, coldness doesn't cause her pain or discomfort," he assured me, "but if you ever feel she is uncomfortable, let us know, and we can give something to her for relief." He covered her feet with the blanket.

"She's doing well," he said with a gentle smile.

I heard a quiet knock on the door. It was Nurse Misayo.

"I'm sorry, I didn't mean to interrupt."

"No, I was just leaving," said the doctor.

"Susan, may I have a few minutes with your mother?" she asked. "I won't be long. I want to tidy her up."

"Yes, yes, of course." As I left the room, I heard Nurse Misayo speak to my mother in Japanese.

The nurse called out to her patient. "Helen-san, ohayogozaimasu. Soredewa imakara okarada o fukasete itadakimasu. Yokomuki ni sasete itadakimasune. Yoroshiidesuka?" (Good morning, Helen, I'm going to freshen you up and turn you over, okay?)

I smiled, knowing the comfort my mother must have felt hearing those words in Japanese. I gave a silent "thank you" to her excellent team of doctors and nurses.

Later that day, I called the Midwest Buddhist Temple.

"Hello, Reverend Miyamura?" I asked over the phone.

"Yes?" I heard a pleasant voice answer.

"My name is Susan Rakstang. My mother had my father's memorial service at Midwest Buddhist Temple—before you became the reverend there. My mother is in hospice now, and my brother and I think she would want her service there too. Can we meet to talk about the arrangements?"

"Yes, certainly, Susan. Is her time near?" asked the reverend.

"I don't know." My voice caught. "I'm not sure how to plan the service when everything is so uncertain."

"Will she be cremated?" he asked.

"Yes."

"Then we can plan her memorial service at any time. Don't worry, my schedule is very flexible, but I want to let you know that I'll be delivering a sermon in Cleveland this coming weekend. Will that be okay?"

"Yes, thank you," I said. "I'll call you after the weekend so we can talk. Thank you very much."

Hearing is the last sense lost before a person dies, so Dennis brought over my mother's boom box with Okinawan music and a cassette tape her sister, Aiko, sent of my mother's favorite song by Patti Page, "Red Sails in the Sunset."

"Mom, Aiko sent this tape to you. Do you remember the song?" I asked.

I didn't expect her to respond. She was in a coma. But then I saw a single tear roll down her cheek as Patti Page sang.

The next day, Marcia and John visited my mother at the hospice center. Marcia, her Irish hair still a flaming red, went straight to my mother and took her hand.

"Hi, Helen, it's me, Marcia. You look very pretty—they're taking good care of you!" Marcia said.

She continued, "I was only seventeen when we met. I can't believe we've known each other for so long—

"You've always been so special to me. Do you remember we have the same name? My middle name is Helen!—

"Thank you for including us at all your parties, especially New Year's. Your cooking was so good, and we loved being with you. Remember how we used to complain about our husbands?—

Marcia smiled as her eyes welled with tears.

"We had so much fun. I'll be right here, so rest now. I love you, Helen."

Marcia and I left the room as she wept. She turned to me and whispered, "You need to give your mother permission to die."

I gasped.

"You know she'll do anything for you, Susan, anything, even if it means hanging on to her life longer than she wants. Tell her you're going to be all right if she leaves, so she can feel free to go whenever she's ready."

"Oh my god, Marcia. I don't know that I can say that to her."

"You have to. Your mother needs your permission. This is not about you. This is about your mother and what she needs to hear from you."

I nodded. After Marcia and John left, I checked my mother's legs. *"When the red mottling reaches her knees, her time may be near,"* the doctor had said.

I saw the mottling had expanded from her ankles onto her calves.

Sitting by my mother's side, I had both my hands lightly wrapped around her right hand while Nurse Misayo tidied up the room. My mother released her hand from mine to explore her left (paralyzed) arm.

Her eyes remained closed as she squeezed her unfamiliar arm, up and down, and shook it as if to awaken it. Grasping her left arm, she raised it, and let it fall. She found my hand, took it firmly into hers, and used it to hit her left arm. I was shocked. I couldn't speak, and my mind moved fast.

What's going on? Is she lucid? Can she think? Maybe she's not dying after all!

She's dying.

But what if——?

I could feel my heart pound faster, and my eyes were hot and full. Nurse Misayo saw what my mother was doing and quickly went to her.

"Helen, your arm feels heavy, doesn't it?" she said. Her voice was calm. "Don't worry. You will be okay."

Nurse Misayo, as she left the room, nodded to me and smiled as if to say, "She'll be all right." My mother stopped exploring.

I looked at my mother's legs and saw the red splotches around her calves had expanded upward. My heart was no longer beating quickly but felt very, very heavy. I turned to her and held her hand.

"Mom, I needed more time to be with you, and you gave it to me. It's been seven days since you fainted. You gave all of us the time we needed to understand what was happening to you. Dennis, his family, and my family are grateful for that, thank you very much—

"Do you remember when we went to Sturgeon Bay for Dad's fishing trip? You taught me how to float on my back. You held your hand under me, and I was so afraid you'd let go—

"You promised you wouldn't let go until I was ready. And then, I floated, and you let go—

"I love you, Mom. I'm ready for you to let go now, whenever you want—

"You know, when you go, you'll be able to throw away your walker and dance with your father again! He's waiting for you, yes. And so is Dad, and your mother, and your sisters, too, so when you're ready, you can let go. We'll be all right."

I cried without making a sound.

Saying those words to my mother brought a knot in my stomach.

"When she passes, where will she go?" I asked Reverend Miyamura in an email. I was working very hard at accepting my mother's death but still feared for her.

Reverend Miyamura wrote back to me.

"One passes into the Pure Land. Think of life as an ocean—this is the Oneness of life. In the ocean, there are waves, which have a shape and form for a limited duration. Our lives are like a wave—we have a shape and a form for a limited time; we think we are unique and separate (which would be our ego or image of ourselves). When the wave hits the shore, it disappears, yet we all know that the wave was always part of the ocean. Each wave comes from the ocean and returns to the ocean—this is Oneness. So, where do we go? We return to the Oneness of all life—the Pure Land is that Ocean of Oneness—it is not a place, rather it is a realm in another dimension."

The red mottling on her legs was rising closer to her knees.

That day, Dennis brought up an issue. "Jane told me that her aunt said we should have a 'pillow service' ceremony performed by a Buddhist minister at bedside just before, or right after Mom dies."

"Like last rites or something?" I asked.

"I guess so—that's what it sounds like."

"But how can we possibly make that happen? I mean, how does Mom pass away at precisely the time when the reverend just happens to be here? We can't schedule her death, and we can't schedule Reverend Miyamura—he's in Cleveland!"

Dennis sighed. "I don't know. I guess we try the best we can. I don't know."

A "pillow sutra" or Makura-gyo, I learned, is a brief ceremony performed by a Shin Buddhist minister, when Amida Buddha will appear as a person to welcome the dying soul—a new Buddha—to the Pure Land.

A few days had passed since I'd initially spoken to the reverend. My mother's breathing had become weaker, and her carotid artery along the side of her neck, once pumping vigorously, was now barely pulsing.

One of my mother's nurses went through great effort to locate the reverend and somehow contacted him as he drove from Cleveland back to Chicago. But I feared my mother would be unable to wait for him.

Reverend Miyamura called me from his car and said he was driving directly to the hospice center and was minutes away.

I whispered to my mother, "You're the luckiest girl in the world. Reverend Miyamura will come to see you soon! Please give him just a little more time if you can."

With short notice, many miles between us, and impossible timing, Reverend Miyamura arrived. A gentle man in his middle years, of average height, with a kind, round face, he spoke to us in my mother's quiet, darkened room.

Her breathing was shallow, her carotid artery, ever weaker.

The family gathered around her.

In his black wa-gesa, the reverend gently tapped a bell, representing the voice of Buddha, and commenced with traditional Japanese chanting in a low, cathartic pitch.

After a few minutes of the reverend's chanting, Dennis peered down at my mother.

He bent over her.

He felt her neck.

Her carotid artery was still.

He looked at us, and closing his eyes, he nodded.

My mother had taken her last breath, passing from her life's journey on earth. I believed that Reverend Miyamura's presence helped my mother take her final step. She was gone. My mother had let go.

And a tear, her final one, slowly rolled down her cheek.

When he finished chanting, Reverend Miyamura paused, and then sounded the bell again. He continued the makura-gyo ritual in Japanese, resolving and embracing her passing, releasing her from this changing world, and welcoming her into the Ocean of Oneness—the Pure Land.

I was numb. My mind was full and moving fast, trying to comprehend all that had happened. How did the hospice nurse, not knowing the reverend and on a late Sunday evening, manage to contact him? How did my mother hang onto her life and die just as the reverend started to chant? Makura-gyo is intended to be performed shortly before or after a person dies. And my mother had lived and died through both intentions—how could that be? I was grateful for the nurse who had made it possible, and for Reverend Miyamura's Makura-gyo ceremony that he performed for my mother and family. And I was thankful for my mother, who let go in peace with gentleness, and in the most gracious, noble, and selfless way possible—for us. That was who she was.

After the reverend finished the ceremony, and we said our goodbyes to my mother, we left her room and walked down the corridor. But I excused myself and went back to see her again. I put her hand on my hot, tearful face.

"Mom? Are you dancing with your father now?—

"I'm going to miss you and will love you always—

"You've been with me every step of my life. I'm so sad, and don't know how I'll manage without you—

"But don't worry, I'll be strong—

"So long, for now."

I kissed her and looked at her beautiful face, one last time.

Does she see the glint of the sun on the ice, in all its glistening, shimmering splendor? Yes, of course—she's in the Pure Land.

I had no idea that when I decided to retire, it would be one of the most important decisions I'd ever made. During that last year of my mother's life, she and I were entwined in our world of laughter, respect, support, and magical love. I had been my mother's daughter, her mother, friend, nurse, piano teacher, and now I was, and will always be forever, daughter of Humiko Helen Higa Uehara.

When I got home that evening, I called Margaret and told her my mother had died.

"Oh, no, Susan! I'm so sorry, I'm so sad," she cried. "I hope her passing was peaceful."

"Yes, it was very peaceful."

"Margaret, she passed a sakura branch to you for good health so that you can finish your own journey."

That was what my mother would have wanted me to tell her.

Margaret was frail and ravaged by her cancer treatment. She wore a scarf to keep her bare head warm. Her face was heavy without expression, her eyes hollow, and her voice so weakened, she could barely speak over a whisper. Margaret had trouble walking, but with the help of her sister-in-law, Marge Hoglin, she mustered the will and energy to attend my mother's memorial service. I was grateful she was able to bid farewell to my mother, her friend, her kindred spirit.

As with my father's memorial service at the Midwest Buddhist Temple, my mother's service was humble and comforting. The familiar fragrance of mild incense, symbolic of gratitude, and burning away life's impurities, was soothing. When the *Kansho*[2] called, with its deep, yet soft-edged calming sound, Reverend Miyamura commenced with the service, giving a *Kanzen Dokkyo*.[3] Presenting the *Homyo*[4] came next, after which Kristin, with a gesture of offering, placed the Mala prayer beads my mother had given her, onto the altar in front of my mother's photograph. When the reverend began the *Sutra chanting*,[5] my brother and his family approached the incense burner pot, followed by my family and me, and we each pinched loose incense from a small dish and dropped it into the bowl of burning incense. Her many friends, including those from The Breakers, lined the center aisle, waiting to offer their incense.

Chanting by the reverend, family, and friends helped my mind clear in a meditative way, replacing sadness with tranquility. Kevin, Dennis's son, expressed a heartfelt eulogy, Reverend Miyamura gave his Dharma Talk, and finally, Bob shared his words of appreciation to the congregation on behalf of our family.

What profoundly resonated with me was Reverend Miyamura's presentation of the Homyo. He told us all that he chose a Homyo, a symbolic Buddhist name, my mother would use in the Pure Land. He used the Japanese characters representing "eat" and "joyful." 食楽. The Romanized characters translated into the words, SHOKU-RAKU.

I'm sure my mother's eyes lit brightly, and she would embrace her new name with a broad smile and a hearty laugh.

Such a perfect name, befitting this beautiful Okinawan woman.

Days after my mother's memorial service, my family and I cleaned her apartment, boxed possessions, and bagged and sorted items for refuse or donations. By late afternoon, after a flurry of activity doing a yeoman's job of cleaning and clearing, my family left for the day. I stayed behind.

My job was to take care of her bedroom, the place she spent most of her time. It was her sanctuary, and I saw her everywhere—fabric for her next project, a dress form wearing a half-altered dress, her jar of buttons, clothes, jewelry, make-up, and a bed quilt her sister Nobuko made her. Hanging from the corner of the mirror, I saw a kukui nut lei, a cherished gift from her friend, Alice.

I'd remembered visiting mother's sisters, Nobuko, Se, and Aiko in Hawai`i. My mother was very close to them, even though they lived miles apart. They told me about how my mother, as their older sister, sewed for them when they were kids.

"You know, Susie, your mother sewed beautifully. She made jackets and dresses for us when we were growing up," Nobuko told me. Nobuko had become an accomplished sewer herself and appreciated the work my mother put into her sewing.

"Yes, and she made us the prettiest book bags when we were in school," Se said, as she sketched a picture of the book bags. Se continued, "And she always knew how to make us laugh, too! We had such fun with her. And even though she lived in Chicago for so many years, she never lost her Hawai`i roots. She loved Hawai`i."

"Right after she arrived in Chicago," Aiko remembered, "she wrote me a letter. In it, she said, 'The ink is smeared, not from a beautiful sun shower, but from my tears.' Oh, I felt so sad for her! She missed Hawai`i!"

"Most of my top teeth were knocked out in a playground accident," Alice, my mother's best friend, told me. "Children made fun of how I looked, and no one wanted to be my friend except Helen." Alice continued. "Her whole family later moved from Waipahu to Honolulu, and I lost my only friend. Then one day, when I was doing my daily chores, I saw her from my kitchen window, walking up the road to my house. She came from so far away to see me! I ran out of my house, and we hugged and cried, and she told me she would be my friend forever. Helen had a big heart. Your mother was a good woman."

A story that moved me was from my Auntie Nobuko. She told me my mother had a boyfriend before meeting my father.

"I don't remember his name, but he often came by the house," Auntie said, "A nice guy and good looking, too! The two planned to marry, but his parents forbade him to marry your mother because she was Okinawan."

On hearing this, my heart ached with empathy for her. Presumably, as a plea for forgiveness, the young man gave my mother a gift—a broach, which my mother rejected and threw away. Her older sister, Norma, retrieved it and had it converted to a pendant. Before Norma died, she asked Auntie Nobuko to give me the pendant, which Auntie did while I visited.

The pendant, composed of translucent jadeite coveted for its spiritual energy, has a lavender $5/8$" diameter, half-dome stone set with a thin gold rim, flanked vertically by $1/2$" diameter, light green dome stones with a similar setting. I was intrigued by the story and the pendant that validated it. Was it the story, or was it merely the sheer beauty of the object that transfixed me? My mother never told me about this young mystery man, and why would she?

But knowing these stories satisfied my search for her, not the person I knew as my mother, but the independent, kind, and beautiful woman who had loved and was loved, had heartbreak, gained strength from her setback, and lived a fulfilled life.

Yes, she was a good woman.

I sighed and continued sorting my mother's belongings. Her sewing workspace was familiar to me. When I worked on my sewing projects at her place, I found it well equipped with every possible tool I needed to complete my task. She had a Bernina sewing machine with all kinds of attachments, a serger machine, threads plentiful in every color, needles, measuring tapes, large, sharp scissors for general work, and tiny ones for delicate work. I was often in her sewing drawers when I came over to work on one of my sewing projects. With her drawers and shelves well organized, I knew in which drawer to find whatever I needed.

Boxing up her sewing things, I was stunned to find a mysterious letter. Its envelope, light blue stamped Par Avion, with bold red and royal blue diagonal stripes along the edges and matching stationery as thin as tissue paper, looked old and fragile. It lay in one of my mother's sewing drawers, right in front, on top of her scissors. It was from Sam.

Of my mother's five sisters, Norma, the oldest, had three sons: firstborn was Sadao (Sam), then Susumu (Richard), and her youngest son, Tamotsu (Norman).

Norma was pregnant with Tamotsu at the same time that the sisters' mother, Kame, was pregnant with Aiko, the youngest of all the sisters. So, the sisters and Norma's boys were contemporaries of sorts and bonded closely growing up.

I carefully unfolded the letter and read it.

Sam, a soldier in the U.S. Army serving in the Korean War, thanked my mother for the care package she'd sent him full of her homemade cookies and her famously delicious fruitcake cups. He wrote about everyday life in the army and seemed in good spirits. But the family later learned the North Koreans captured Sam and sent him to a prison camp. The U.S. Army designated him as a prisoner of war, but en route to the prison camp, he contracted dysentery and died. This news, of course, tore up the family, making every letter received from Sam a treasured memory.

My mother had never mentioned this letter to me. So why, suddenly, was it in such a conspicuous place? I had been through those sewing drawers dozens of times, and it was never there, so why now?

Did my mother put it there for me to find?

Yes, I believed she did and placed it where she knew I would find the letter and keep it safe. With resolve, I knew what she wanted me to do. I sent the letter to Norman, Sam's youngest brother, and the last survivor of Norma and her sons.

The strain of sadness and remembrances left me exhausted. Leaving my mother's bedroom, the low, west sun from her window shone on the wall I was passing. Something on the wall glistened. I walked up to it.

Time stopped.

It was an imprint of my mother's hand. I remembered how she used this wall to steady herself as she walked to her bedroom. I remembered how, with much regret, I admonished her for not using her walker. I slowly aligned my hand on top of her handprint, and they matched perfectly—I had her long fingers. I didn't know our hands were alike. "Mom—" I whispered.

Over the next few months, rivulets of sadness spilled from my eyes and down my cheeks. Unaccompanied by sobbing or anguish, they were just small, slow rivulets, like a gentle spring rain against a window—one drop merging with another then another, meandering slowly down the glass. My rivulets spilled when I least expected—at the grocery store, walking Tony, washing the dishes, or cooking a meal. I ached for my mother.

※

One evening, I was trying to make dinner. My motions used to flow as I cooked, but lately, I moved in fits and starts from the sink to the fridge and back again, having forgotten what I'd planned to do.

"I'm so lonely," I told Bob. "She's been here for me all my life. I don't know how to *be* without her." My voice matched my feeling of flatness.

"I miss her, too," Bob said.

Yes, but you don't understand. You don't know what it's like to not hear her voice on the phone every day. Or remember all the things she taught me. Or understand how she cheered me on in my life.

Bob was fully present and attentive through my grief, trying to console my inconsolable sadness, but I could not mend.

"Your mother was my mother, too," he said. "I met her when I met you. I was nineteen years old. She always believed in me, and I loved her for that."

Although he tried, Bob couldn't hold back his tears and wrapped his arms around me. My arms remained heavy, hanging from my shoulders, with little strength or will to wrap around him.

I regret I was absent for Bob. He and my mother were simpatico, and he grieved for her. My mother loved him. She loved that he loved me. She loved that he embraced her foods, her culture, and was joyous when he cooked her recipes. And he loved her back. They were so similar in temperament—cheerful and positive by nature, loving, patient, supportive, and enthusiastic over any accomplishment or endeavor I pursued. And they both knew how to make me laugh. I believe while many women marry men like their father, I married a man like my mother.

She visited me in my dreams. Each time I woke up and realized it was just a dream, the rivulets spilled.

In the morning, I was awakened by my mother's percussion concerto in the kitchen, like the ones I heard as a child—except it was Bob, who was the solo percussionist. I listened to his fork tapping staccato against a glass bowl as he whisked eggs, the sound of pebbles falling through a rain stick as bacon fried, and cowbells ever so softly tinged, dinged and clinked as he quietly handled plates and glasses while preparing breakfast.

I heard the sound of love again. And it brought me solace and peace.

PART III

Exhausted, I sought
a country inn, but found
wisteria in bloom
　　　　—Bashō[1]

REFLECTING ON THE PAST six months of the dark days laden with fear and sadness when in January, I struggled with angst and denial of my mother's declining health, and in February, Margaret received her diagnose of squamous cell carcinoma. I faced the fragility of life and the incomprehensibility of death. I had no compass to follow and nothing but my professional instincts on which to rely—keep a cool head, know my resources, be tactical, and take action. I knew I couldn't alter the inalterable, which only heightened my despair, but with denial in overdrive, I persevered. My breath shallow, back and shoulders tense, a knot in my stomach, worry and fear trapped in my head, I'd felt weak, frustrated, and helpless knowing two important women in my life were in profound peril. My stress was high, and time was running out. I'd promised Margaret I would make one hundred meals to stock her freezer with food for all her homestays during the months of her cancer treatment.

My thoughts traveled back to Margaret's first homestay in March when I'd begun preparing her meals. But it wasn't until after my mother had passed away in June and Margaret had completed her cancer treatment in July, that I'd had time to recall the steps I took, using specific techniques to create meals for my friend.

It was months before our local farmers' market opened, so I'd gone to Whole Foods to buy perfectly beautiful, organic ingredients. Chemicals from chemotherapy and a myriad of medications barraged Margaret's body, so I chose Whole Foods' meats and poultry as they were raised without animal by-products in their feed and were antibiotic and growth hormone-free. And all her veggies would be certified organic.

Because radiation would cause open sores in Margaret's mouth and throat, I didn't use seasonings or spices of any kind, including flavorings like garlic or onions, nor acids such as lemon juice, orange juice, vinegar, or tomatoes. In other words, only the true flavors of pureed whole foods would come through in all of her meals.

I'd hoped cooking veggies, pureeing and pouring the delicious mixture into a soup bowl, would be food for her soul, and a warm (or chilled) pureed soup would slip smoothly down Margaret's throat without causing pain.

Preparing for a dinner party years earlier, I discovered the beauty of a recipe for "Eclipse Soup" in Chef Cary Neff's cookbook, *Conscious Cuisine*.[2] The contrasting colors of black bean, butternut squash, and red pepper purees, poured into a single soup bowl, presented a visually stunning and tasty soup. Chef Neff's technique of using foods like an artist uses her paint palette was to become a platform from which my preparation and presentation of Margaret's meals evolved.

Planning her menus, I'd decided on "comfort foods" as the theme for cooking. I'd hoped meals like beef stew, hamburgers, and French fries, pork chops, roasted chicken, meatloaf with mashed potatoes and gravy, green beans, and salads would beckon Margaret to eat. Each meal will be beautiful—striking colors would be imperative, and three-dimensional forms, a must. Although Margaret needed all foods finely pureed, the appearance of varied textures would be a whimsical "trompe l'oeil," fool the eye, component of the meals. And because Margaret's taste buds would be temporarily lost, I'd decided to cook for her eyes.

On that first evening in March, I put Chopin Nocturnes on the stereo. Stepping into my kitchen, I retrieved my folded, white chef's apron from the drawer, flicked it to bellow and unfold in the air, put the top loop around the back of my neck, tied the strings around my waist with a half-bow in the front, and secured a white flour sack dishtowel under the string. I was ready to cook.

Handling the food, I felt empowered. My kitchen provided me the respite I desperately needed. Like meditation, my mind cleared itself of anguish. As I worked on making Margaret's meals, I focused on the tasks at hand so intently that, while worries of my mother and Margaret still emerged in my mind, I was able to let them pass, allowing my creative thoughts awaken and evolve. There was no time to waste. The purees were fresh and fragile, and I needed to work quickly.

For her soups, I pureed each vegetable and created a visual design of swirls, squiggles, and color bursts. The soup bowl was my canvas, and the veggies were my media. The soups still looked like soup but were playful and more fun to see. (*See back cover for color photographs*).

BEET SOUP SWIRL (1)

My first project was beet soup. I ladled purees of red beets and golden beets into separate paper cups and poured the purees simultaneously into the bowl. Inserting a skewer about halfway down into the darkest color, in this case, the red beets, and starting near the edge of the bowl, I dragged the skewer in a continuous spiral motion until the skewer reached the center. As a result, the red beets were pulled into the golden beets, creating delicate swirl lines. The green burst was a teaspoon of pureed beet greens poured into a puddle on top of the red beets. I pulled the red beets toward the center of the greens with my skewer, creating a pinwheel. I marveled at how a few simple strokes of a skewer could transform three static puddles of vegetables into an image in motion.

Soups were stand-alone meals or served as a base into which I added three-dimensional elements using ingredients with contrasting colors to bring out distinct designs.

To create three-dimensional elements, I pureed fully cooked proteins and vegetables using just enough thinning liquid—usually the water they were boiled in or plain water—so a toothpick stood up in the mixture. After lining a cookie sheet with aluminum foil, I evenly spread the puree to about ⅜-inch thick and placed the cookie sheet in the freezer. When the mixture was partially frozen, I worked quickly so the food would not defrost. I used a cookie cutter or sharp knife to cut the food into strips, rounds, triangles, or diamonds.

Keeping the cut pieces separated from each other with plastic wrap, I put them back in the freezer until they were frozen solid. I saved excess scraps and used them for "tossed salads."

With few exceptions, I kept the shapes abstract. Rather than trying to make the pureed chicken look like a drumstick, peas to look like a scoop of peas, or broccoli to look like florets, would have been too time-consuming and would likely fail at trompe l'oeil, fool the eye. I preferred to use abstract shapes, so those foods visually stood on their own and not try to "fake" realism.

I'd determined what heightened safe food practices were necessary because of Margaret's weakened immune system during her cancer treatment. At the UCMC, diagrams of "hands" posted in its public restrooms, delineated the most commonly missed areas after washing. Interestingly, they included the thumbs, fingertips, between the fingers, and the backs of hands. I found this information very instructive and took heed.

Avoiding cross-contamination of foods weighed heavily on my mind, so I only worked with one food type at a time. For instance, after working with chicken and before turning to another food type such as veggies, I washed all kitchen utensils, tools, cutting boards, small appliances, and counters with hot water, soap, followed by Clorox Clean-up spray and rinsed thoroughly. As my final step, I poured boiling water on the tools. My dishwasher had a "sanitation" setting, and I often used that instead of manual washing. As always, I handled food with gloved hands.

PORK CHOPS (2)

Like all good comfort foods, this meal of pork chops, applesauce, and vegetables is no exception—pureed pork chop spears over pureed broccoli, butternut squash, roasted red beets and applesauce.

LUCKY SOUP (3)

Lucky Soup is pureed asparagus and sweet potatoes. The four-leaf clover is green beans, and the triangular protein is roasted chicken garnished with rosemary sprigs.

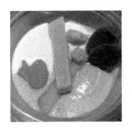

SALMON MOUSSE (4)

Creamy broccoli is next to the salmon mousse along with purees of sliced red beet rounds and sweet potato "fries." The "catsup" is roasted red bell pepper."

HAMBURGER DINNER (5)

I made the top of the bun by pureeing white bread, and thinned it with a little milk. I spread the mixture in a plastic-lined, small, shallow bowl and froze it.

I spread additional bread puree on a cookie sheet and when workably frozen, used a round cookie cutter the same diameter as the shallow bowl to create the bottom half of the bun. After both sides of the bun were frozen, I brushed on some sweet potato puree to give it color. The French fries are pureed potatoes spread on a cookie sheet, and when it became partially frozen, I cut it into strips, then brushed a little sweet potato glaze for color. The cheese, lettuce, and catsup are all veggie purees of roasted yellow bell pepper, broccoli, and roasted red bell pepper.

COBB SALAD (6)

Cutting frozen pureed shapes led to frozen scraps of food. Instead of throwing them out, I saved them in the freezer until ready for use. I cut those frozen scraps into various geometric shapes and called it "tossed salad." For this Cobb Salad, I used scraps of pureed green beans, red lentils, cube cut carrots, roasted red beets, roasted chicken, and asparagus. The "egg" is pureed white rice poured in a plastic-wrap lined egg mold and when frozen to a workable state, I scooped out a half-sphere depression in the rice and poured in golden beets for the "yolk."

During those turbulent months of January through June, confusion, sadness, and fear over my mother's declining health and Margaret's enormous challenges of squamous cell carcinoma dominated my life. But in those few weeks I spent preparing meals for Margaret, I felt as if time suspended itself for me when I entered my kitchen. I was in a world of total immersion of planning, designing, problem-solving, and preparing her meals. There, I discovered the true beauty of food as a nurturer not only for eating but for cooking as well. With a simple stroke of a knife, frozen sheets of pureed food turned into funky geometric shapes of protein, and with a skewer, puddles of pureed vegetables emerged as free-form art.

It may seem like a lot of work to prepare one hundred puree meals for my friend, but I viewed it more as a privilege. People remarked, "what a good friend," I was, or "how lucky" Margaret was for my help. But I didn't see it that way. Anyone who helps someone, knows the truth—the treasures reaped by helping others are greatest for the helper.

I communed with the foods spiritually as we worked together. They beckoned me to make them into something beautiful, much like a lump of clay implored me to give it a form and purpose each time I sat at the potter's wheel. While designing and making these meals each night, my mind demanded I stretch my creative thought, and I felt cleansed and sated. I took in the air with deep breaths again. I felt energized and strengthened and could step back into the real world of life and death. And with courage, I went to my mother and Margaret with a sense of calm and acceptance. So no, cooking for Margaret was not work, nor was she lucky to have me as a friend. Cooking her meals saved me from stepping too close to the edge of the bluff.

I hadn't seen Margaret for over a month after my mother passed away. Margaret had finished her cancer treatment, blood tests, and CT scan. She was ready for follow-up consultations with her doctors. It was a warm, sunny July day when I picked her up for her meetings at UCMC with her oncologist, Dr. Villaflor, and otolaryngologist, Dr. Portugal.

I clapped my hands together when she got into the car.

"Oh, my god Margaret, you look fantastic!" Her beautiful brown eyes were softened, opened wide, and twinkling.

"Thanks! I feel great!"

"Look at you, you have good color in your face, and what's that I see on your head, a little peach fuzz? And you're smiling again!" I said.

"Yes, my hair is growing back," she laughed, patting the top of her head. "And how are you?"

"Better, thank you."

"You must miss her, huh?"

"Yeah, very much. But today is going to bring exciting news to us. I know it!" I said.

The purpose of the meetings was to learn the findings of her tests and CT scan she'd recently taken and would reveal the status of her tumor—whether it was the same size, larger, smaller, or gone altogether.

Dr. Villaflor welcomed us into her office and reviewed the CT scan report and digitally scanned images of Margaret's tongue and head area.

The doctor read the radiologist's report to us in a language seemingly more Pig Latin than English. But in spite of the doctor's enthusiasm with what she learned, the words "the tumors were reduced significantly," rang loud.

Margaret asked, "Wait. Don't we want the tumors to be—gone?"

Dr. Villaflor smiled and patiently explained that "reduced significantly" is radiologist-speak for an unidentified mass that could likely be scar tissue or dead cells left behind. The doctor digitally aligned the side-by-side images of the "before and after" treatment scans. I saw her cursor quickly scampering across the computer screen here, there, and everywhere as she pointed to unidentifiable, amorphous forms that were a hundred shades of gray.

"See over here?" The doctor's eyes were bright and gleeful. "The tumor in the "before" scan is asymmetrical and now look at it on the "after" scan: you can barely see it!"

I squinted and willed myself to see what the doctor was pointing out. Margaret bristled and asked again why the mass was not gone. Dr. Villaflor framed her answer in different ways, and we were half-convinced that what she told us was good news. But what we wanted to hear was, "Congratulations! You no longer have a mass on your tongue!"

Before Dr. Villaflor sent us off to Margaret's next appointment with Dr. Portugal, she told us that his exam would further clarify the radiologist's findings. Each image slice of the CT scan is two-dimensional and very informational, but Dr. Portugal's "live" exam would give us a comprehensive understanding of that remaining mass.

Dr. Portugal waved us into the exam room, and we settled in. He looked cheerful.

Margaret frowned. "I don't understand why I still have a mass on my tongue and what that means."

"Well, let me take a look," he said. "I'm going to perform a nasal endoscopy. It's a painless procedure involving a narrow tube with a lighted camera at the tip. Do you remember I did this before?"

She nodded.

The endoscope, tethered to a computer and monitor screen, was inserted in Margaret's nose and carefully guided into her throat area. The doctor saw the condition of her tongue and throat area on the computer screen in real-time. We watched along with him. It was not two-dimensional but rather a video-like format allowing him to guide the camera in and around as necessary.

"I don't know what I'm looking at, but everything looks nice and pink!" I said.

Dr. Portugal had a broad grin. "Margaret, I see a healthy tongue and throat. No mass, no tumor. I'd say you are officially cancer-free!" He removed the endoscope.

Looking like she was on the brink of crying and laughing at the same time, Margaret took a big breath and let out a sigh of relief.

"Oh, Doctor Portugal, thank you, I'm so happy! So, my treatment is done?" She beamed.

"Yes, your treatment is done!" the doctor said.

I turned to Margaret, and we hugged tightly—longer than usual. The kind of hug two people shared when one of them had just come home after a long journey. Our tears fell, and we laughed.

We chattered away as I drove Margaret home.

"You worked so hard. You won this wretched battle!" I said.

Margaret smiled. "I can't believe it's over—I couldn't have done it without you. So many people helped me—I didn't know they loved me." She looked out the window. "I can't believe it's finally over."

Throughout her cancer, Margaret maintained her conviction to survive and pressed forward day after each terrible day. Her energy was increasing, her spirit lifted higher, and she was on the mend. All the puzzle pieces were now in place, and it was picture perfect!

※

I drove home, basking in the glow of Margaret's good news. Tony greeted me—his tail wagging like a windshield wiper on high speed, whimpering with happiness. I picked him up and we hugged. He kissed the space between us profusely, and I laughed. Tony's kisses were more like air licks than smooches, thank god—he was a pretty tidy guy, not slobbery.

"Yeah, I missed you too, Tony. What's it been, four hours?" I giggled.

I carried him to the den, and we sank into the sofa. I sighed. I was tired, and thoughts collided in my mind.

I closed my eyes, and as exhaustion dissolved, I slipped into a twilight state—

Had my mother lived, her happiness over the news of Margaret's good health would have been over the moon.

"Ahhhh!" she would have squealed. "Oh, Susie! Susie! I knew Margaret would get healthy and strong again!" My mother would have laughed, hands on her cheeks, and tears would have filled her eyes.

I would have wrapped my arms around her soft, full body, feeling her warmth and positive energy transfusing into me.

Yes, that's what my mother and I would have done. And then the rivulets flowed. My heart ached for her. My mind floated to the Art Center from years ago when my heartbeat quickened, and I felt lightheaded. I steadied myself.

"*Mom—I'm going to fall down the bluff!*"

"*You won't fall, Susie. I'm with you—I'll never let you go,*" she promised.

EPILOGUE

Since 2012, when Margaret was first diagnosed and treated for squamous cell carcinoma, she has been cancer-free. Except for sensitivity to strong spices, her restored taste buds allow her to enjoy the foods she always loved, and she is designing and baking beautiful cakes once again. Her life is as it was before cancer, with one significant difference. She met her soulmate, Bill Lilly. He is a good man—caring, kind, smart, and together, they were a beautiful couple. Margaret and Bill had their wedding ceremony and brunch reception in Bob's and my loft. Bob made an "after-ceremony" music compilation—its first song was Etta James's "At Last," to which Margaret and Bill danced. Mr. and Mrs. Lilly have good health, happiness, and love—indeed, at last.

Midwest Palliative & Hospice CareCenter, Skokie, Illinois, where my mother spent her final days, so inspired Kristin with their mission, work, and compassion, she decided to pivot from her career in business marketing to pursue a nursing degree. During graduate school, Kristin was a student volunteer in the Veterans Administration's No Veteran Dies Alone program. After two grueling years of nursing studies, she earned her master's degree and passed her nursing boards. Midwest Palliative & Hospice CareCenter subsequently merged with another organization and was renamed JourneyCare, Barrington, Illinois, where Kristin followed her dream and accepted a position. Kristin is a hospice nurse.

During the dog days of constant chaos and rehabilitation of our house during our family's early years, Jonathan defiantly declared he didn't like construction. After his professional studies and working a few years, though, he decided to build a weekend getaway home in the foothills of the Ozarks. Jonathan used his instincts in architecture to design and prepare sketches for his contractor and found his project successful and satisfying. He likes construction now, thank goodness—I guess our never-ending home construction projects didn't mess up his mind after all. Jonathan did not become an architect. But the youngster who didn't know boys could grow up to be doctors, chose dentistry and orthodontics as his life's work—well done, Dr. Rakstang.

Bob and I continue to live in our "emerging" neighborhood in Chicago's West Loop although it's undergoing a remarkable transition since we arrived before the turn of the millennium. Most of the one and two-story light industrial buildings surrounding our loft are replaced with new condos and apartment buildings ranging from eight stories to high rises. Across the street from us, where the abandoned building full of pigeons once resided, is now the Mary Bartelme Park, a modern urban green space. Upscale restaurants and high-profile corporate headquarters replaced most of Fulton Market's meatpackers, produce purveyors, and fishmongers. The West Loop, once our colorful, scrappy, odd little neighborhood with a strange past, is now officially sanitized, which some call "progress." But Bob and I still love living there anyway.

As for me, now seventy years old, I'm contending with issues of aging's effect on the quality of my mind, body, and spirit, as well as struggling with facing death. With both my Okinawan parents living well into old age, as did their parents, I may have inherited their legacy of longevity. The irony, though, is I'm not all that certain *my* end of life is what troubles me. Losing my parents, still painful in my heart, created a fear of losing others I love. Longevity may assure that, which may be ultimately what I must learn to accept. I have time on my side—presumably—to learn.

ACKNOWLEDGMENTS

I was blessed to have had two women in my life. Each of them handling their compromised health with dignity and strength—one, accepting her destiny with elegant grace and tranquility, the other, fighting with the courage of a warrior for a life she felt she earned and deserved. They leaned on me, sharing their innermost thoughts and hearts during their darkest, as well as joyous days of our journeys together, for which I was honored and privileged to be a part. With open arms, they allowed me into their lives and accepted my help, which was the most precious gift they could give me. With sincere gratitude and love, I offer my prayers of unending peace for my mother, Helen Humiko Higa Uehara, and my friend, Margaret Lastick Lilly.

Mr. Richard Goode's masterful interpretation of Beethoven's Piano Sonata No. 8 in C minor, Opus 13, drew me into his glorious music, inspiring me to transcribe the sonata into my written voice. I am indebted to maestro Beethoven for his music that resonated with me so profoundly, and to Mr. Goode, for unleashing his music into my mind and heart.

Working with my editor, Erin Brown made writing this story a fascinating, albeit daunting journey. Like piano lessons, writing tests one's mental acuity, memory, intellect, and, most of all, courage. More like a coach, Ms. Brown lured me into the complex world of writing, challenging me to dig deeper into myself and my memory, with detail, color, and accuracy. My thanks to Ms. Brown for her masterful editing, corrections, and comments, and for helping me summon up the courage to express my thoughts and remembrances in a way I never thought I could or would. My sincerest gratitude.

As a young student of music, I loved playing the piano. My hands, able to span beyond an octave, afforded me fundamental potential, but alas, I lacked the talent and resolve to continue my studies past my mid-teen years. As an adult, I turned to piano teacher Mr. Joseph Cisar, whose performance technique and teaching skills were unmatched. He taught me how to hear music and play the piano, and through those lessons, a window in my mind opened letting in, like a whoosh of autumn leaves, long-forgotten memories of music in my life that had sat dormant for so many years. My thanks to Mr. Cisar for his teachings. They were gifts that strengthened my love of music and influenced this story.

Ms. Nomi Epstein, music theory professor, performer, and composer with unparalleled knowledge of music, guided me through the analysis of every note, chord, bar, phrase, and movement of Pathetique. Without Ms. Epstein's expertise, generous patience, and steadfast attention to detail, I could not have understood, nor fully appreciate the depth and breadth of Beethoven's powerful masterpiece. My heartfelt thanks to Ms. Epstein for instilling an understanding of the intricacies of the maestro's work, so that I could organize the structure of my story.

As a novice author, the process of turning thoughts into words and words into a book was a fascinating journey, and although writing is a solitary activity, it was heartening to know that my book designer, Mr. John Hubbard, was just a few keystrokes away. His sharp eye for design and typography, precision, wit, and steadfast commitment to his work, made our seamless collaboration enlightening and great fun. My sincerest thanks to Mr. Hubbard for his patience with me, all his creative gifts, and much appreciated support.

My mother's sisters, Nobuko (Nancy) Tamashiro, Setsuko, Se (Agnes) Yamaguchi, and Aiko (Jeanette) Ekimura, and my mother's life-long friend, Alice Kuba, shared their stories of life growing up in Hawai`i through pre and post WWII. Their loving remembrances of my mother helped me paint a picture of her youth and gave me insight into her young life as a minority in the island of paradise. My aunties gave me books, newspaper articles, and photos, teaching me about all things Okinawan, our proud heritage. With sincere gratitude, I send my love and warmest thanks to them.

With humble gratitude, I thank Reverend Ron Miyamura, Midwest Buddhist Temple, for comforting my mother through her end of life journey. And with his kind, steady, spiritual hand, he shepherded me through an understanding of Buddhist beliefs. Without his lessons, I could not have experienced or written about my mother's peaceful, final voyage.

Thinking about Kristin and Jonathan in their youth brought me welcomed respite while writing about the painful realities of life and death. As they shared their memories with me, I was reminded of our loving experiences together and burst with pride for the adults they've become.

I'm indebted to my husband, Bob Rakstang. He was my fact and memory checker of this story, digital guru, mate for life, and partner in all things we share. He stood with me throughout our lives together, lifting my heart when I needed it most, and helping me hear again, the exquisite, consoling sounds of a percussion concerto—my love to you, Gassho (palms together with gratitude).

REFERENCES

Japanese Death Poems, Kaisho. Tuttle Publishing, ©1986 Charles E. Tuttle Publishing.

From *The Sound of Water: Haiku by Basho, Buson, Issa, and Other Poets*, translated by Sam Hamill, ©1995 by Sam Hamill. Reprinted by arrangement with The Permissions Company, LLC on behalf of Shambhala Publications, Inc., Boulder, Colorado, Shambhala.com.

Neff, Cary. *Conscious Cuisine A New Style of Cooking from the Kitchens of Chef Cary Neff*. Naperville, Illinois: Sourcebooks, Inc., 2002.

BIBLIOGRAPHY

Achatz, Grant and Nick Kokonas. *Life, on the Line: A Chef's Story of Chasing Greatness, Facing Death, and Redefining the Way We Eat*. New York: Gotham Books, Penguin Group (USA) Inc., 2011

Ekimura, Aiko and Jonathan Rakstang. *Sukenori Higa, Kamanaka Higa, Shingo Higa: A Family Celebration*. Honolulu, Hawai`i, 1995.

Hui O Laulima. *Chimugukuru—the soul, the spirit, the heart Okinawan Mixed Plate II Generous Servings of Culture, Customs, and Cuisine*. Honolulu, Hawai`i: Mutual Publishing, LLC, 2008.

EastWest Magazine Co., Editor. *Uchinanchu: A Pictorial Tribute to Okinawans in Hawai`i*. Honolulu, Hawai`i: EastWest Magazine Co., Ltd., 1990.

Solomon, Maynard. *Beethoven*. New York, New York: Schirmer Books, an Imprint of Simon & Schuster Macmillan, 1998, 1977.

Tamura, Eileen H. *Americanization, Acculturation, and Ethnic Identity: The Nisei Generation in Hawai`i*. Urbana and Chicago, Illinois: The University of Illinois Press, 1994.

Tovey, Donald Francis. *A Companion to Beethoven's Pianoforte Sonatas*. London: ABRSM (Publishing) Ltd, a wholly owned subsidiary of ABRSM, 2004, 2005, 2010, 2012.

Ethnic Studies Oral History Project, University of Hawai`i at Manoa, United Okinawan Association of Hawai`i. *UCHINANCHU A History of Okinawans in Hawai`i*. ©1981 Ethnic Studies Oral History Project, Ethnic Studies Program, University of Hawai`i.

APPENDIX

ANALYSIS OF
Sonata No. 8 in C minor Op. 13
(Pathetique)
LUDWIG VAN BEETHOVEN

1ST MOVEMENT

2ND MOVEMENT

3RD MOVEMENT

INTRODUCTION

I structured this memoir as Beethoven structured his Piano Sonata No. 8, C minor, to ground my story in a way that inspired me most—through music. The full score shown above is separated into three sections delineating its three movements. Using ink markers on architects' bumwad (tracing) paper overlaid on the score, I color-coded most key modulations so I could refer, at-a-glance, to the score's organizational structure. (See back cover for color photographs). This method helped me match my story to the tempo, tenor, and emotion of the music.

The first movement begins and ends in its tonic, C minor (magenta), where *Grave* marks the beginning of the end of my story. I took the opportunity of the brief key modulation to E♭-III (violet), a less ominous tone, lengthened its presence, and took the reader back in time to set up my story. Beethoven modulated from key to key (shown in varying colors) expressing his main themes and its development, creating musical instability, agitation, and tension. As such, I, too, was unstable while dealing with the speeding and ever-changing status and fear for the future of two women I loved.

While this form appears highly structured, they were, some say, a guideline for Beethoven, who exercised flexibility and artistic license to find the best-suited elements such as modulation, theme, order, phrase length, as vehicles for expressing his emotion and passion.

I also, did not use these forms as a rigid tenet or prescription for the story, but rather on a macro level as a guideline for order, connecting and sequencing events, and expressing my own emotions. For example, the powerful, Cm (i) opening notes of the first movement, evoked the moment I entered a hospice room and realized the finality of Time and impermanence of life. Although this scene occurred later in the actual sequence of events, Beethoven's stunning chords of the *Grave* introduction inspired me to begin my story as such.

My analysis is, indeed, a broad-brush overview of the sonata and how my story relates to it. I do not profess to be a music theorist—I'm just a humble writer wanting to express myself through music.

PART I
1st Movement

Grave

The Cm (C minor) introduction opens with bars of inauspicious, directionally opposing chords of the treble and bass, as I try to reconcile the speed of Time.

Anxiety and fear, some conscious, some tucked away profoundly rooted in my psyche, wove in and out of the story, as does this melody. I struggled with emotional denial colliding with reality, persistent, haunting angst, reminding me that time was running out. Like the pleading treble, I made a last-ditch effort to negotiate with my mind, for more time:

Must she?

She must.

But I need more time.

The Cm melody repeats, this time in E♭-III and "calls," with a tone of voice in the treble, not as intense and oppressive as Cm, eliciting remembrances of less troubled times, while the "response" of the falling bass is a sobering reminder of the challenges of life with which I struggled. Only a bar long, I used this short, unthreatening mood of E♭-III treble chords to introduce context, history, and main characters, stretching the section to many pages.

The Introduction returns to Cm with two, pensively played cadential bars that end with a raised note. It was as if the music asked the question—"Why would Dr. Forbes order a CT scan for a routine sore throat and earache?"—before the fast descent of chromatic half-stepped notes down the keyboard arrives at *Allegro di molto e con brio*.

EXPOSITION

Allegro di molto e con brio (Fast, with vigor)

Allegro symbolized the speed of changing events, my state of mind racing with worry, and inability to calmly process medical information regarding the failing health of my mother and my friend, Margaret.

In Cm, the Exposition introduces Theme 1, a powerful and fast two-part theme. I heard the first part, ascending notes, as the "call" of the doctor's diagnosis about Margaret's ill health, and the second part, descending staccato chords, as the "response" of Margaret's incredulity and horror over the news. With tension rising, my anxiety grew like the ominous rising bass tremolos. Modulating from Cm to its dominant, the Exposition continues its intensity with the persistent high G sforzando followed by a falling treble that punctuated the frenzy of emotions. Finally, a place of relief came when the score passes through modulations to E♭m for Theme 2, as I began to teach my mother to play the piano. But my respite was short-lived, realizing the gravity of my mother's profoundly declining cognitive skills.

The Exposition modulates to E♭-III, where it stabilizes as I continued my journey with Margaret, steeped in meetings with doctors about her imminent cancer treatment, and with my mother, who was bewildered over her failing health. I decided to cook meals for Margaret, and she came over for a taste-test. I promised I would make one hundred meals for her. She completed a dreaded test, as Exposition ends in the tonic's dominant. (No repeats).

DEVELOPMENT

The somber *Grave* tempo returns, this time in Gm, as I received a phone call with unexpected news about my mother. I went to the hospital where a doctor gave me his unsettling observations.

Grave is again followed by *allegro di molto e con brio*, in Em. The instability of its many key modulations is metaphoric of how I spent my time, back and forth, tending alternately from my mother to Margaret and feeling the angst of emotional instability and uncertainty about their future.

Margaret continued going through a plethora of tests and struggled with counterintuitive emotions over the test results. My mother experienced uncharacteristic agitation. Margaret found solace in thoughtful words from a Buddhist abbot, began her cancer treatment, and suffered its effects, including a stubborn fever.

My mother had a remembrance of her father that she found perplexing. And she had a dream that frightened us both.

RECAPITULATION

Theme 1 reappears in Cm, when Margaret's persistent fever, requiring repeated hospital admissions, refused to yield to medical protocol. Through several key modulations, Theme 2 returns, this time in Fm, as I shopped for my mother's garden and spent a day with her, planting the flowers. The following morning, although I planned to revisit my mother, I changed my mind and decided to visit Margaret first.

Returning to Cm, while visiting Margaret, I received notification that my mother's health had taken a catastrophic turn and rushed to the hospital. I left Margaret to be with my mother. While driving, the doctor called me. Trying to process what the doctor said, filled me with conflict, denial, and horror over my mother's imminent future.

When *Grave* again revisits, I attempted to surrender to reality. *Allegro con di molto e con brio* returns with fierceness as I desperately tried to keep up with the ambulance transporting my mother to the hospice center. Finally, catching up with the ambulance and arriving at the hospice facility, I ran inside the lobby. I saw my mother being wheeled into the elevator just as its doors closed.

PART II
2nd Movement

Adagio Cantabile (Slow, songlike)
The 2nd movement, structured in rondo form, follows ABACA Coda. The story opens where I left off in the Introduction, *Grave*, of the 1st movement:
Must she?
She must.
But I need more time.

A) Rondo (A♭ M)
Arriving in my mother's hospice room, I was relieved by its quiet, tranquil environment but lamented that I hadn't asked my mother more questions about her youth growing up in Hawai`i. Why did she change her Japanese birth name to an Anglo name? How did she feel moving from the idyllic life in Hawai`i to Chicago? How did she meet my father?" But we had run out of time for those questions.

B) First episode (Fm to E♭)
The music modulates through Fm to E♭, where I wove a story in 3rd person point of view. I answer those and other questions based on anecdotal conversations with my mother's sisters, her life-long friend, reading books on Hawai`i history, family photos, and my remembrances.

A) Rondo
(A♭ M)
When the music returns to the tonic, so, too, the story returns to my mother's hospice room. From the counsel of the hospice doctor, nurses, and my mother's Buddhist minister, I learned about the process of death.

C) Second episode (A♭ m to E♮)
My dearest friend, whose mother died a few years earlier, told me I must give my mother permission to die. Not ready to say those difficult words to my mother, I waited. My mother's breath became shallow, and the pulse of her carotid artery weakened. I spoke to my mother. When the minister arrived and began the Makura-gyo ceremony, my mother took her final breath. Margaret attended my mother's memorial service. During the ceremony, my mother's minister gave her a symbolic Buddhist name, most befitting of her.

A) Rondo (A♭ M)
The music returns home to A♭ M, as did I, to my mother's home. I discovered a letter in her sewing drawer and believed she left it there for me to return it to its rightful owner. I noticed a handprint on the wall and had remembrances.

Coda: Months later, still grieving and still in A♭ M, Bob expressed his grief, and I realized how similar he and my mother were. I awakened to the sounds of a percussion concerto. I finally had a sense that I would recover from my despair.

PART III
3rd Movement

Allegro (quickly, bright)
The movement, structured in sonata-rondo form, follows ABACABA Coda. The tempo is quick, just as I must handle fragile foods, fresh and frozen, quickly.

EXPOSITION
A) Rondo (Cm) In the rondo's Cm tonic, I reflected on the previous six months and recalled my despair over my mother's and Margaret's health crises. So, too, the melody of this rondo harkens back to the first movement, Exposition, Theme 2 in E♭ m, providing a common thread of remembrances.

B) First episode (E♭-III)
It wasn't until after my mother passed away in June, and Margaret's cancer treatment completed in July that I finally had time to explain how and why I cooked for her. While planning and designing her meals, I discovered the natural beauty and simplicity of whole foods, and knowing her immune system would be severely compromised during treatment, I researched safe-food preparation practices. I had a remembrance of a dish I'd seen in a cookbook and used that method as a platform for designing Margaret's meals.

A) Rondo (Cm)
Returning to the tonic, I was ready to fulfill my cooking commitment to Margaret.

DEVELOPMENT
C) Second episode (A♭-VI)
Cm modulates to A♭-VI, time was of the essence, and I needed to work quickly so the frozen protein would not defrost as I handled them. I created two-dimensional and three-dimensional foods, shown through photos, and described my techniques.

A) (Cm)
Again, in tonic, I recalled the turbulent months past but found my kitchen a respite—a wondrous world where I could forget my troubles and focus on cooking.

RECAPITULATION
B) (CM)
Margaret and I reunite and visit the doctors for a follow-up consultation.

A) CODA (Cm to A♭-VI to Cm)
In Cm, Dr. Villaflor showed us arcane film images of Margaret's tongue and throat area and mentioned the radiologist's report indicated that the tumor significantly reduced. Margaret was disappointed and thinks it's terrible news. The doctor attempted to clarify the findings.

Modulating to A♭-VI, Dr. Portugal confirmed her throat was free of cancer, and her treatment was a success, was completed, and I took her home. She and I hugged with joy.

Heading back to my home as the score modulates back to tonic, I was exhausted and imagined how my mother would have reacted to Margaret's good news.

DESCRIPTIONS OF MOTHER'S NEW YEAR'S FEAST

Sumi Salad
Finely shredded cabbage, uncooked broken ramen noodles, green onions, almonds, w/sweetened rice vinegar dressing.

Namasu Salad
Cucumber, carrot salad w/sweetened rice vinegar, ginger, sesame dressing.

Cold soba noodle salad
Lettuce, bean sprouts, carrots, cucumber, shrimp, green onions, thinly sliced egg crepes, and nori strips w/sweetened rice vinegar, sesame oil and soy sauce dressing over soba noodles.

Gobo salad
Braised matchstick-cut burdock root and carrots in sweetened dashi, shoyu, sake, mirin sauce.

Purple Okinawa sweet potatoes
Steamed and sliced.

Seaweed salad
Reconstituted sea vegetable salad mix with a dressing of miso, shoyu, grated ginger, mirin, rice wine vinegar, sugar, sesame oil, and garnished with black and white sesame seeds.

Chow Mein with pan-fried noodles
Stir-fried carrots, celery, white and green onions, red bell pepper, bean sprouts, pea pods with oyster sauce to taste, served over pan-fried Chinese noodles.

Fried rice with vegetables
As noted in the story.

Charcoal-grilled teriyaki chicken and vegetable kabobs
Bite-sized chicken, red and green bell pepper, yellow onions, mushrooms,

pineapple chunks in teriyaki marinade of shoyu, mirin, brown sugar, ginger, garlic, skewered and grilled. (Teriyaki marinade noted in text).

Tonkatsu
Deep-fried pork loin breaded in panko breadcrumbs with katsu sauce of catsup, Worcestershire sauce, shoyu, mirin, sugar, and Dijon mustard.

Oven-roasted char siu short-ribs finished on the grill:
Short ribs marinated in store-bought char siu sauce and finished on the grill.

Tabletop-cooked Sukiyaki
Beef tenderloin strips, tofu cubes, leeks, shiitake mushrooms, spinach in teriyaki sauce over cellophane noodles.

Vegetable and Shrimp tempura:
Shrimp, sweet potatoes, green beans, onions, carrots, bell peppers, and mushrooms battered in flour/ice water, then breaded in panko breadcrumbs and deep-fried.

Nishime
A Japanese village stew, prepared Hawaiian style, of carrots, celery, bamboo shoots, lotus root, gobo, konnyaku, shiitake mushrooms, chicken chunks, kombu, simmered in a dashi-shoyu broth.

Inari sushi
Rice in sweetened rice vinegar tucked into store-bought, deep-fried tofu pockets.

Chirashizushi (scattered sushi)
Shiitake mushrooms chopped kampyo gourd strips, pickled lotus root, thinly sliced egg crepes, blanched/shocked pea pods, thinly sliced green onions over sushi rice infused with sweetened rice vinegar and garnished with strips of nori.

Mochi
Sticky rice cakes (store bought) made from sweet rice, cooked, pounded, and formed into small balls sometimes stuffed with anko wsweet red bean paste) or formed into cubes.

Haupia
A gelatin-like, coconut-based dessert often served in blocks or cubes (similar to *Jello* squares) and with fruit.

Andagi
Sweet, deep-fried Okinawan donuts, looking similar to larger donut holes.

ENDNOTES

AUTHOR'S NOTE
1. Beethoven, Ludwig van. "Sonata No. 8, C minor, Opus 13 (Pathetique)." 1993. *BEETHOVEN The Complete Sonatas Richard Goode*, Richard Goode, ©1993, Elektra Entertainment, a division of Warner Communications Inc. CD.

PART I
1. From *The Sound of Water: Haiku by Basho, Buson, Issa and Other Poets*, translated by Sam Hamill, ©1995 by Sam Hamill. Reprinted by arrangement with The Permissions Company, LLC on behalf of Shambhala Publications, Inc., Boulder, Colorado, shambhala.com.
2. Sakura: Cherry tree.
3. (Paraphrased), *Immortal Beloved*, Film, Directed by Bernard Rose, 1994: Icon Productions, Icon Entertainment, Majestic Films International.
4. Timbre: Tone, color of sound.
5. Gobo: Burdock root.
6. Konnyaku: From the Konjac potato, comes in the form of slices or noodles. Also known as the "miracle noodle."
7. Dashi: Broth made from water, kombu (dried kelp) and bonito fish flakes.
8. Shoyu: Soy sauce.
9. Hai: Japanese for "yes."
10. See Description of Mother's New Year's Eve Feast in the Appendix.
11. Jook: Chinese rice soup.
12. Wiki wiki: A term used in Hawai`i, meaning quick quick!
13. Kawaii, neh?: So cute, don't you agree?

14 Hapa haole: Hapa, pronounced "hoppa," means half, and haole, pronounced how-lee, means Caucasian—so hapa haole means half Caucasian.
15 Chawan: Rice or tea bowl.
16 Atama: Brain, mind.
17 Pyrometric cones: Small, three-sided, pyramid-shaped, ceramic composite cones that gauge the level of heat inside the kiln. Each cone, designated to bend (melt) at a specific temperature, allows the potter to determine when the kiln reaches proper and intended milestone temperatures.
18 Loop area: Elevated trains that track around a square loop within Chicago's downtown area.
19 Crit: critique of student work.
20 En Charette: French for cart or wagon. In the 1800s, Parisian architecture students would continue to work on their drawings and models as they were being transported by cart to their crit. The phrase is known as intense, final efforts on a project just before a deadline.
21 HVAC: Heating, ventilating, and air conditioning.
22 MLTW: Moore Lyndon Turnbull Whitaker, architectural firm, Berkeley, CA.
23 Kawaiso, neh?: Poor thing, yes?
24 Okai: Rice porridge. Also known as okayu.
25 Chotto: A little bit.
26 Sisyphus: In Greek mythology, a cruel king's punishment was that Sisyphus push a boulder up a hill, and just as the boulder approached the top of the hill, it would roll back down requiring the king to repeat his task, for eternity.

27 Red lines: A process where an architect writes notes and revisions in red pencil or pen on a check-set of construction drawings, and hands it over to a lower level architectural graduate to transfer onto the next iteration of drawings.
28 "L": Short for trains elevated above the streets.
29 Program: In architecture, it is generally the architect's document of findings in the first phase of a project. After interviews with the client, the architect identifies building and user needs, scope, financial, and client objectives, site opportunities and restrictions, and local, state, and federal requirements.
30 Gohan o mazeru: Fluff up the rice.
31 Umami: Savoriness. Umami is the fifth basic taste next to sweet, sour, salty, bitter.
32 Oak Leaves: Newspaper focusing on news and events in Oak Park, Illinois.
33 Udon: Thick diameter wheat flour noodle often served in soup.
34 Hondo: Main room in a Buddhist temple.
35 Kansho: Tolling bell.
36 Ochazuke: Green tea, hot rice, and an assortment of savory small plates.
37 Otolaryngologist: Medical specialist who treats ear, note, and throat concerns.
38 Ophthalmologist: Medical specialist in the treatment of disorders and diseases of the eye.
39 Baka: Stupid, silly. Short for bakatare.
40 PET-CT scan: Positron emission tomography-computer tomography scans to better diagnose and assess condition of Margaret's cancer.
41 Yakamashii: Noisy.
42 Pruncus Incisa Little Twist: Flowering cherry tree.

PART II

1. *Japanese Death Poems*, Kaisho. Tuttle Publishing, ©1986 Charles E. Tuttle Publishing.
2. Kansho: Tolling of the bell.
3. Kanzen Dokkyo: Sutra Chant.
4. Homyo: Presentation of a Buddhist name.
5. Sutra Chanting: "Shoshinge" chanting by the minister and congregation.

PART III

1. From *The Sound of Water: Haiku by Basho, Buson, Issa and Other Poets*, translated by Sam Hamill, ©1995 by Sam Hamill. Reprinted by arrangement with The Permissions Company, LLC on behalf of Shambhala Publications, Inc., Boulder, Colorado, shambhala.com.
2. Neff, Cary. *Conscious Cuisine A New Style of Cooking from the Kitchens of Chef Cary Neff*. Naperville, Illinois: Sourcebooks, Inc., 2002.

AUTHOR BIOGRAPHY

Born in Hawaii and raised in Chicago, Susan Uehara Rakstang, a retired architect, lives in Chicago's West Loop with her husband, Bob, and their Cockapoo, Tony.

Visit the author's websites:
Cooking For Her Eyes
https://cookingforhereyes.com

The Art and Architecture of Puree
https://theartandarchitectureofpuree.com